.NET 4.0 Generics

Beginner's Guide

Enhance the type safety of your code and create applications easily using Generics in the .NET 4.0 Framework

Sudipta Mukherjee

BIRMINGHAM - MUMBAI

.NET 4.0 Generics
Beginner's Guide

First published: January 2012

Production Reference: 1190112

Published by Packt Publishing Ltd.
Livery Place
35 Livery Street
Birmingham B3 2PB, UK.

ISBN 978-1-84969-078-2

www.packtpub.com

Cover Image by Asher Wishkerman (a.wishkerman@mpic.de)

Credits

Author
Sudipta Mukherjee

Reviewers
Atul Gupta
WEI CHUNG, LOW
Antonio Radesca

Acquisition Editor
David Barnes

Lead Technical Editor
Meeta Rajani

Technical Editors
Veronica Fernandes

Copy Editor
Laxmi Subramanian

Project Coordinator
Vishal Bodwani

Proofreader
Joanna McMahon

Indexer
Monica Ajmera Mehta
Rekha Nair

Graphics
Manu Joseph

Production Coordinator
Alwin Roy

Cover Work
Alwin Roy

Foreword

It is my pleasure to write the foreword to a book which will introduce you to the world of generic programming with C# and other .NET languages. You will be able to learn a lot from this book, as it introduces you to the elegant power of generic programming in C#. Through it, you will become a better C# programmer, and a better programmer in all future languages you might choose to use.

It is now almost 10 years since .NET Generics was first described in publications from Microsoft Research, Cambridge, a project I was able to lead and contribute to, and six years since it was released in product form in C# 2.0. In this foreword, I would like to take a moment to review the importance of .NET Generics in the history of programming languages, and the way it continues to inspire a new generation of programmers.

When we began the design of C# and .NET Generics, generic programming was not new. However, it was considered to be outside the mainstream, and attempts to change that with C++ templates and proposals for Java Generics were proving highly problematic for practitioners. At Microsoft Research, we pride ourselves on solving problems at their core. The three defining core features of .NET Generics as we designed them were efficient generics over value types with code generation and sharing managed by the virtual machine, reified run-time types, and language neutrality.

These technical features are now widely acknowledged to represent the "right" fundamental design choices for programming language infrastructure. They are not easy to design or build, and they are not easy to deliver, and when Microsoft Research embarked on this project, we believe we put the .NET platform many years ahead of its rivals. The entire credit goes to Microsoft and people such as Bill Gates, Eric Rudder, and Anders Hejlsberg for taking the plunge to push this into our range of programming languages. However, without the prototyping, research, engineering, and incessant advocacy by Microsoft Research, C# and .NET Generics would never be in their current form.

Let's take some time to examine why this was important. First, .NET Generics represents the moment where strongly typed and functional programming entered the mainstream. .NET Generics enabled C# to become more functional (through LINQ, Lambdas, and generic collections), and it enabled a new class of strongly typed, fully functional .NET languages (such as F#) to thrive. Further, .NET Generics also enabled new key programming techniques, such as Async programming in F# 2.0 and C# 5.0, and Rx programming for reactive systems. Even though you may not realize it, you'll have learned a lot of functional programming by the end of this book.

Next, .NET Generics categorically proved that strongly typed object-oriented programming can integrate seamlessly with generic programming. It is hard to describe the extent to which .NET Generics managed to defeat the "object fundamentalists" of the 1990s (who want a world where there is nothing but classes). These people, many still occupying powerful positions in the software industry, seemed satisfied with a world where programmers are less productive, and programs less efficient, in the name of orthodoxy. Today, no practicing programmer or language designer with experience of .NET Generics would design a strongly typed programming language that does not include Generics. Further, almost every .NET API now features the use of .NET Generics, and it has become an essential weapon in the programmer's toolkit for solving many problems.

Finally, and for me most importantly, .NET Generics represents the victory of pragmatic beauty over pragmatic ugliness. In the eyes of many, alternative solutions to the problem of generic programming such as Java's "erasure" of Generics are simply unpleasant "hacks". This leads to reduced productivity when using those languages. In contrast, .NET Generics is perhaps the most smoothly integrated advanced programming language feature ever constructed. It integrates with reflection, .NET NGEN pre-compilation, debugging, and run-time code generation. I've had many people e-mail me to say that .NET Generics is their favorite programming language feature. That is what language research is all about.

I trust you will learn a great deal from this book, and enjoy the productivity that comes from C#, and .NET languages such as F#.

Dr. Don Syme
Principal Research,
Microsoft Research, Cambridge, U.K.

Generic types are more than just lists of `T`. Functional programmers have known this for a long time. C++ programmers who use templates knew this too. But 10 years ago when Don Syme and I first designed and prototyped the Generics feature of the .NET run-time, most mainstream developers were constrained by the rudimentary type systems of languages such as Visual Basic and Java, writing type-generic code only by resorting to casting tricks or worse. In that space, it's hard to conceive of myriad uses of generic types beyond lists and simple collections, and it's fair to say that there was some resistance to our design! Fortunately, some forward thinkers in Microsoft's .NET run-time team regarded Generics in managed languages as more than an academic indulgence, and committed substantial resources to completing a first-class implementation of Generics that is deeply embedded in the run-time languages and tools.

We've come a long way in 10 years! Managed code frameworks make liberal use of generic types, ranging from obvious collection types such as List and Dictionary, through `action' types such as Func and IEnumerable, to more specialized use of Generics such as Lazy initialization. Blogs and online forums are full of discussions on sophisticated topics such as variance and circular constraints. And if it weren't for Generics, it's hard to see how newer language features such as LINQ, or even complete languages such as F#, could have got off the ground.

Coming back, Generics really does start with `List<T>`, and this book sensibly begins from there. It then takes a leisurely tour around the zoo of generic types in the .NET Framework and beyond, to Power Collections and C5. The style is very much one of exploration: the reader is invited to experiment with Generics, prodding and poking a generic type through its methods and properties, and thereby understand the type and solve problems by using it. As someone whose background is in functional programming, in which the initial experience is very much like experimenting with a calculator, I find this very appealing. I hope you like it as much as I do.

Andrew Kennedy
Microsoft Research, Cambridge, U.K.

About the Author

Sudipta Mukherjee was born in Kolkata and migrated to Bangalore, the IT capital of India, to assume the position of a Senior Research Engineer in a renowned research lab. He is an Electronics Engineer by education and a Computer Engineer/Scientist by profession and passion. He graduated in 2004 with a degree in Electronics and Communication Engineering. He has been working with .NET Generics since they first appeared in the .NET Framework 2.0.

He has a keen interest in data structure, algorithms, text processing, natural language processing ,programming language, tools development, and game development.

His first book on data structure using the C programming language has been well received. Parts of the book can be read on Google Books at `http://goo.gl/pttSh`. The book was also translated into Simplified Chinese available on Amazon at `http://goo.gl/lc536`.

He is an active blogger and an open source enthusiast. He mainly blogs about programming and related concepts at `sudipta.posterous.com`. Inspired by several string processing methods in other languages, he created an open source string processing framework for .NET, available for free at `stringdefs.codeplex.com`.

He lives in Bangalore with his wife. He can be reached via e-mail at `sudipto80@yahoo.com` and via Twitter at `@samthecoder`.

Acknowledgement

Books like this cannot be brought to life by the author alone. I want to take this opportunity to thank all the people who were involved in this book in any way.

First of all, I want to thank Microsoft Research for bringing Generics into the .NET Framework. Great work guys. I have used STL in C++ and Collections in Java. But I can say without being biased that Generics in .NET is the smartest implementation of generic programming paradigm that I have ever come across. Without that, I wouldn't have anything to write about.

I owe a big "Thank You" to the Senior Acquisition Editor and Publisher David Barnes at Packt Publishing for offering me this opportunity to write for them. I want to thank Vishal Bodwani and Meeta Rajani, also from Packt Publishing, for their great support. Everytime I missed a deadline, they helped me get back on track. Thanks for bearing with me. Last but not the least, I want to thank my Technical Editors Snehal and Veronica who painstakingly corrected all the mistakes, did all the formatting, without which the book would not have been possible. Thanks a lot.

I have no words to express my gratitude towards Don and Andrew for taking time off to read the manuscript and their kind words. Thank you Don. Thank you Andrew.

I want to thank all the reviewers of the book. Thanks for all your great feedback. It really made the book better.

My wife, Mou, motivated me to write this book. She stood by me when I needed her throughout all these months. Thank you sweetheart. Last but not the least, I can't thank my mom Dipali and dad Subrata enough for finding the love of my life and always being supportive. Thank you mom. Thank you dad.

About the Reviewers

Atul Gupta, is currently a Principal Technology Architect at Infosys' Microsoft Technology Center. He also has close to 15 years of experience working on Microsoft technologies. His expertise spans user interface technologies, and he currently focuses on Windows Presentation Foundation (WPF) and Silverlight technologies. Other technologies of interest to him are Touch (Windows 7), Deepzoom, Pivot, Surface, and Windows Phone 7.

He recently co-authored the book "*ASP.NET 4 Social Networking*", *Packt Publishing* (`http://www.packtpub.com/asp-net-4-social-networking/book`). His prior interest areas were COM, DCOM, C, VC++, ADO.NET, ASP.NET, AJAX, and ASP.NET MVC.

He has also authored papers for industry publications and websites, some of which are available on Infosys' Technology Showcase (`http://www.infosys.com/microsoft/resource-center/pages/technology-showcase.aspx`). Along with colleagues from Infosys, Atul is also an active blogger (`http://www.infosysblogs.com/microsoft`). Being actively involved in professional Microsoft online communities and developer forums, Atul has received Microsoft's Most Valuable Professional award for multiple years in a row.

WEI CHUNG, LOW, a Technical Lead in BizTalk and .NET, and a MCT, MCPD, MCITP, MCTS, and MCSD.NET, works with ResMed (NYSE: RMD), at its Kuala Lumpur, Malaysia campus. He is also a member of PMI, certified as a PMP. He started working on Microsoft .NET very early on and has been involved in development, consultation, and corporate training in the areas of business intelligence, system integration, and virtualization. He has been working for the Bursa Malaysia (formerly Kuala Lumpur Stock Exchange) and Shell IT International previously, which prepared him with rich integration experience across different platforms.

He strongly believes that great system implementation delivers precious value to the business, and integration of various systems across different platforms shall always be a part of it, just as people from different cultures and diversities are able to live in harmony in most of the major cities.

Antonio Radesca has over 15 years of programming experience. He has a degree in Computer Science and is interested in architectures, programming languages, and enterprise development. He has worked at some of the most important Italian companies, especially at Microsoft .NET Framework as a Developer and an Architect. His expertise spans .NET programming to mobile development on iOS, Android, and Windows Phone.

www.PacktPub.com

Support files, eBooks, discount offers and more

You might want to visit www.PacktPub.com for support files and downloads related to your book.

Did you know that Packt offers eBook versions of every book published, with PDF and ePub files available? You can upgrade to the eBook version at www.PacktPub.com and as a print book customer, you are entitled to a discount on the eBook copy. Get in touch with us at service@packtpub.com for more details.

At www.PacktPub.com, you can also read a collection of free technical articles, sign up for a range of free newsletters and receive exclusive discounts and offers on Packt books and eBooks.

http://PacktLib.PacktPub.com

Do you need instant solutions to your IT questions? PacktLib is Packt's online digital book library. Here, you can access, read and search across Packt's entire library of books.

Why Subscribe?

- Fully searchable across every book published by Packt
- Copy and paste, print and bookmark content
- On demand and accessible via web browser

Free Access for Packt account holders

If you have an account with Packt at www.PacktPub.com, you can use this to access PacktLib today and view nine entirely free books. Simply use your login credentials for immediate access.

Table of Contents

Preface

Thanks for picking up this book. This is an example-driven book. You will learn about several generic containers and generic algorithms available in the .NET Framework and a couple of other majorly accepted APIs such as Power Collections and C5 by building several applications and programs.

Towards the end, several benchmarkings have been carried out to identify the best container for the job at hand.

What this book covers

Chapter 1, Why Generics?, introduces .NET Generics. We will examine the need for the invention of Generics in the .NET Framework. If you start with a feel of "Why should I learn Generics?", you will end with a feeling of "Why didn't I till now?"

Chapter 2, Lists, introduces you to several kinds of lists that .NET Generics has to offer. There are simple lists and associative lists. You shall see how simple lists can deliver amazing results avoiding any typecasting woes and boosting performance at the same time.

Chapter 3, Dictionaries, explains the need for associative containers and introduces you to the associative containers that .NET has to offer. If you need to keep track of one or multiple dependent variables while one independent variable changes, you need a dictionary.
For example, say you want to build a spell check or an autocomplete service, you need a dictionary. This chapter will walk you through this. Along the way, you will pick up some very important concepts.

Chapter 4, LINQ to Objects, explains LINQ to objects using extension methods. LINQ or Language Integrated Query is a syntax that allows us to query collections unanimously. In this chapter, we will learn about some standard LINQ Standard Query Operators (LSQO) and then use them in unison to orchestrate an elegant query for any custom need.

Chapter 5, Observable Collections, introduces observable collections. Observing events on collections has been inherently difficult. That's going to change forever, thanks to observable collections. You can now monitor your collections for any change; whether some elements are added to the collection, some of them are deleted, change locations, and so on. In this chapter, you will learn about these collections.

Chapter 6, Concurrent Collections, covers concurrent collections that appeared in .NET 4.0. Multi-threaded applications are ubiquitous and that's the new expectation of our generation. We are always busy and impatient, trying to get a lot of things done at once. So concurrency is here and it is here to stay for a long time. Historically, there was no inbuilt support for concurrency in generic collections. Programmers had to ensure concurrency through primitive thread locking. You can still do so, but you now have an option to use the concurrent version of generic collections that support concurrency natively. This greatly simplifies the code. In this chapter, you will learn how to use them to build some useful applications such as simulating a survey engine.

Chapter 7, Power Collections, introduces several generic algorithms in `PowerCollections` and some handy generic containers. This collection API came from Wintellect (`www.wintellect.com`) at the time when .NET Generics was not big and had some very useful collections. However, now .NET Generics has grown to support all those types and even more. So that makes most of the containers defined in `PowerCollections` outdated. However, there are a lot of good general purpose generic algorithms that you will need but which are missing from the .NET Generics API. That's the reason this chapter is included. In this chapter, you will see how these generic algorithms can be used with any generic container seamlessly.

Chapter 8, C5 Collections, introduces the C5 API. If you come from a Java background and are wondering where your hash and tree-based data structures, are this is the chapter to turn to. However, from the usage perspective, all the containers available in C5 can be augmented with generic containers available in the .NET Framework. You are free to use them. This API is also home to several great generic algorithms that make life a lot easier. In this chapter, you will walk through the different collections and algorithms that C5 offers.

Chapter 9, Patterns, Practices, and Performance, covers some best practices when dealing with Generics and introduces the benchmarking strategy. In this chapter, we will use benchmarking code to see how different generic containers perform and then declare a winner in that field. For example, benchmarking shows that if you need a set, then `HashSet<T>` in the .NET Framework is the fastest you can get.

Appendix A, Performance Cheat Sheet, is a cheat sheet with all the performance measures for all containers. Keeping this handy would be extremely useful when you want to decide which container to use for the job at hand.

Appendix B, Migration Cheat Sheet, will show you how to migrate code from STL/JCF/PowerCollections/.NET 1.0 to the latest .NET Framework-compliant code. Migration will never be easier. Using this cheat sheet, it will be a no brainer. This is great for seasoned C++, Java, or .NET developers who are looking for a quick reference to .NET Generics in the latest framework.

What you need for this book

You will need the following software to use this book:

- Visual Studio 2010 (any version will do, I have used the Ultimate Trial version)
- LINQPad

Instructions to download this software are given in the respective chapters where they are introduced.

Who this book is for

This book is for you, if you want to know what .NET Generics is all about and how it can help solve real-world problems. It is assumed that readers are familiar with C# program constructs such as variable declaration, looping, branching, and so on. No prior knowledge in .NET Generics or generic programming is required.

This book also offers handy migration tips from other generic APIs available in other languages, such as STL in C++ or JCF in Java. So if you are trying to migrate your code to the .NET platform from any of these, then this book will be helpful.

Last but not the least, this book ends with generic patterns, best practices, and performance analysis for several generic containers. So, if you are an architect or senior software engineer and have to define coding standards, this will be very handy as a showcase of proofs to your design decisions.

Conventions

In this book, you will find several headings appearing frequently.

To give clear instructions of how to complete a procedure or task, we use:

Time for action – heading

1. Action 1
2. Action 2
3. Action 3

Instructions often need some extra explanation so that they make sense, so they are followed with:

What just happened?

This heading explains the working of tasks or instructions that you have just completed.

You will also find some other learning aids in the book, including:

Pop quiz – heading

These are short, multiple choice questions intended to help you test your own understanding.

Have a go hero – heading

These set practical challenges and give you ideas for experimenting with what you have learned.

You will also find a number of styles of text that distinguish between different kinds of information. Here are some examples of these styles, and an explanation of their meaning.

Code words in text are shown as follows: "Suppose, I want to maintain a list of my students, then we can do that by using `ArrayList` to store a list of such `Student` objects."

A block of code is set as follows:

```
private T[] Sort<T>(T[] inputArray)
{
      //Sort input array in-place
      //and return the sorted array
      return inputArray;
}
```

When we wish to draw your attention to a particular part of a code block, the relevant lines or items are set in bold:

```
Enumerable.Range(1, 100).Reverse().ToList()
  .ForEach(n => nums.AddLast(n));
```

Any command-line input or output is written as follows:

```
Argument 1: cannot convert from 'int[]' to 'float[]'
```

New terms and **important words** are shown in bold. Words that you see on the screen, in menus or dialog boxes for example, appear in the text like this: "Then go to the **File** menu to create a console project."

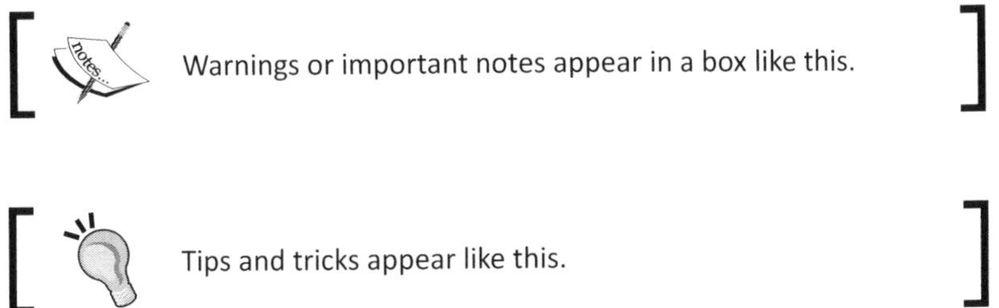

Warnings or important notes appear in a box like this.

Tips and tricks appear like this.

Reader feedback

Feedback from our readers is always welcome. Let us know what you think about this book—what you liked or may have disliked. Reader feedback is important for us to develop titles that you really get the most out of.

To send us general feedback, simply send an e-mail to `feedback@packtpub.com`, and mention the book title through the subject of your message.

If there is a topic that you have expertise in and you are interested in either writing or contributing to a book, see our author guide on `www.packtpub.com/authors`.

Customer support

Now that you are the proud owner of a Packt book, we have a number of things to help you to get the most from your purchase.

Downloading the example code

You can download the example code files for all Packt books you have purchased from your account at `http://www.packtpub.com`. If you purchased this book elsewhere, you can visit `http://www.packtpub.com/support` and register to have the files e-mailed directly to you.

Errata

Although we have taken every care to ensure the accuracy of our content, mistakes do happen. If you find a mistake in one of our books—maybe a mistake in the text or the code—we would be grateful if you would report this to us. By doing so, you can save other readers from frustration and help us improve subsequent versions of this book. If you find any errata, please report them by visiting `http://www.packtpub.com/support`, selecting your book, clicking on the **errata submission form** link, and entering the details of your errata. Once your errata are verified, your submission will be accepted and the errata will be uploaded to our website, or added to any list of existing errata, under the Errata section of that title.

Piracy

Piracy of copyright material on the Internet is an ongoing problem across all media. At Packt, we take the protection of our copyright and licenses very seriously. If you come across any illegal copies of our works, in any form, on the Internet, please provide us with the location address or website name immediately so that we can pursue a remedy.

Please contact us at `copyright@packtpub.com` with a link to the suspected pirated material.

We appreciate your help in protecting our authors, and our ability to bring you valuable content.

Questions

You can contact us at `questions@packtpub.com` if you are having a problem with any aspect of the book, and we will do our best to address it.

1

Why Generics?

A cat and a dog shouldn't share a bed. Neither should integers and floats.

Thanks for picking up the book! This means you care for Generics. This is similar to dropping a plastic bag in favor of our lonely planet.

We are living in an interesting era, where more and more applications are data driven. To store these different kinds of data, we need several data structures. Although the actual piece of data is different, that doesn't always necessarily mean that the type of data is different. For example, consider the following situations:

Let's say, we have to write an application to pull in tweets and Facebook wall updates for given user IDs. Although these two result sets will have different features, they can be stored in a similar list of items. The list is a generic list that can be programmed to store items of a given type, at compile time, to ensure type safety. This is also known as parametric polymorphism.

In this introductory chapter, I shall give you a few reasons why Generics is important.

An analogy

Here is an interesting analogy. Assume that there is a model *hand pattern*:

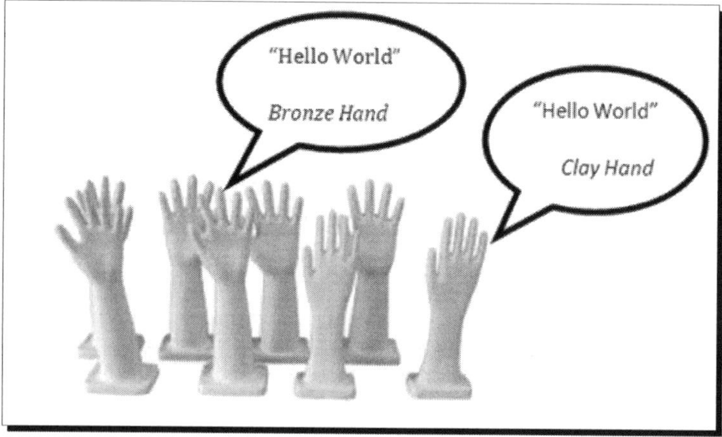

If we fill the pattern with *clay*, we get a *clay-modeled hand*. If we fill it with *bronze*, we get a hand model replica *made of bronze*. Although the material in these two hand models are very different, they share the same pattern (or they were created using the same algorithm, if you would agree to that term, in a broader sense).

Reason 1: Generics can save you a lot of typing

Extrapolating the algorithm part, let's say we have to implement some sorting algorithm; however, data types can vary for the input. To solve this, you can use overloading, as follows:

```
//Overloaded sort methods
private int[] Sort(int[] inputArray)
{
    //Sort input array in-place
    //and return the sorted array
    return inputArray;
}
private float[] Sort(float[] inputArray)
{
    //Sort input array in-place
    //and return the sorted array
    return inputArray;
}
```

However, you have to write the same code for all numeric data types supported by .NET. That's bad. Wouldn't it be cool if the compiler could somehow be instructed at compile time to yield the right version for the given data type at runtime? That's what Generics is about. Instead of writing the same method for all data types, you can create one single method with a symbolic data type. This will instruct the compiler to yield a specific code for the specific data type at runtime, as follows:

```
private T[] Sort<T>(T[] inputArray)
{
      //Sort input array in-place
      //and return the sorted array
      return inputArray;
}
```

`T` is short for **Type**. If you replace `T` with anything, it will still compile; because it's the symbolic name for the generic type that will get replaced with a real type in the .NET type system at runtime.

So once we have this method, we can call it as follows:

```
int[] inputArray = { 1, 2, 0, 3 };
inputArray = Sort<int>(inputArray);
```

However, if you hover your mouse pointer right after the first brace (`(`), you can see in the tooltip, the expected type is already `int[]`, as shown in the following screenshot:

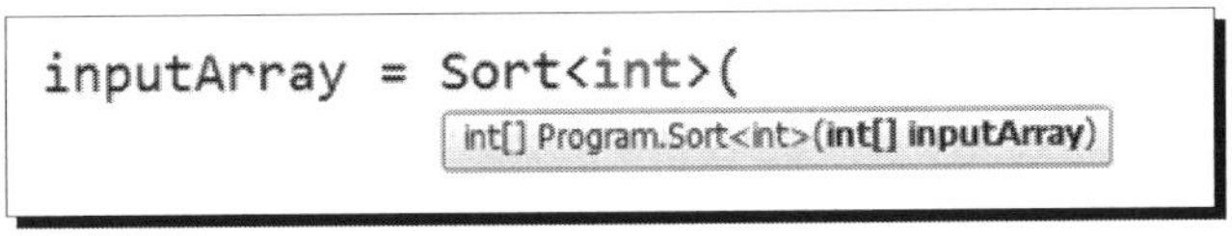

```
inputArray = Sort<int>(
                int[] Program.Sort<int>(int[] inputArray)
```

That's the beauty of Generics. As we had mentioned `int` inside `<` and `>`, the compiler now knows for sure that it should expect only an `int[]` as the argument to the `Sort<T>()` method.

However, if you change `int` to `float`, you will see that the expectation of the compiler also changes. It then expects a `float[]` as the argument, as shown:

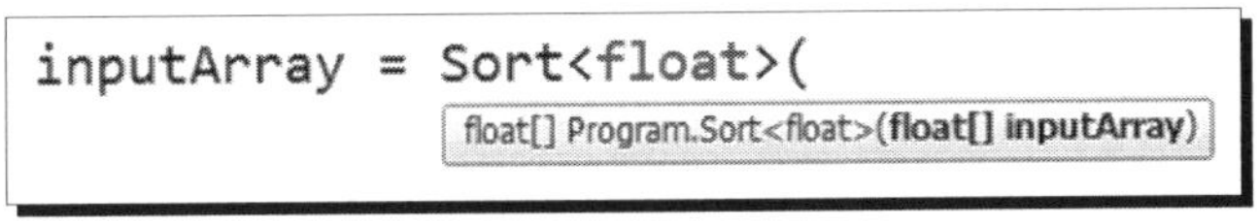

```
inputArray = Sort<float>(
                float[] Program.Sort<float>(float[] inputArray)
```

Now if you think you can fool the compiler by passing an integer array while it is asking for a float, you are wrong. That's blocked by compiler-time type checking. If you try something similar to the following:

```
int[] inputArray = { 1, 2, 0, 3 };
inputArray = Sort<float>(inputArray);
```

You will get the following compiler error:

```
Argument 1: cannot convert from 'int[]' to 'float[]'
```

This means that Generics ensures strong type safety and is an integral part of the .NET framework, which is type safe.

Reason 2: Generics can save you type safety woes, big time

The previous example was about a sorting algorithm that doesn't change with data type. There are other things that become easier while dealing with Generics.

There are broadly two types of operations that can be performed on a list of elements:

1. Location centric operations
2. Data centric operations

Adding some elements at the front and deleting elements at an index are a couple of examples of location-centric operations on a list of data. In such operations, the user doesn't need to know about the data. It's just some memory manipulation at best.

However, if the request is to delete every odd number from a list of integers, then that's a data-centric operation. To be able to successfully process this request, the method has to know how to determine whether an integer is odd or not. This might sound trivial for an integer; however, the point is the logic of determining whether an element is a candidate for deletion or not, is not readily known to the compiler. It has to be delegated.

Before Generics appeared in .NET 2.0, people were using (and unfortunately these are still in heavy use) non-generic collections that are capable of storing a list of objects.

As an object sits at the top of the hierarchy in the .NET object model, this opens floodgates. If such a list exists and is exposed, people can put in just about anything in that list and the compiler won't complain a bit, because to the compiler everything is fine as they are all objects.

So, if a loosely typed collection such as `ArrayList` is used to store objects of type `T`, then for any data-centric operation, these must be down-casted to `T` again. Now, if somehow an entry that is not `T`, is put into the list, then this down-casting will result in an exception at runtime.

Suppose, I want to maintain a list of my students, then we can do that by using `ArrayList` to store a list of such `Student` objects:

```
class Student
{
    public char Grade
    {
        get; set;
    }

    public int Roll
    {
        get; set;
    }

    public string Name
    {
        get; set;
    }
}

//List of students
ArrayList studentList = new ArrayList();

Student newStudent = new Student();
newStudent.Name = "Dorothy";
newStudent.Roll = 1;
newStudent.Grade = 'A';

studentList.Add(newStudent);

newStudent = new Student();
newStudent.Name = "Sam";
newStudent.Roll  = 2;
newStudent.Grade ='B';

studentList.Add(newStudent);

foreach (Object s in studentList)
{
    //Type-casting. If s is anything other than a student
```

```
        //or a derived class, this line will throw an exception.
        //This is a data centric operation.
        Student currentStudent = (Student)s;
        Console.WriteLine("Roll # " + currentStudent.Roll + " " +
                          currentStudent.Name + " Scored a " +
                          curr entStudent.Grade);
    }
```

What's the problem with this approach?

All this might look kind of okay, because we have been taking great care not to put anything else in the list other than `Student` objects. So, while we de-reference them after boxing, we don't see any problem. However, as the `ArrayList` can take any object as the argument, we could, by mistake, write something similar to the following:

```
studentList.Add("Generics"); //Fooling the compiler
```

As `ArrayList` is a loosely typed collection, it doesn't ensure *compile-time type checking*. So, this code won't generate any compile-time warning, and eventually it will throw the following exception at runtime when we try to de-reference this, to put in a `Student` object.

Then, it will throw an `InvalidCastException`:

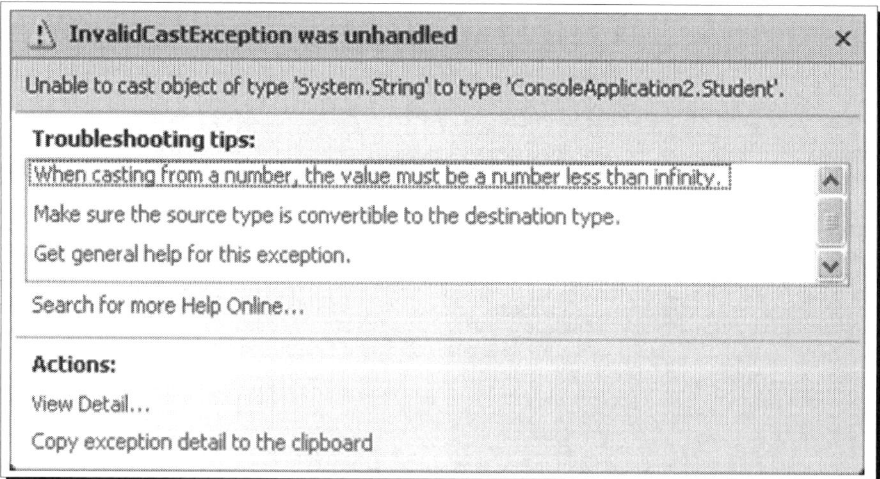

What the exception in the preceding screenshot actually tells us is that Generics is a string and it can't cast that to `Student`, for the obvious reason that the compiler has no clue how to convert a string to a `Student` object.

Unfortunately, this only gets noticed by the compiler during runtime. With Generics, we can catch this sort of error early on at compile time.

Following is the generic code to maintain that list:

```
//Creating a generic list of type "Student".
//This is a strongly-typed-collection of type "Student".
//So nothing, except Student or derived class objects from Student
//can be put in this list myStudents
List<Student> myStudents = new List<Student>();

//Adding a couple of students to the list
Student newStudent = new Student();
newStudent.Name = "Dorothy";
newStudent.Roll = 1;
newStudent.Grade = 'A';

myStudents.Add(newStudent);

newStudent = new Student();
newStudent.Name = "Sam";
newStudent.Roll = 2;
newStudent.Grade = 'B';

myStudents.Add(newStudent);

//Looping through the list of students
foreach (Student currentStudent in myStudents)
{
      //There is no need to type cast. Because compiler
      //already knows that everything inside this list
      //is a Student.
      Console.WriteLine("Roll # " + currentStudent.Roll + " " +
                        currentStudent.Name + " Scored a " +
                        currentStudent.Grade);
}
```

The reasons mentioned earlier are the basic benefits of Generics. Also with Generics, language features such as LINQ and completely new languages such as F# came into existence. So, this is important. I hope you are convinced that Generics is a great programming tool and you are ready to learn it.

Reason 3: Generics leads to faster code

In the .NET Framework, everything is an object so it's okay to throw in anything to the non-generic loosely typed collection such as `ArrayList`, as shown in the previous example. This means we have to box (up-cast to object for storing things in the `Arraylist`; this process is implicit) and unbox (down-cast the object to the desired object type). This leads to slower code.

Here is the result of an experiment. I created two lists, one `ArrayList` and one `List<int>` to store integers:

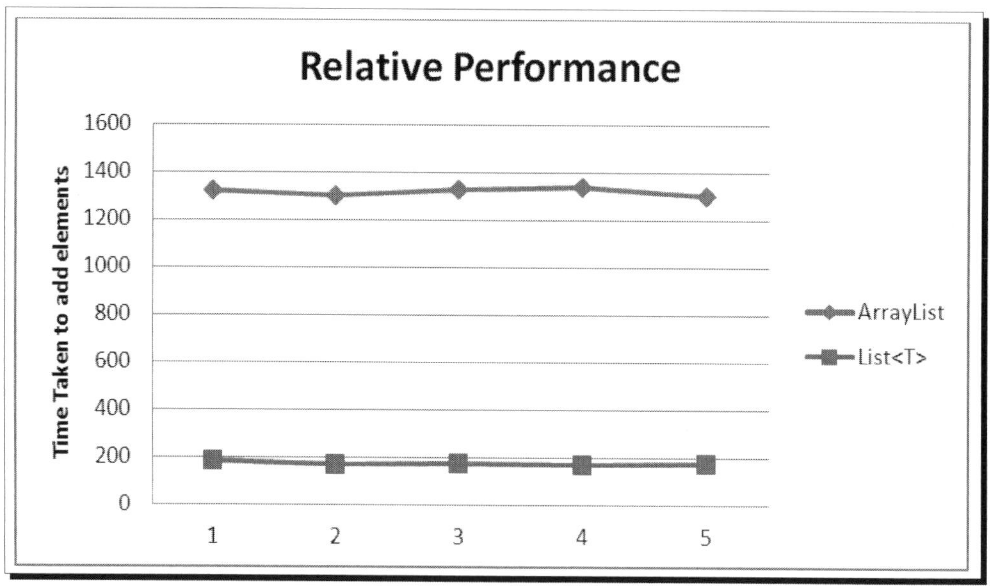

And following is the data that drove the preceding graph:

ArrayList	List<T>
1323	185
1303	169
1327	172
1340	169
1302	172

The previous table mentions the total time taken in milliseconds to add 10,000,000 elements to the list. Clearly, generic collection is about seven times faster.

Reason 4: Generics is now ubiquitous in the .NET ecosystem

Look around. If you care to develop any non-trivial application, you are better off using some of the APIs built for the specific job at hand. Most of the APIs available rely heavily on strong typing and they achieve this through Generics. We shall discuss some of these APIs (LINQ, PowerCollections, C5) that are being predominantly used by the .NET community in this book.

So far, I have been giving you reasons to learn Generics. At this point, I am sure, you are ready to experiment with .NET Generics. Please check out the instructions in the next section to install the necessary software if you don't have it already.

Setting up the environment

If you are already running any 2010 version of Visual Studio that lets you create C# windows and console projects, you don't have to do anything and you can skip this section.

You can download and install the Visual Studio Trial from `http://www.microsoft.com/download/en/details.aspx?displaylang=en&id=12752`.

Once you are done, you should see the following in your program menu:

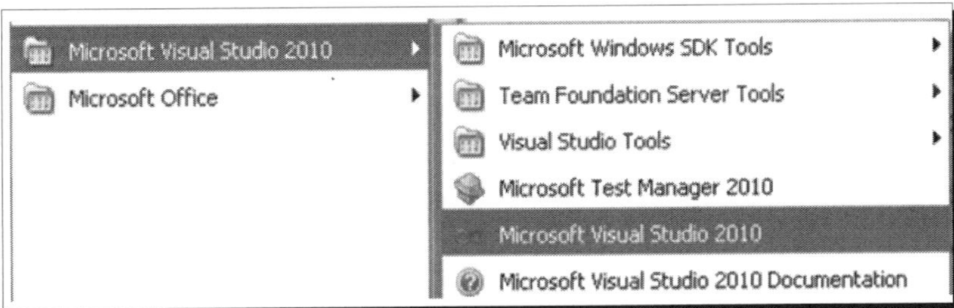

After this, start the program highlighted in the preceding screenshot **Microsoft Visual Studio 2010**.

Then go to the **File** menu to create a console project:

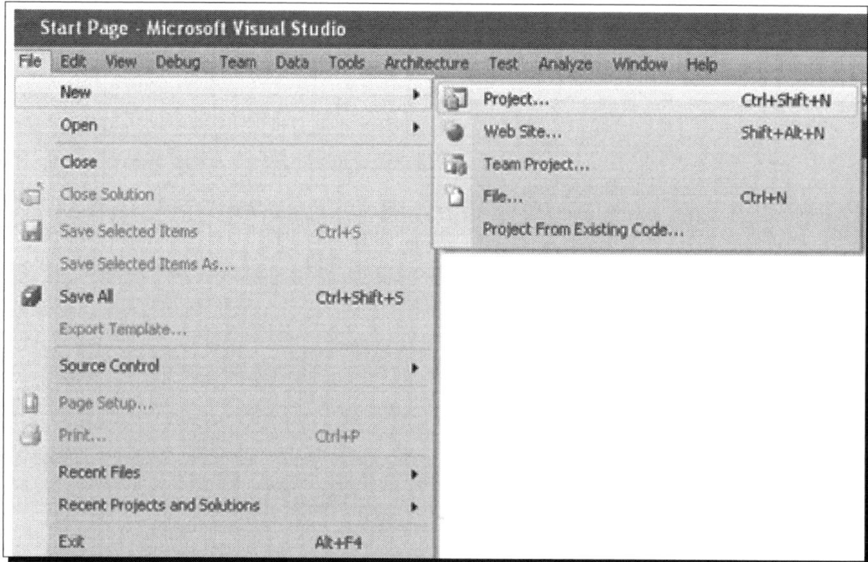

Now, once that is created, make sure the following namespaces are available:

```
using System;
using System.Collections.Generic;
using System.Collections.
using System.Linq;          {} Concurrent
using System.Text;          {} Generic
                            {} ObjectModel
                            {} Specialized
```

If these are available, you have done the right setup. Congratulations!

Summary

My objective for this chapter was to make sure you get why Generics is important. Following are the points again in bullets:

- It ensures compile-time type checking, so type safety is ensured.
- It can yield the right code for the data type thrown at it at runtime, thus saving us a lot of typing.
- It is very fast (about seven times) compared to its non-generic cousins for value types.
- It is everywhere in the .NET ecosystem. API/framework developers trust the element of least surprise and they know people are familiar with Generics and their syntax. So they try to make sure their APIs also seem familiar to the users.

In the end, we did an initial setup of the environment; so we are ready to build and run applications using .NET Generics. From the next chapter, we shall learn about .NET Generic containers and classes. In the next chapter, we shall discuss the Generic container `List<T>` that will let you store any type of data in a type safe way. Now that you know that's important, let's go there.

2
Lists

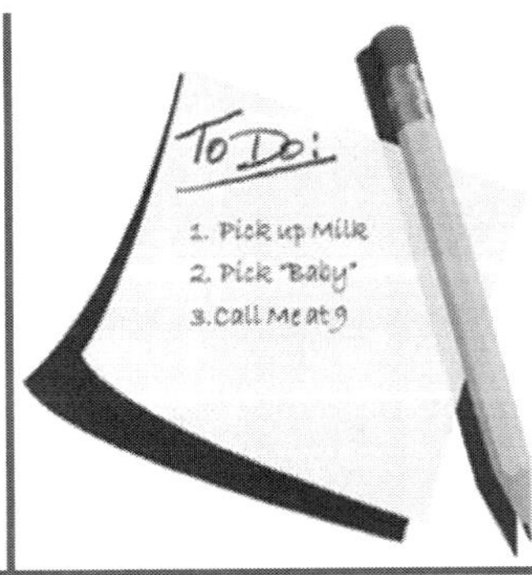

Don't forget the milk, honey!

Lists are everywhere, starting from the laundry list and grocery list to the checklist on your smartphone's task manager. There are two types of lists. Simple lists, which just store some items disregarding the order allowing duplicates; and other types which don't allow duplicates. These second types of lists which don't allow duplicates are called sets in mathematics. The other broad category of list is associative list, where each element in some list gets mapped to another element in another list.

In this chapter, we shall learn about these generic containers and related methods. We shall learn when to use which list-based container depending on the situation.

Reading this chapter and following the exercises you will learn the following:

- Why bother learning about generic lists?
- Types of generic lists and how to use them

- Give proper rationale for choosing a generic list such as one container over the other
- How to create custom generic list-based containers

So let's get on with it...

Why bother learning about generic lists?

Let us see why generic lists are important:

- It ensures compile-time type checking. So type-unsafe code becomes a thing of the past.
- It saves us a lot of typing, because compiler can generate type-safe code for generic types at runtime. So the same code works for different data types.
- It is faster in many cases than its non-generic cousins, because it removes the need to box and unbox (also known as type-casting) from the code.
- It makes source code much cleaner than its older, non-generic, unsafe cousins.

In this chapter, you shall find examples of how generic list-based containers make these possible. Happy listing!

Types of generic lists

There are mainly three types of lists you can imagine or would ever need:

1. Simple list: It allows duplicates by default.
2. Sets: It doesn't allow duplicates by default.
3. Associative list: It helps to represent a relationship between two types of entities.

A simple list is just a collection of items. Say a laundry list, a grocery list, a task list, a list of courses. The elements in a simple container don't associate them with any other element. There are several generic container classes to represent simple lists. They are Stack<T>, Queue<T>, List<T>, LinkedList<T>, and SortedSet<T>. These are generic implementations of classic data structures. So Stack<T> is a **Last In First Out** (**LIFO**) list, Queue<T> is a **First In First Out** (**FIFO**) list, List<T> is a simple unordered list, and so is LinkedList<T>. But List<T> supports random integer indexing natively, while the others don't.

Sets are simple lists that don't allow duplicates. All sets implement the interface ISet<T>. There are two set implementations HashSet<T> and SortedSet<T>. HashSet<T> doesn't maintain the order of elements, while SortedSet<T> keeps the elements sorted, if it knows how to sort the type. For custom types, you can pass a custom IComparer<T> instance to delegate the task of comparing. For HashSet<T>, you can pass IEqualityComparer<T> for custom equality comparison.

An associative list, as the name suggests, brings in an association between two different entities and represents them in a single list for example, marks obtained by a student in a different semester of a course, share values for a company over the years, and so on. To represent these type of lists, there is an interface IDictionary<TKey,TValue> and SortedList<TKey,TValue> is a derived class that implements this interface. So we can use SortedList<TKey,TValue> to represent any associative list in .NET Generics. SortedList<TKey,TValue> is also a list. This is implemented using an array. So unlike other IDictionary<TKey,TValue> implementations, SortedList<TKey,TValue> supports indexing over keys and values. So the order of insertion in a SortedList determines the order of elements; unlike other IDictionary<TKey,TValue> implementations, as we shall see in the next chapter.

If you were wondering what the heck are TKey and TValue, they are short and quite traditional ways of representing the type of key and type of value respectively. As generic lists can support any type, they are represented in this way. So at runtime the compiler generates appropriate code for the specified data type. This greatly helps to reduce code duplication and type mismatch issues.

In a nutshell:

Stack<T>	This is a generic Stack implementation. This is first in last out.
Queue<T>	This is a generic Queue implementation. This is a first in first out list.
List<T>	This is a generic implementation of a simple list. This offers native random zero based integer indexing like an array.
LinkedList<T>	This is a generic implementation of a classic double-linked list. No native random indexing is offered.
HashSet<T>	This is a generic Set implementation. The elements are not sorted. For custom equality comparison, you can pass the IEqualityComparer<T> instance.
SortedSet<T>	This is a generic Set implementation. The value type elements remain sorted, by default. For reference types, we have to pass custom-comparer objects for custom element sorting; you can use the IComparer<T> instance.
SortedList<T>	Sometimes you want an associative container, but you still want to be able to access each key-value pair, like you do in a plain old array using the index. Then all you need is a SortedList<T>.

Now that we have some basic idea about these generic list based containers, we shall see how these can be used to solve some real-world problems. Let's get started with a fun app!

A generic collection can contain objects of value and reference types. This means you can create nested types.

For example, if you want a list of stacks, you can get that by declaring `List<Stack<T>>`.

If you want a `SortedList` of integer keys and associate a list of string values with each such integer key, you can write `SortedList<int,List<string>>`.

Checking whether a sequence is a palindrome or not

All the following sequences share a common attribute. They all read the same both ways, save for the punctuations

"Madam I'm Adam"

"A Man, A Plan, A Canal, Panama!!"

12321

Detroit-Chicago-Detroit (This reads same word by word backwards, unlike others that read the same character by character.)

A Toyota

These types of sequences are called palindromes. A sequence is palindromic too, if the contents read the same both ways, for example, A-B-A. In this example, we shall see how a generic stack (that is, a `Stack<T>` instance) can be used to implement this, so that we can detect whether a given sequence is a palindrome or not for any given type that knows how to compare itself (that is, implements the `IComparable` interface).

So the task at hand is to build a generic palindrome checker that can check whether any sequence is a palindrome or not. All we have to do is let it know the type of the sequence at runtime.

The algorithm to find whether a sequence is a palindrome or not is really simple. If we arrange the tasks to be done in order to check whether the given sequence is a palindrome or not, it will be like:

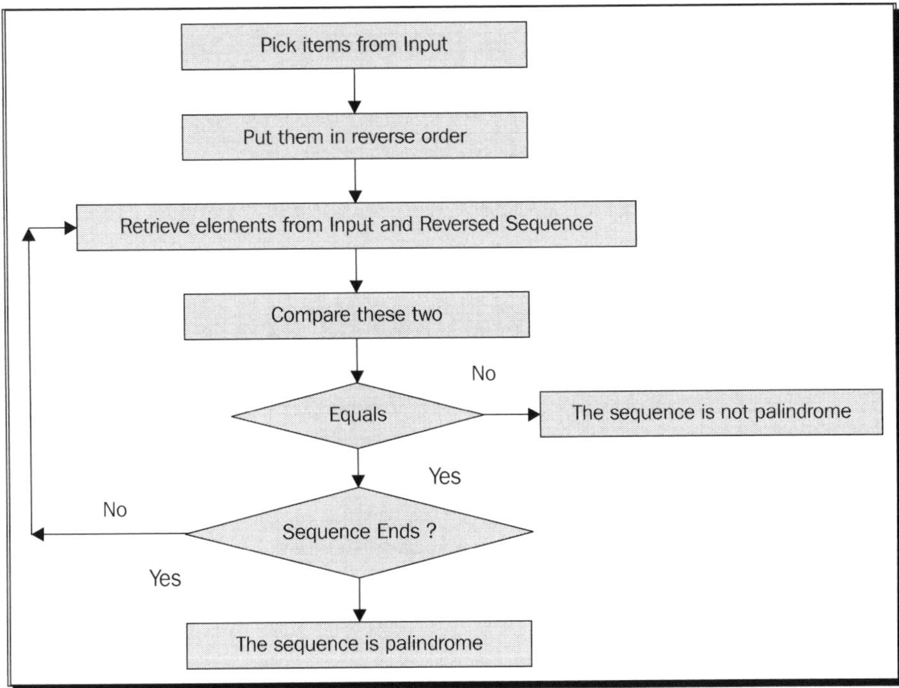

The sequence can be of any type; char, string, integer, float, and so on to name a few. Also, note that the algorithm is not different for all these different types. However, we shall have to write several methods for supporting several data types.

However, if we use Generics we can avoid this code duplication for each type. We can write a single method (also known as **Generic Method**) that can write the data type-specific code at runtime depending on what type of data type we want. The tradition is to use the letter *T* (which is short for Type) to create the generic method. When we consume this method, we pass concrete Types that conform to the standard expectations from the Type; like in this case, we expect the Type to implement `IComparable`.

The heart of the solution is to reverse the elements of the input sequence. This can be done by a stack. Since we want to make the method generic, we need a generic stack.

Time for action – creating the generic stack as the buffer

Follow the given steps:

1. Create a console application project. Call it `Palindrome Checker`.
2. Create a method called `IsPalindromic()` with the following signature:

   ```
   public static bool IsPalindromic<T>(IEnumerable<T> inputSequence)
               where T:IComparable
   {
        Stack<T> buffer = new Stack<T>();
        return true;
   }
   ```

3. Add the following code in the `Main()` method:

   ```
   static void Main(string[] args)
   {
        bool status = IsPalindromic<char>(new int[] { 1, 2, 2, 1 });
   }
   ```

4. Try to compile the program.

What just happened?

You will see a compiler error as shown in the following screenshot:

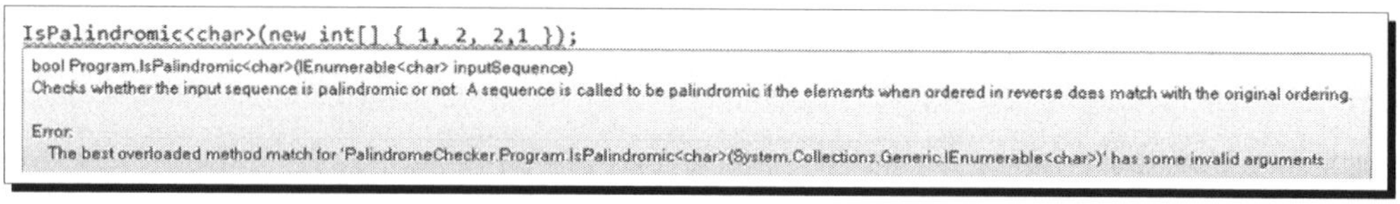

```
IsPalindromic<char>(new int[] { 1, 2, 2,1 });
bool Program.IsPalindromic<char>(IEnumerable<char> inputSequence)
Checks whether the input sequence is palindromic or not. A sequence is called to be palindromic if the elements when ordered in reverse does match with the original ordering.

Error:
  The best overloaded method match for 'PalindromeChecker.Program.IsPalindromic<char>(System.Collections.Generic.IEnumerable<char>)' has some invalid arguments
```

Let's see why that compile-time error occurred. Before that, let's learn a little more about generic stacks.

Creating a generic stack is very easy. Here is how:

```
Stack<T> myGenericStack = new Stack<T>();
```

So if you want a generic stack to be used to store a stack of string, then you change `T` with string as follows:

```
Stack<string> myCDs = new Stack<string>();
```

If you want a stack of integers, you just say:

```
Stack<int> opCodes = new Stack<int>();
```

If you are dealing with reference types, then you can declare a stack of base types and put derived types in that. Say if `D` is a class that implements an `ID` interface, then if you create a stack of `ID` objects, you can put `ID` objects in the `Stack` as follows:

```
Stack<ID> somethings = new Stack<ID>();
Somethings.Push(new ID());
```

However, the method needs to know how to compare the elements in the buffer. So now the obvious question you might have is, if we write the code using a generic place holder (`T` in this case) which gets replaced by the original data type at runtime, how will the method know at compile time how to compare variables of such data type?

Well, that's a very good question and the answer lies in the very first line of the method. Let's take a close look at it:

```
public static bool IsPalindromic<T>(IEnumerable<T> inputSequence)
where T:IComparable
```

The keyword `where` is used to constrain the types that can be used as a valid argument in the generic method `IsPalindromic<T>()`, we just created. `where T:IComparable` means `T` has to be a type that implements the `IComparable` interface. This syntax is known as **Constraints in Generics**.

Now, let's get back to the compilation error part. Generics ensure compile-time type checking as follows:

```
bool status = IsPalindromic<char>(new int[] { 1, 2, 2, 1 });
```

In this code, `IsPalindromic<char>` promises that everything that follows in the argument to this method will be of type character. However, we have an integer array as the input sequence. This is causing a type mismatch and thus is caught at compile time.

We are passing an array as the parameter, where the method expects something of type `IEnumerable<T>`. This is possible because `IEnumerable<T>` inherits from `IEnumerable` and good old arrays implement `IEnumerable` too. Thus, `IEnumerable` serves as a bridge between pre-generic collections and generic collections.

Time for action – completing the rest of the method

Follow the given steps:

1. Add the following code after the initialization of the buffer in the source, as carried out previously in step 2:

```
foreach (T element in inputSequence)
{
  buffer.Push(element);
}
```

   `Count()` and `ElementAt()` are extension methods and are available at `System.Linq` namespace in .NET Framework 3.5 and above. You can get it with Visual Studio 2008 and above. So please include that namespace:

```
for (int i = 0; i < inputSequence.Count(); i++)
{
  if(buffer.Pop().CompareTo(inputSequence.ElementAt(i))==0)
    continue;
  else
    return false;
}
```

   Make sure you retain the last `return true;` statement.

2. Replace the content of the `Main()` method with the following:

```
static void Main(string[] args)
{
  //Checking if a string (Which is basically a sequence of
  //characters)
  bool status1 = IsPalindromic<char>("LIRIL");
  //Checking if an array of string is palindromic
  bool status2 = IsPalindromic<string>(new string[]
    {"mango","apple","mango"});
  //Checking if an array of int is palindromic
  bool status3 = IsPalindromic<int>(new int[]
    { 1,2,3,4,5,6,0,6,5,4,3,2,1 });
  //Checking if an array of float is palindromic
  bool status4 = IsPalindromic<float>(new float[]
    { 1.34F,2.34F,43.1F});
  Console.WriteLine(status1 + " " + status2 + " " +
    status3 + " " + status4);
}
```

3. Run the program.

What just happened?

The program shall print the following to the console:

```
True True True False
```

The following looping construct:

```
foreach (T element in inputSequence)
{
  buffer.Push(element);
}
```

pushes all the elements in the input sequence to a stack. The stack is a last in first out list. It keeps the elements in reverse order. So if you want to add an element to the top of the stack, you should use the push method.

So when the method is called by `bool status1 = IsPalindromic<char>("GENERICS");` it stores the characters of the input sequence in the internal generic stack buffer as follows:

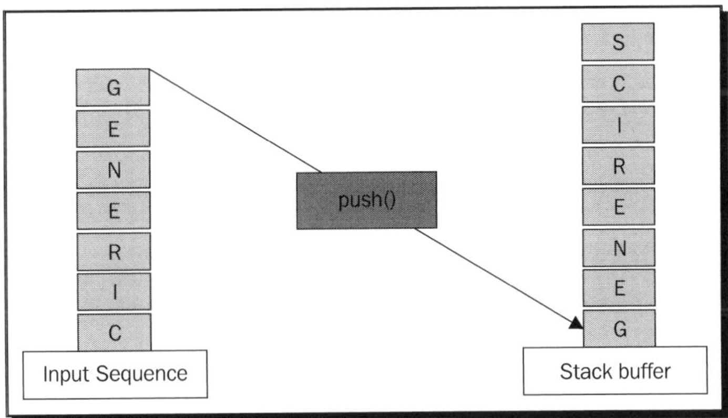

`buffer.Pop()` returns the top-most element from the stack and removes that from the stack. The `ElementAt()` method returns the *ith* element from the input sequence. As long as these two are equal, the sequence might be a palindrome. So, we must continue going through the input sequence. However, if they mismatch at any point, it becomes evident immediately that the input sequence is not a palindrome. Thus, we can return `False`. However, if we can get to the end of the input sequence without encountering a mismatch, the input sequence is a palindrome and thus we have to return `True`.

Let's now try to decode the output. Among four input sequences in the `Main()` method, the first three are palindromes. However, the last one doesn't read the same both ways and surely isn't a palindrome. Output matches that. We get `True` for the first three input sequences and `False` for the last one.

Any type that implements `IComparable` would work. Other types will fail.

Designing a generic anagram finder

Generics are not limited to lists and you can even mix parameterized types with specialized types as well. For instance, what if you want to store the frequency of occurrence of a string, number, or a symbol. While the type of what you keep the frequency of is unknown or undecided, however you see that the frequency itself is always a number. Let's take a look at how we can implement that using anagrams as an example.

Anagrams are as fascinating as palindromes. Two sequences are said to be anagrams of each another, when they share the same number of elements in the same frequency.

For example, two strings "The eyes" and "They see" both have the same number of characters, and the frequency of each character in these two strings is the same. Both of them have a single "T", a couple of "e"s, and so on. Thus, they are anagrams of each other.

`http://www.anagrammy.com/` organizes a competition for the best anagrams each month. Assume your friend wants to participate and is now seeking your help to develop a program that can find anagrams of a given word. Let's get into action and help your buddy.

A strategy to check whether two sequences are anagrams of each other or not is really simple. We need a container that would let us store each unique element of the sequence and their frequency of appearance in the sequence.

For example, the string "The eyes" will be stored in such a container as follows:

Element	Frequency
T	1
H	1
E	3
Y	1
S	1

If another string stored in the same way shares the same frequency of characters, then that will be an anagram of "The eyes". So, if we deduct 1 from the frequency as soon as we get the same character in the second string; we shall have all zeros in the frequency column of the preceding table at the end of scanning the second string; in this case, we are dealing with two anagrams.

This algorithm is applicable to any type of anagram sequence, not only for strings. So, we can write a generic method to check whether two sequences are anagrams of each other or not, for any type.

Time for action – creating the method

Follow the given steps:

1. Create a console application called `Ganagram` (short form for generic anagram). This is a showcase of `SortedList<TKey,TValue>`, solving a real problem.

2. Add the following method in the `Program.cs` file:

```
public static bool IsAnagram<T>(IEnumerable<T> first,
IEnumerable<T> second)
{
  SortedList<T, int> val = new SortedList<<T, int>();

  foreach (T element in first)
  {
    if (!val.ContainsKey(element))
      val.Add(element, 1);
    else
      val[element]++;
  }

  foreach (T element in second)
  {
    if (val.ContainsKey(element))
      val[element]--;
    else
    return false;
  }
  foreach (T element in val.Keys)
  {
    if (val[element] != 0)
    return false;
```

```
    }
    return true;
}
```

3. Call this method from the `Main()` method of the console application as follows:

```
static void Main(string[] args)
{
  bool status  = IsAnagram<char>("dream", "armed");
  bool status2 = IsAnagram<string>("yesterday today tomorrow".
    Split(' '),

  "tomorrow today yesterday".Split (' '));
  bool status3 = IsAnagram<int>(new int[]{1,2,3},
    new int[]{ 3,4,1});

  Console.WriteLine(status + " " + status2 + " " + status3);
}
```

4. Compile and execute the program.

What just happened?

As you execute the program, you will see the following output:

```
True True False
```

`"dream"` and `"armed"` are anagrams of each other so the first one returned `True`. So are the sentences where the words `"Yesterday"`, `"Today"`, and `"Tomorrow"` appear in different locations. However, the last sequence of integers are not anagrams of each other because the second one has a four and the first one doesn't. That's why the generic method returns `False` for that one.

Ok. So the method works well. Let's see how it works.

`SortedList<T, int>` means a sorted list where the data type of the key is `T` and that of the value is an integer, there is no duplicate entry, and the entries in the `SortedList<T,int>` are sorted.

`SortedList` can be used to store key-value pairs as long as the keys are unique. This is the condition imposed by `IDictionary` and thus has to be followed by all `IDictionary` implementations. A sequence can be expressed as a list of key-value pairs as shown earlier. Keys are the individual elements of the sequence and the value for each key is the frequency of that particular element in the sequence.

At runtime, when we pass two strings, the compiler generates code for `SortedList<char, int>`.

In the next loop, we are adding all the elements from the first sequence to this `SortedList`. The `ContainsKey()` method returns `true` if the key is present in the sorted list. Otherwise it returns `false`.

> **Warning!**
>
> As the `SortedList` can only store key-value pairs with unique keys, it is good practice to check for the existence of the key before trying to add it. If the key is already present, it will throw the following exception:

The following screenshot shows the exception that occurs when we want to add a duplicate key:

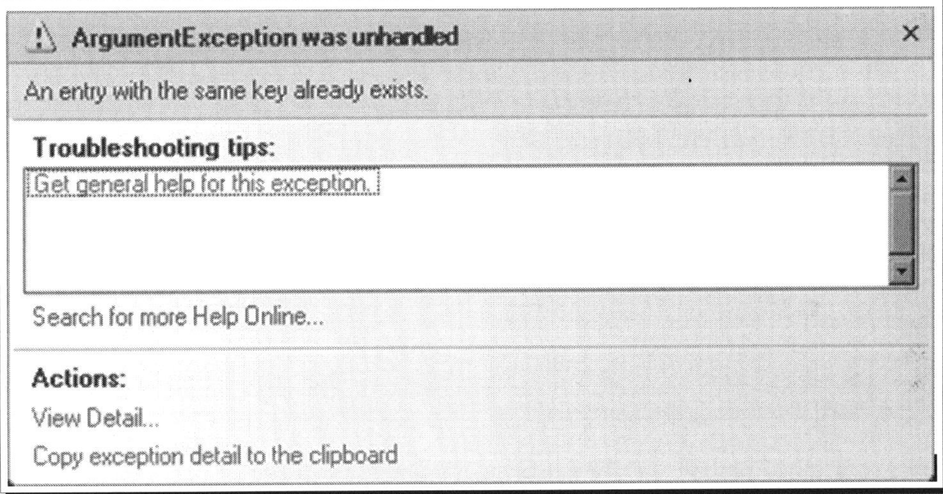

`val.Add(element, 1);` adds the element for the first time, when it is not present in the `SortedList`. However, from the second time onwards the frequency of the element is increased by the code snippet `val[element]++;`.

The `SortedList` class implements the `IDictionary<TKey,TValue>` interface. So there is a concrete implementation for `SortedList` of the interface indexer:

```
TValue this[TKey key] { get; set; }
```

This is why the corresponding value can be obtained by passing the key in square brackets. So in the statement `val[element]++; val[element]` refers to the corresponding frequency of the key, whose value is stored in the element. Thus, `val[element]++` means increasing the corresponding element by unity.

In the third loop, we are iterating over the second sequence. If the sequence contains an element not present in the `SortedList` already, we don't need to look any further. They can't be anagrams. However, if the current element of the second sequence is present in the `SortedList` as a key, then we must decrease the frequency by unity; and continue to do so as long as we don't hit the end of the second sequence or encounter an element that is not present as a key in the `SortedList` already.

The last loop checks whether all the values of the `SortedList` are zero or not. If they are, both the sequences are anagrams to each other, otherwise they aren't. We return the status accordingly.

Have a go hero – use this method to find anagrams from a dictionary

Now that we have the method that can find whether two given sequences are palindromes to each other or not, can you write a program that uses this method and finds all the anagrams of the given word? You can use any dictionary you want. You can verify your program by several word anagram duos listed at `http://sudipta.posterous.com/found-these-word-beauties-on-the-taxi-ride-ho`.

Life is full of priorities, let's bring some order there

As gadget addicts, there are so many gadgets we desire to buy, but often our budget is limiting. So, let's keep a prioritized list of gadgets we hope to buy.

Priority queues come to our help here.

Let's see how we can create our own implementation of the generic priority queue. .NET doesn't offer a built-in generic priority queue.

As there can be more than one gadget that you want with the same zest, so the shopping list can have more than one element with the same priority. We shall represent the priority queue as a `SortedList<TKey,TValue>`, where the priority will be represented by any type that can be compared for equality and the values will be represented by a list of values of type `TValue`.

Time for action – creating the data structure for the prioritized shopping list

Follow the given steps:

1. Create a console application.
2. Add a class called `PriorityQueue` to the project. Change the signature of the class header as follows:

   ```
   public class PriorityQueue<Tkey, TValue> where Tkey : IComparable
   ```

3. The heart of this `PriorityQueue` is a `SortedList`. I want to call it `innerDS`, add this private variable as follows:

   ```
   private SortedList<Tkey, List<TValue>> innerDS;
   public PriorityQueue()
   {
     innerDS = new SortedList<Tkey, List<TValue>>();
   }
   ```

4. Go to the `Main()` method of the console app and add the following code:

   ```
   PriorityQueue<int, string> gadgets = new PriorityQueue<int,
   string>();
   ```

5. Try to compile. You will see that it compiles. It will run too. But don't expect any visible output yet.

What just happened?

When you run the console application, you will see nothing happens. But in the background the compiler created a type-safe copy of the generic priority queue, where the priorities are of type integer and the values are of type string.

Now, go and change the priority queue declaration as follows:

```
PriorityQueue<TimeZone, string> set = new PriorityQueue<TimeZone,
string>();
```

and try to compile. You will get the following compile-time error:

```
There is no implicit reference conversion from 'System.TimeZone' to
'System.IComparable'.
```

This will happen because the `TimeZone` class doesn't implement the `Compare()` method of the `IComparable` interface.

Time for action – let's add some gadgets to the list and see them

Follow the given steps:

1. Add the following code, in the same `PriorityQueue` class:

```
/// <summary>
/// Adds a new entry to the priority queue
/// </summary>
/// <param name="key">priority of the item.</param>
/// <param name="value">the item itself.</param>
public void Enque(Tkey key, TValue value)
{
  if (!innerDS.ContainsKey(key))//O(log n)
  {
    List<TValue > vals = new List<TValue>();
    vals.Add(value);
    innerDS.Add(key, vals);
  }
  else
  if (!innerDS[key].Contains(value))
  innerDS[key].Add(value);
}
```

2. Add this method in the `PriorityQueue` class as follows:

```
/// <summary>
/// Gets elements of given priority
/// </summary>
/// <param name="priority">Given priority</param>
/// <returns>A list of elements that has this priority</returns>
public IEnumerable< TValue > GetElemenets(Tkey priority)
{
  try
  {
    return innerDS[priority];
  }
  catch (KeyNotFoundException ex)
```

```
    {
      //return empty list. So the caller wouldn't crash.
      return new List<TValue>();
    }
  }
```

3. Go to the `Main()` method and replace the existing content with the following:

```
PriorityQueue<int, string> gadgetShoppingList = new
PriorityQueue<int, string>();

gadgetShoppingList.Enque(1, "iPhone");
gadgetShoppingList.Enque(2, "iPad");
gadgetShoppingList.Enque(1, "MacBook");
gadgetShoppingList.Enque(3, "Amazon Kindle");

var gadgetsIWantMost = gadgetShoppingList.GetElemenets(1);
foreach (string gadgetName in gadgetsIWantMost)
         Console.WriteLine(gadgetName);
Console.ReadLine();
```

What just happened?

This will print the following output. Can you explain why?

```
iPhone

MacBook
```

Now, let's see what caused this. The first line in the `Main()` method: `PriorityQueue<int, string> gadgetShoppingList = new PriorityQueue<int, string>();` creates a specific copy of a generic priority queue, where the priorities are of type integer, and data types of objects to be stored as values are set to string. I wanted to assign integer priorities to the gadgets I want to buy. This call internally replaces the `TKey` with `int` and `TValue` with `string` at runtime, in the generic implementation of the `PriorityQueue<TKey,TValue>` defined previously.

Note that the internal data structure is a sorted list, where each key of the list maps to a list of values depicted by `List<TValue>`. So, with the four calls to the `Enque()` method, the internal `SortedList` will look as follows:

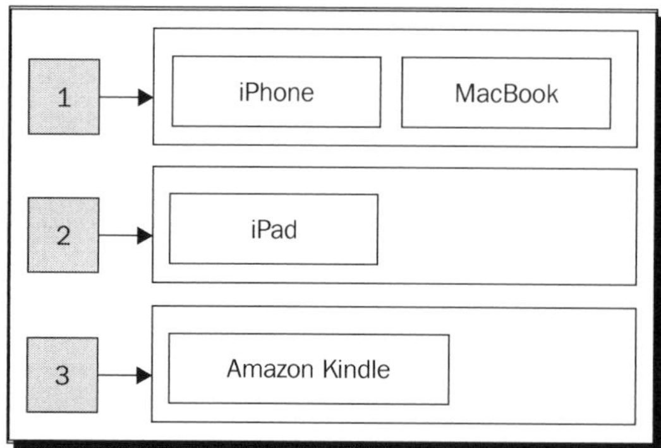

In the `Enque()` method, the elements are entered, if the priority attached to the element is not already present in the `innerDS.Keys`. However, users might get over-enthusiastic and add the same element twice or more. That will result in duplicate entries in the prioritized list. In order to avoid that `innerDS[key].Contains(value)` is used to check whether this gadget is already there or not.

Now that we know how the elements made their way to the inner list, let's see what happens when we try to retrieve the elements for a given priority.

As described earlier, the value for a corresponding key from a `SortedList` is found by indexing over the key. So in the method `GetElements()` `innerDS[priority];` shall return all the gadgets that were added with the given priority. However, if no element exists with that priority, it will throw a `KeyNotFoundException`. In such a case, we shall return a blank list of `TValue` to match the method signature. In order to validate this point, do a little experiment.

Add the following code in the `Main()` method:

```
Console.WriteLine(gadgetShoppingList.GetElemenets(4).Count());
```

This will print "0" to the console as there is no element in the `ShoppingList` with priority `4`.

Tips!

If we get an exception of type `KeyNotFoundException` and the caller method is expecting a list of items, it is best practice to return an empty list so that the caller method doesn't have to do anything special with the return value.

Now suppose you have enough money to buy a few of the top gadgets you wanted, it's time to strike them off the `ShoppingList`. Let's see how.

Time for action – let's strike off the gadgets with top-most priority after we have bought them

Follow the given steps:

1. Add the following method in the `PriorityQueue` class:

```
/// <summary>
/// Removes the first element with top priority
/// </summary>
public void Deque()()
{
  if (innerDS.Count > 0)
  {
    int i;
    for (i = 0; i < innerDS.Count; i++)
    if (innerDS[innerDS.Keys[i]].Count > 0)
    break;
    try
    {
      innerDS[innerDS.Keys[i]].RemoveAt(0);
    }
    catch (KeyNotFoundException ex)
    {
      return;
    }
  }
}
```

2. Add the following property in the `PriorityQueue` class:

```
/// <summary>
/// This is a port between other functionalities that are omitted.
/// This returns a Queue implementation of the Prioritized Queue.
/// </summary>
public Queue<TValue> OriginalQueue
{
  get
  {
    Queue<TValue> actual = new Queue<TValue>();
    foreach (Tkey key in innerDS.Keys)
    {
      foreach (TValue value in innerDS[key])
      {
        actual.Enqueue(value);
      }
    }
    return actual;
  }
}
```

This `OriginalQueue`, read-only property, flattens the `SortedList<TKey,TValue>` instance and arranges all the elements in the `PriorityQueue` maintaining the order using a `Queue<TValue>` instance.

3. Add the following property in the `PriorityQueue` class:

```
/// <summary>
/// The first element with top priority
/// </summary>
public TValue First
{
  get
  {
    try
    {
      int i;
      for (i = 0; i < innerDS.Count; i++)
      if (innerDS[innerDS.Keys[i]].Count > 0)
      break;
      return innerDS[innerDS.Keys[i]][0];
    }
```

```
      catch (Exception ex)
      {
        return default(TValue);
      }
    }
  }
```

4. Add the following code in the `Main()` method:

```
static void Main(string[] args)
{
  PriorityQueue<int, string> gadgetShoppingList =
    new PriorityQueue<int, string>();
  gadgetShoppingList.Enque(1, "iPhone");
  gadgetShoppingList.Enque(2, "iPad");
  gadgetShoppingList.Enque(1, "MacBook");
  gadgetShoppingList.Enque(3, "Amazon Kindle");

  //Returning the first element from the prioritized Shopping List
  string gadgetIWantTheMost = gadgetShoppingList.First;
  Console.WriteLine("Buying {0}",gadgetIWantTheMost );


  Console.WriteLine("Bought " + gadgetIWantTheMost);
  //Bought the first gadget. Let's strike it off the list.
  gadgetShoppingList.Deque();

  //Let's see what else I can buy if I get some more dollars ;)
  Console.WriteLine("Need more cash to buy ");
  Queue<string> gadgets = gadgetShoppingList.
  OriginalQueue;
  foreach (string gadgetName in gadgets)
  Console.WriteLine(gadgetName);
}
```

5. Compile and run the program.

What just happened?

This will print the following output to the console:

```
Buying iPhone
Bought iPhone
Need more cash to buy
MacBook
iPad
Amazon Kindle
```

Let's see how we got there.

The property `First` returns the value of the first element of the `PriorityQueue` or in this case the gadget I want most.

`innerDS[innerDS.Keys[i]].count` returns the list of gadgets, where the priority is the *ith* key of the inner `SortedList`. So first in the list of gadgets that has at least one element are the gadgets of top-most priority. The first item (which is located at index zero of such a list) is the item with top-most priority and entered in the `ShoppingList` first. So, technically that's the first element with top-most priority. This is referenced by `innerDS[innerDS.Keys[i]][0]`.

The method `Deque()` just removes this first element from the priority queue. The property `OriginalQueue` returns a queue of gadgets in order of their priority.

Using this generic `PriorityQueue`, we can deal with other priorities of our life too. Say we want to schedule our meetings and appointments. This is how we can do it.

Time for action – let's create an appointment list

Follow the given steps:

1. Add the following code to the `Main()` method:

```
//Creating a priority queue to store the appointments.
PriorityQueue<DateTime, string> myAppointments = new
PriorityQueue<DateTime, string>();

//Adding appointments
```

```
myAppointments.Enque(DateTime.Today.AddDays(1),
  "Dental checkup @ Doctor Smiley :)");
myAppointments.Enque(DateTime.Today.AddDays(3),
  "Weekly grocery shopping");
myAppointments.Enque(DateTime.Today.AddDays(1),
  "Trip to Art Gallery.");
myAppointments.Enque(DateTime.Today.AddDays(2),
  "Son's football tournament at school");

//Listing all appointments as per they are scheduled
foreach (string task in myAppointments.OriginalQueue)
  Console.WriteLine(task);
```

2. Compile and run the program.

What just happened?

This will print the following output:

```
Regular dental checkup @ Doctor Smiley :)
Trip to Art Gallery.
Son's football tournament at school
Weekly grocery shopping
```

Note that the tasks are scheduled as per the date.

Live sorting and statistics for online bidding

Imagine you work for an online bidding company such as eBay. Your company deals in several product lines. On the company website, live bidding prices for all the products have to be displayed. In this example, we shall see how `LinkedList<T>` can be used to offer such functionalities.

There are a lot of hits on the server per second, so sorting the data at regular intervals is not an option. You have to come up with a structure such that the bidding prices get inserted in a list in the sorted order as the user submits them from the site console. This is what I like to call **live sorting**. Moreover, as two or more people can quote the same bid amount, so the list where you store the bidding values must allow duplicates. Your boss is interested to know the following:

- What are the actual bid amounts submitted for any product?
- What is the range of bid amounts (minimum and maximum) for any product?
- What is/are the common bidding amounts across different product lines?

Besides this, your boss would be happy to see whether you can design a system to capture the demographics of the bidders. This will help your company distribute targeted advertisements. For example, which newspaper is mostly read by people who bid for smartphones and MP3 players?

Thankfully, .NET can help and we can build a couple of generic structures to solve this problem. First, we shall build a structure that will help us solve the live sorting challenge. Later, we shall use this and some other generic .NET classes to solve the remaining demographics issues.

Time for action – let's create a custom class for live sorting

Follow the given steps:

1. Create a class library project. Call it `LiveSortedListAPI`.
2. Change the name of the class from `Class1.cs` to `LiveSortedList.cs`.
3. Change the header of the class as follows:

   ```
   public class LiveSortedList<T>  where T:IComparable
   ```

4. Add the following private variables and properties:

   ```
   LinkedList<T> innerDS;
   LinkedList<T> innerDSDesc;
   LinkedList<T> actualValues;

   public List<T> LiveSortedValues
   {
     get
     {
       return new List<T>(innerDS);
     }
   ```

```
}
public List<T> LiveSortedValuesDesc
{
  get
  {
    return new List<T>(innerDSDesc);
  }
}

public List<T> ActualValues
{
  get
  {
    return new List<T>(actualValues);
  }
}
```

5. Add the constructor as follows:

```
public LiveSortedList()
{
  innerDS = new LinkedList<T>();
  innerDSDesc = new LinkedList<T>();
  actualValues = new LinkedList<T>();
}

/// Add the following method to add elements in the Live Sorted
/// List
/// <summary>
/// Adds a new element in the LiveSortedList
/// </summary>
/// <param name="val">The value to be added.</param>
public void Add(T val)
{
  //Adding to the actual list
  actualValues.AddLast(val);
  //If there is no item in the list,
  //This is the first item in the list
  if (innerDS.Count == 0)
  {
    //Adding the first item to the ascending values list
    innerDS.AddFirst(val);
    //Adding the first item to the descending values list
```

```
        innerDSDesc.AddFirst(val);
      }
      else
      {
        //If the current value is less than first value
        //in the ascending list
        if (innerDS.First.Value.CompareTo(val) >= 0)
        {
          //Add this as the first item in the ascending values list
          innerDS.AddFirst(val);
          //Add this as the last item in the descending values list
          innerDSDesc.AddLast(val);
          //return the control
          return;
        }
        //If the current value is more than the last value
        //in the ascending list
        if (innerDS.Last.Value.CompareTo(val) <= 0)
        {
          //Add this as the last item in the ascending values list
          innerDS.AddLast(val);
          //Add this as the first item in the descending values list
          innerDSDesc.AddFirst(val);
          //return the control
          return;
        }
        //For all other range of values of the current value
        else
        {
          T temp = default(T);
          //Iterate over the current ascending collection to
          //find the proper place of insertion.
          foreach (T t in innerDS)
          {
            if (t.CompareTo(val) > 0)
            {
              //Temp is the value Just greater than the current value
              temp = t;
              break;
            }
          }
          //Add this value before temp in the ascending list
          innerDS.AddBefore(innerDS.Find(temp), val);
```

```
            //Add this value after temp in the descendng list
            innerDSDesc.AddAfter(innerDSDesc.Find(temp), val);
        }
    }
}
```

6. Add a console application project to this solution, where you created the class library.

7. In the `Main()` method of the console application, add the following code:

```
LiveSortedList<double> bids = new LiveSortedList<double>();

//Say, Adding bidding amount for a iPod
bids.Add(12.50);
bids.Add(11.50);
bids.Add(11.32);
bids.Add(13.35);
bids.Add(11.50);
bids.Add(12.60);
bids.Add(18.40);
bids.Add(19.50);
bids.Add(11.65);

foreach (double bidAmount in bids.LiveSortedValues)
  Console.WriteLine(bidAmount.ToString("$00.00"));
```

8. Compile and run the program. Don't forget to set the console application as the start-up project.

What just happened?

As you execute the program, you will see the following output:

```
$11.32
$11.50
$11.50
$11.65
$12.50
$12.60
$13.35
$18.40
$19.50
```

`LinkedList<T>` is a generic linked list that stores elements of type `T` in `LinkedListNode<T>`. A linked list offers several methods to insert nodes in several parts of the list. The names of these methods are very straightforward. `AddFirst()` lets you add an element at the start of the linked list. `AddLast()` lets you add an element at the end of the linked list. `AddBefore()` lets you add an element before a particular node in the linked list, whereas `AddAfter()` lets you add an element after a particular node in the linked list.

The properties `First` and `Last` represent the first and the last node of a linked list. `First.Value` returns the value of the first node. `Last.Value` returns the value of the last node. These nodes are of type `LinkedListNode<T>`.

The `Add()` method of `LiveSortedList<T>` class works very simply. If the element to be added is less than the first value, then we have to add it as the first element. If, however, the element to be added is more than the last value, then we have to add it as the last element. However, if the element's value is somewhere in between, we need to find the `LinkedListNode<T>` whose value is just greater than the element's value.

The `Find()` method of the `LinkedList<T>` class returns the `LinkedListNode<T>` that has the value passed as an argument of `Find()`. So in the call `innerDS.AddBefore(innerDS.Find(temp), val); innerDS.Find(temp)` returns the `LinkedListNode<T>` whose value is `temp`. So this call will insert `val` before `temp` in the `LinkedList<T> innerDS`.

Why did we have three LinkedList<T> as part of the data structure?

1. One for keeping the bid values/elements to be added as they appear (in order).
2. One for keeping the bid values/elements in ascending order.
3. One for keeping the bid values/elements in descending order.

Pop quiz

1. Fill in the blank to insert 3 after 1.

```
LinkedList<int> numbers = new LinkedList<int>();
numbers.AddLast(1);
numbers.AddLast(11);
numbers.AddAfter(____________);
```

An attempt to answer questions asked by your boss

For now, assume that your company deals with bidding on iPad, iPhone, MacBook, and iPod. So you shall have to keep an eye on the bidding prices of these products. This means we would need a way of associating product name/ID to the live sorted bid amount values. `SortedList<TKey,TValue>` as discussed earlier, fits the bill perfectly. Let's see how.

Time for action – associating products with live sorted bid amounts

Follow the given steps:

1. Stay in the class library project, where we defined `LiveSortedList<T>`. Add a different class. Call it `MultiLiveSortedList.cs`.
2. Change the class header as follows:

```
public class MultiLiveSortedList<TKey,TValue>
       where TKey:IComparable
       where TValue:IComparable
```

3. Add the following variable and the constructor:

```
SortedList<TKey, LiveSortedList<TValue>> innerDS;

public MultiLiveSortedList()
{
  innerDS = new SortedList<TKey, LiveSortedList<TValue>>();
}
```

4. Add the following method to the class to add elements in the list:

```
public void Add(TKey key, IEnumerable<TValue> values)
{
  if (!innerDS.ContainsKey(key))
  {
    innerDS.Add(key, new LiveSortedList<TValue>());
    foreach (TValue val in values)
    innerDS[key].Add(val);
  }
  else
  {
    foreach (TValue val in values)
    innerDS[key].Add(val);
  }
}
```

5. Add the following method to return bid values for a particular product:

```
public List<TValue> BidAmountsFor(TKey key)
{
  try
  {
    return innerDS[key].LiveSortedValues;
  }
  catch
  {
    throw new KeyNotFoundException("No such product exist");
  }
}
```

6. Create a console app and attach the reference of this class library to that. Add the following code in the `Main()` method:

```
MultiLiveSortedList<string, double> categorizedBidValues =
  new MultiLiveSortedList<string, double>();
//Adding live sorted bid amounts for each product
```

```
categorizedBidValues.Add("iPod",
  new List<double>(){12.50,11.50,11.32,13.35,11.50});
categorizedBidValues.Add("iPad",
  new List<double>() { 212.50, 211.50, 211.32, 213.35, 213.50 });
categorizedBidValues.Add("MacBook",
  new List<double>() { 212.50, 211.50, 300, 223, 320 });
categorizedBidValues.Add("iPhone",
  new List<double>() { 333, 242, 302, 301.40, 310 });

//Finding Bid Amounts for the product "iPad"
List<double> BidsForIPad = categorizedBidValues.
  BidAmountsFor("iPad");
//Maximum Bid Amount for "iPad"
double MaxBidForIPad = BidsForIPad[BidsForIPad.Count - 1];
//Minimum Bid Amount for "iPad"
double MinBidForIPad = BidsForIPad[0];

Console.WriteLine("iPad bid amounts are between " + MinBidForIPad.
  ToString ("$.00") +  " and " + MaxBidForIPad.ToString ("$.00"));
```

7. Compile and run the program.

What just happened?

As you execute the program, the following output will be printed to the console:

```
iPad bid amounts are between $211.32 and $213.50
```

The new class created is basically a `SortedList<TKey,TValue>` in disguise where the `TValue` will be a `LiveSortedList<TValue>`. So, you saw how two different generic collections are used together to solve a problem. `LiveSortedList` ensures that the bid amount values being added are always in a sorted order and the `SortedList` class ensures that these `LiveSortedLists` are kept indexed by the product name.

`innerDS[key]`, in this case, returns the `LiveSortedList<TValue>` for the given key.

`innerDS[key].LiveSortedValues`, as shown earlier, returns a list of sorted `TValue` values.

Now is the time to take a look at the other questions your boss had. How to find common bidding amounts. That's conceptually different. That's actually a set theory problem. We have a list of values representing the bidding amount for several products. Now we need to find common values among these lists. This can be solved using an intersection of these two lists of values. .NET makes breathing easy with the introduction of the `SortedSet<T>` class in the `System.Collections.Generics` namespace. Let's see how we can use this.

Time for action – finding common values across different bidding amount lists

Follow the given steps:

1. Stay in the `MultiLiveSortedList` class. Add the following methods:

```
public SortedSet<TValue> CommonAcross
{
  get
  {
    SortedSet<TValue> com;
    com = new SortedSet<TValue>(innerDS.Values[0].
      LiveSortedValues);
    for (int i = 1; i < innerDS.Count; i++)
    com.IntersectWith
    (new SortedSet<TValue>(innerDS.Values[i].LiveSortedValues));
    return com;
  }
}

public SortedSet<TValue> CommonAmong(TKey key1, TKey key2)
{
  SortedSet<TValue> com;
  com = new SortedSet<TValue>(innerDS[key1].LiveSortedValues);
  com.IntersectWith(new SortedSet<TValue>(innerDS[key2].
    LiveSortedValues));

  return com;
}
```

2. Go to the console app previously created. Add the following snippet after the previous code in the `Main()` method. Then compile and run the program:

```
SortedSet<double> mostCommonBiddingAmounts =
  categorizedBidValues.CommonAcross;

SortedSet<double> commonBidAmountForIPadAndMacBook =
  categorizedBidValues.CommonAmong("iPad","MacBook");

Console.WriteLine("Common Bid amounts for iPad and MacBook are ");

foreach (double commonBidAmount in
  commonBidAmountForIPadAndMacBook)
Console.WriteLine(commonBidAmount.ToString("$.00"));
```

What just happened?

As you execute the program, you will see the following output:

```
Common Bid amounts for iPad and MacBook are
$211.50
$212.50
```

`SortedSet<T>` has several methods. The `IntersectWith()` method accepts another `SortedSet<T>` as an argument and modifies the caller `SortedSet<T>` object content with the intersection result. So this is an in-place operation.

`SortedSet<T>` has an overloaded constructor that can take an `IEnumerable<T>` instance and create a sorted set out of it. It removes the duplicates as a set can't have duplicates. In the method `CommonAmong()`,`innerDS[key1]` returns a `LiveSortedList<T>` instance. Thus, `innerDS[key1].LiveSortedValues` is a `List<T>` instance that implements `IEnumerable<T>`. So, this is a valid argument to the `SortedSet<T>` constructor.

Have a go hero – finding common demographic statistics for the bidders

Using these new generic container classes, design a system to capture vital statistics about the demographics of the bidders. For example, you can store the product name/ID and the newspaper bidders as the values in an `MultiLiveSortedList` instance, as shown in the preceding example.

You will win every scrabble game from now on

I was playing the following word-making game with one of my friends. I lost a couple of times:

`http://www.eastoftheweb.com/games/index.php?p=games/multieight/1`

So, I decided to write a program that will help me find all the words from the characters of a given word. This task is not very easy. But with Generics, this becomes lightweight.

In this example, we shall create a console app, where the computer finds all the possible words from the T9 dictionary that uses a subset of the alphabet used in the given word. The following is a sample run:

```
Enter the word or phrase
every
0. eve
1. ever
2. every
3. eye
4. rev
5. rye
6. veer
7. very
```

So, you see how it works. Let's see how we can build it.

Time for action – creating the method to find the character histogram of a word

Follow the given step:

1. Create a console application and add the following method in the program:

```
/// <summary>
/// Finds the histogram of the characters of the word.
/// </summary>
/// <param name="word">The word for which the histogram of
/// characters has to be found.</param>
```

```
/// <returns>Histogram of charactres</returns>
private static SortedList<char, int> GetWordHistogram(string word)
{
  SortedList<char, int> wordHistogram =
  new SortedList<char, int>();
  foreach (char c in word.ToArray())
  {
    if (!wordHistogram.ContainsKey(c))
    wordHistogram.Add(c, 1);
    else
    wordHistogram[c]++;
  }
  return wordHistogram;
}
```

Time for action – checking whether a word can be formed

Follow the given step:

1. Add the following method in the `Program.cs` file:

```
/// <summary>
/// A word can be formed using a set of characters, if one of
/// their histogram is a
/// subset of the other in terms that they share some of the
/// characters and
/// occurrence of characters is not more than in the other one.
/// </summary>
/// <param name="firstOne">The first character histogram</param>
/// <param name="secondOne">The second histogram</param>
/// <returns></returns>
private static  bool CanIFormAWord(SortedList<char, int> firstOne,
  SortedList<char, int> secondOne)
{

  int count = 0;
  bool status = false;
  foreach (char c in firstOne.Keys)
  {
    //In order to be a subset all the characters
    //in this first SortedList has to be there
    //in the second one.
    if (secondOne.ContainsKey(c))
    {
```

```
        //The frequency of these characters should not be exceeding
        //that of the other one.
        if (secondOne[c] >= firstOne[c])
        {
          status = true;
          continue;
        }
        else
        {
          status = false;
          break;
        }

      }
      else
      {
        status = false;
        break;
      }

    }
    return status;
  }
```

Time for action – let's see whether it works

Follow the given step:

1. Add the following code snippet in the `Main()` method:

```
static void Main(string[] args)
{
  //Save the T9.txt file in the applications bin/debug directory.
  StreamReader sr = new StreamReader("T9.txt");
  Console.WriteLine("Enter the word or phrase");
  string word = Console.ReadLine();
  //Stores the histogram of the current given word
  SortedList<char, int> soughtWordHistogram =
    GetWordHistogram(word);
  //Stores histogram of all words in the SortedList
  SortedList<string, SortedList<char, int>> allWordHistogram =
  new SortedList<string, SortedList<char, int>>();
```

```
string line = string.Empty;
while ((line = sr.ReadLine()) != null)
{
  foreach (string w in line.Split(' '))
  {
    string x = w.Trim();
    if(x.Length > 0)
    if(!allWordHistogram.ContainsKey(x))
    allWordHistogram.Add(x, GetWordHistogram(w));
  }
}
sr.Close();
foreach (string w in allWordHistogram.Keys)
{
  //Checks If the current word can be formed using the letters
  //of the given word
  if (CanIFormAWord(allWordHistogram[w], soughtWordHistogram))
  {
    //If yes, print that
    Console.WriteLine(count.ToString() + ". " + w);
    count++;
    //print 20 words or less per page
    if (count % 20 == 0)
    {
      Console.WriteLine();
      Console.WriteLine("---More--");
      Console.WriteLine("---Hit <Enter> to proceed --");

      Console.ReadLine();
    }
  }
}
//Wait for a final keystroke
Console.ReadLine();
      }
```

Pop quiz

1. What will be the value of `x` in the following code snippet:

   ```
   SortedSet<int> set = new SortedSet<int>(new List<int>() { 1, 2, 3,
   2 });
   int x = set.Count;
   ```

   a. 1

   b. 2

   c. 3

   d. 4

2. What will be the content of `set1` after these following calls:

   ```
   SortedSet<int> set1 = new SortedSet<int>(new List<int>() { 1, 2,
   3, 2 });
   SortedSet<int> set2 = new SortedSet<int>(new List<int>() { 2,4,6
   });
   set1.IntersectWith(set2);
   ```

Have a go hero – explain the code!

Can you explain how the program works? Everything used in this example is discussed earlier in another example app in the chapter. You can download the T9 dictionary from the book's website.

Also, as an extension, can you use whatever you learned in this chapter to create a system that offers predictive text suggestions as the user types.

Trying to fix an appointment with a doctor?

The last time I went to see a doctor, I wished I could have seen a specialist the same day. We can build a system that can answer very important questions (such as the ones shown in the following list) that patients might have:

- When is doctor A available?
- When are both doctor A and doctor B there?
- Does doctor A work on all the days that doctor B does and vice versa?
- Which are the days when either of the doctors is available?
- When either of these two doctors available, but not both?
- Which doctor is available over the weekends?

- Whether doctor A is available on the given date?
- Who is more available, doctor A or doctor B?
- When is doctor B available save the weekends?

Time for action – creating a set of dates of the doctors' availability

Follow the given steps:

1. Create a console application. Add the following variables:

```
HashSet<DateTime> AvailabilityOfDoctorA = new HashSet<DateTime>()
{
  DateTime.Today, DateTime.Today.AddDays(-1),
    DateTime.Today.AddDays(1)
};

HashSet<DateTime> AvailabilityOfDoctorB = new HashSet<DateTime>()
{
  DateTime.Today.AddDays(-3), DateTime.Today.AddDays(1),
  DateTime.Today.AddDays(1)
};
```

2. Add the following code in the `Main()` method:

```
Console.WriteLine("Doctor A is avilable on these days ");
Console.WriteLine();
foreach (DateTime d in AvailabilityOfDoctorA)
  Console.WriteLine(d.ToLongDateString());
```

3. Execute the program.

What just happened?

You will see a similar output:

```
Doctor A is available on these days


Sunday, May 08, 2011
Saturday, May 07, 2011
Monday, May 09, 2011
```

We are looping through all the dates in the `HashTable` that holds the dates `Doctor A` is available. That's not very interesting. But let's see how we can do a lot more with sets.

You see here in this list `Sunday` appeared before `Saturday`. If you want to keep your entries sorted, then please resort to a sorted set implementation such as `SortedSet<T>`.

Time for action – finding out when both doctors shall be present

Follow the given steps:

1. Go back to the `Main()` method and change its content as follows:

```
Console.WriteLine("Doctor A and Doctor B both shall be
  available on ");
Console.WriteLine();
HashSet<DateTime> commonDates = AvailabilityOfDoctorA;
commonDates.IntersectWith(AvailabilityOfDoctorB);
foreach (DateTime d in commonDates)
  Console.WriteLine(d.ToLongDateString());
```

2. Execute this new program.

What just happened?

You will see the following output:

```
Doctor A and Doctor B both shall be available on
Tuesday, May 10, 2011
```

Before we dig deep to see what caused the output, please note that every time you run this snippet, you shall see different results because the example uses `DateTime.Today` that will change every second if you are right on the 11th hour of a day.

The `IntersectWith()` method returns the set representing the intersection of two sets. Or in other words, sets with common elements in two sets.

`IntersectWith()` is a method that modifies the caller instance of the `ISet<T>` implementation; in place. So, after the call to `IntersectWith()`; `commonDates` will contain only this: `Tuesday, May 10, 2011` entry. So, if you don't want to modify the `HashSet` in place, try copying that to a temporary variable as I did in this case, in the `commonDates HashSet<T>` instance.

All the methods of `ISet<T>` that end with a `With` are in place. So be careful while calling them. If you want to use a method that returns a new set without modifying the caller set instance; you have to use the extension method `Intersect<T>` available on the `System.Linq` namespace.

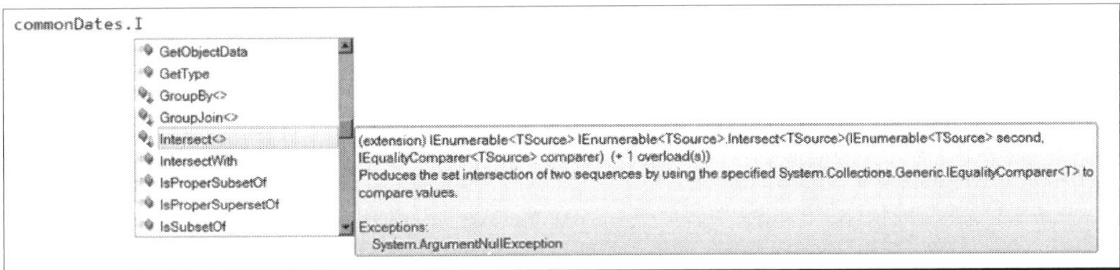

We shall learn more about extension methods in *Chapter 4, LINQ to Objects.* For now it would be enough to know that native `ISet<T>` implementations are in place, while the extension methods are not.

Pop quiz

1. What will be the content of `Set A` after the following calls:

```
HashSet<string> A = new HashSet<string>() { "a", "b", "c", "d" };
HashSet<string> B = new HashSet<string>() { "d","e" };
A.IntersectWith(B);
```

2. What will be the content of `Set B` after the following calls:

```
HashSet<string> A = new HashSet<string>() { "a", "b", "c", "d" };
HashSet<string> B = new HashSet<string>() { "d","e" };
B.UnionWith(A);
```

Revisiting the anagram problem

We solved the anagram problem earlier, so let's take a second look. An anagram duo results in the same sorted collection. For example, consider the following two strings:

"The Eyes"

"They See"

When sorted and any special character (including whitespace) is removed; these two strings result in the following string:

"eeehsty"

or in other words that can be written as follows:

"e3h1s1t1y1"

where the digits next to each character represents the frequency of that character in the phrase.

Time for action – re-creating the anagram finder

Follow the given steps:

1. Create a class library project. Call it `GenEx`.
2. Add the following class there:

```
/// <summary>
/// A Set that allows multiple copies of the same element.
/// It keeps a count of how many elements are present.
/// </summary>
/// <typeparam name="T"></typeparam>
public class MultiSet<T>
{
  private SortedList<T, int> innerDS;

  /// <summary>
  /// Creating a multiset instance from an IEnumerable of T
  /// </summary>
  /// <param name="input">The input from which we want to
  /// create the multiset instance.</param>
  public MultiSet(IEnumerable<T> input)
  {
```

```
    innerDS = new SortedList<T, int>();
    foreach (T item in input)
    {
      if (!innerDS.ContainsKey(item))
      {
        innerDS.Add(item, 1);
      }
      else
      innerDS[item]++;
    }
  }
  /// <summary>
  /// The flattend value combining all the elements.
  /// </summary>
  public IEnumerable<T> Value
  {
    get
    {
      List<T> vals = new List<T>();
      foreach (T item in innerDS.Keys)
      {
        for (int i = 0; i < innerDS[item]; i++)
        vals.Add(item);
      }
      return vals;
    }
  }
}
```

3. Add a console application to this project. Name it `GenExTest`. Add a reference of the class library project to this one.

4. Add the following to the `Main()` method:

```
static void Main(string[] args)
{

  MultiSet<char> firstPhrase = new MultiSet<char>
    ("theeyes".ToCharArray());
  MultiSet<char> secondPhrase = new MultiSet<char>
    ("theysee".ToCharArray());

  bool isAnagram = firstPhrase.Value.SequenceEquals
    (secondPhrase.Value);
```

```
        Display("The Eyes", "They See", isAnagram);

        MultiSet<string> firstSentence = new MultiSet<string>
        ("nay nada nay".Split(' '));
        MultiSet<string> secondSentence = new MultiSet<string>
        ("nada nay nay".Split(' '));

        isAnagram = false;

        isAnagram = firstSentence.Value.SequenceEquals
          (secondSentence.Value);

        Display("nay nada nay", "nada nay nay", isAnagram);

        Console.ReadKey();
    }
```

5. Add the following `Display()` method:

```
private static void Display(string a, string b, bool isAnagram)
{
  Console.WriteLine("\"{0}\" and \"{1}\" are {2}", a, b,
    isAnagram == true ? "Anagrams" : "Not Anagrams");
}
```

6. Compile and run the program.

What just happened?

As you execute the program, you will see the following output:

```
"The Eyes" and "They See" are Anagrams
"nay nada nay" and "nada nay nay" are Anagrams
```

Now, let's see how we got here. The constructor of the `MultiSet` class creates an element histogram.

The public read-only property `Value` flattens the histogram by returning an enumerable of type `T`.

For example, the entry "the eyes" histogram will look like this:

Element	Frequency
e	3
h	1
s	1
t	1
y	1

And the `Value` property will be `eeehsty`.

So, we get these sorted versions of the input from two sources in the `Value` property and then compare those using the `SequenceEquals()` extension method.

Warning!

The extension method `SequenceEquals()` and the native method `SetEquals()` expects inputs to be in order, otherwise they return false. It is kind of misleading for `SetEquals()`, because ideally `SetEquals()` should check whether two sets contain the same elements or not, disregarding the order of elements.

If you are familiar with `multiset` in C++, then you shall be able to co-relate with this structure we have just built.

Lists under the hood

So far in this chapter, we have learnt about many generic containers. This is the perfect time to know how they fit in to the entire ecosystem of .NET Generics. Different list-based implementations implement different interfaces. These relationships are shown as follows:

Generic collection	Interfaces it implements	What's the significance?
Stack<T>	IEnumerable<T> ICollection IEnumerable	Stack is a generic collection that has to be enumerable. It is also a collection, so any collection can be converted to Stack. For that ICollection is implemented.
Queue<T>	IEnumerable<T> ICollection IEnumerable	From compiler's standpoint Stack and Queue are identical. Only their concrete implementation for these interface methods make them distinct from one another.
List<T>	IList<T> ICollection<T> IEnumerable<T> IList ICollection IEnumerable	It is a list. So IList is implemented. It is also a generic list so IList<T> is implemented. Everything else is common, because it is also a collection. Because of IList and IList<T> it can provide random indexing over the contents.
LinkedList<T>	ICollection<T> IEnumerable<T> ICollection IEnumerable ISerializable IDeserializationCallback	This is a generic implementation of a classic LinkedList data structure.
HashSet<T>	ISerializable IDeserializationCallback ISet<T> ICollection<T> IEnumerable<T> IEnumerable	This is a Hash-based set implementation. The fastest of its kind. As with mathematical sets, no duplicates are allowed. Elements are not sorted.

Generic collection	Interfaces it implements	What's the significance?

`SortedSet<T>`	`ISet<T>`
	`ICollection<T>`
	`IEnumerable<T>`
	`ICollection`
	`IEnumerable`
	`ISerializable`
	`IDeserializationCallback`
		This is a tree-based set implementation. Entries remain sorted for value types, for reference the default comparer implementation is used.

`SortedList<TKey,TValue>`	`IDictionary<TKey, TValue>`
	`ICollection<KeyValuePair<TKey, TValue>>`
	`IEnumerable<KeyValuePair<TKey, TValue>>`
	`IDictionary`
	`ICollection`
	`IEnumerable`
		This is a list as well as a dictionary that offers indexing over its contents and values can be obtained by key indexing.

Summary

We learned a lot in this chapter about .NET Generics' list-based containers. We have learnt which generic container to use depending on the task at hand. The main idea of this chapter was not to be yet another API reference; but to learn how to use these generic list-based containers to solve real-world problems.

Although some of the applications built in the chapter might look trivial, they share the same pattern of several other problems in other domains.

Some concepts such as constraints and extension methods are used, but not explained here. Constraints shall be discussed in the appendix and extension methods in *Chapter 4, LINQ to Objects*.

In this chapter, we have learnt about a list-based associative container `SortedList`. However, that's not much use for performance issues. In the next chapter, we shall discuss tree-based `IDictionary` implementations that are much faster than `SortedList`.

3

Dictionaries

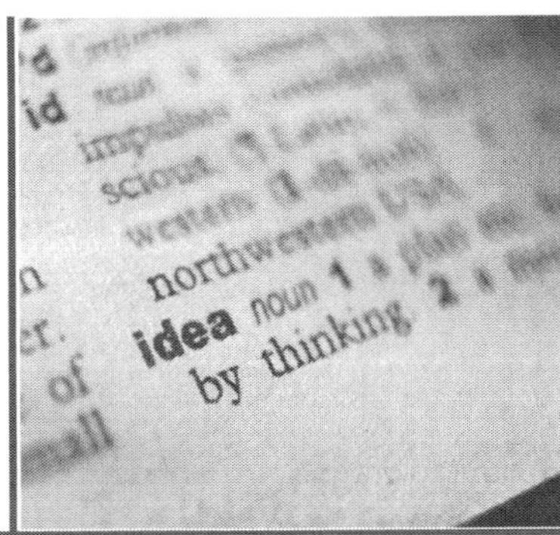

"To one" or "To many" that's the question.

In the last chapter, we have learnt about different generic list-based containers. Those are great for maintaining simple lists. However, they are not the best for storing associative relationships among different entities.

For example:

- *You might want to know how many electronic gadgets are available from* `amazon.com` *that are below $20*
- *A football fanatic friend of mine wants to keep a count of how many times Real Madrid won over other teams in recent times*
- *Your friend at the local electronics store dreams about a system that can auto-complete electronic part names*

These are some of the examples you can think of, where you would need a mechanism to associate one variable with another. The fun factor is that all these situations can be represented conceptually using the same structure—the same structure where some fields will be accessible very quickly using some other unique variable. This structure is known as **Dictionary** *in C#. Using Generics, you can build a common structure that can be used in different applications.*

Reading this chapter and following the exercises, you shall learn the following:

- Types of **Generic Associative Structures** and how to use them
- How to create your own custom generic associative structure

Types of generic associative structures

There are two types of associative containers/structures available in .NET Generics. They are as follows:

1. Key-value pairs
2. Tuples

Key-value pairs can be of two types. One type allows duplicate keys. These are represented by a collection of KeyValuePair<TKey,TValue> objects. The other type doesn't allow duplicate keys. These are represented by Dictionary<TKey,TValue> and SortedDictionary<TKey,TValue>. SortedDictionary<TKey,TValue> keeps the keys in sorted order unlike Dictionary<TKey,TValue>, where the keys are not stored in any particular order.

Tuples are a new inclusion to the .NET 4.0 Framework and like KeyValuePair<TKey,TValue> they also allow duplicate keys. However, KeyValuePair<TKey,TValue> can be viewed as a special case of a Tuple. A Tuple allows you to store the relationship between *n* different variables (they may be of different types). However a Key-value pair is what the name suggests. It's a pair. Only one variable is associated with the other. If you need to store a relationship between three or more variables, you need a Tuple.

Creating a tag cloud generator using dictionary

Tag cloud is a fascinating way to visualize content. Tag clouds, generated from text sources, give an impression about the text. It speaks for the text.

Here is a tag cloud that I generated pointing my program to Apple's iPad page. It's almost evident from the tag cloud that the Apple iPad will arrive at the store from April and you can pre-order. All this without even rolling our eyeballs over the page:

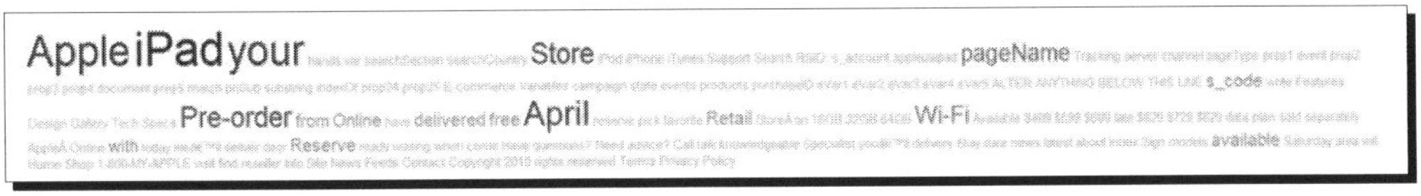

Time for action – creating the word histogram

Follow the given steps:

1. Create a console application. Call it `TagCloud`.
2. Add the following in the `Main()` method of `Program.cs`:

```
Dictionary<string, int> wordHistogram = new Dictionary<string,
int>();
wordHistogram.Add("Apple",33);
wordHistogram.Add("Orange",85);
wordHistogram.Add("Strawberry",20);
wordHistogram.Add("Watermelon",150);
wordHistogram.Add("Guava", 52);
wordHistogram.Add("Grape", 80);
ShowCloud(wordHistogram);
```

3. Copy the `Sample Code` from the following location and save it as `TagCloudData.txt` in the `C:\` drive:

```
http://visapi-gadgets.googlecode.com/svn/trunk/termcloud/doc.
html
```

4. Replace the highlighted part of this file (as shown in the following screenshot) with a place holder `!DATA!`:

```
TagCloudData - Notepad
File Edit Format View Help
<html>
  <head>
    <link rel="stylesheet" type="text/css" href="http://visapi-gadgets.googlecode.com/svn/trunk/termcloud/tc.css"/>
    <script type="text/javascript" src="http://visapi-gadgets.googlecode.com/svn/trunk/termcloud/tc.js"></script>
    <script type="text/javascript" src="http://www.google.com/jsapi"></script>
  </head>
  <body>
    <div id="tcdiv"></div>
    <script type="text/javascript">
      google.load("visualization", "1");
      google.setOnLoadCallback(draw);
      function draw() {
        data = new google.visualization.DataTable();
        data.addColumn('string', 'Label');
        data.addColumn('number', 'Value');
        data.addColumn('string', 'Link');
        data.addRows(3);
        data.setValue(0, 0, 'First Term');
        data.setValue(0, 1, 10);
        data.setValue(1, 0, 'Second');
        data.setValue(1, 1, 30);
        data.setValue(1, 2, 'http://www.google.com');
        data.setValue(2, 0, 'Third');
        data.setValue(2, 1, 20);
        var outputDiv = document.getElementById('tcdiv');
        var tc = new TermCloud(outputDiv);
        tc.draw(data, null);
      }
    </script>
  </body>
</html>
```

Delete the highlighted lines and replace these with `!DATA!`.

So, after replacement it will look something similar to the following screenshot:

```
TagCloudData - Notepad
File Edit Format View Help
<html>
  <head>
    <link rel="stylesheet" type="text/css" href="http://visapi-gadgets.googlecode.com/svn/trunk/termcloud/tc.css"/>
    <script type="text/javascript" src="http://visapi-gadgets.googlecode.com/svn/trunk/termcloud/tc.js"></script>
    <script type="text/javascript" src="http://www.google.com/jsapi"></script>
  </head>
  <body>
    <div id="tcdiv"></div>
    <script type="text/javascript">
      google.load("visualization", "1");
      google.setOnLoadCallback(draw);
      function draw() {
        data = new google.visualization.DataTable();
        data.addColumn('string', 'Label');
        data.addColumn('number', 'Value');
        data.addColumn('string', 'Link');
        !DATA!
        var outputDiv = document.getElementById('tcdiv');
        var tc = new TermCloud(outputDiv);
        tc.draw(data, null);
      }
    </script>
  </body>
</html>
```

5. Add the following method in `Program.cs`:

```
private static void ShowCloud(Dictionary<string,int>
  wordHistogram)
{
  //Creating the data to replace the placeholder
  StringBuilder cloudBuilder = new StringBuilder();

  cloudBuilder.AppendLine("data.addRows(" + wordHistogram.Keys.
    Count.ToString() + ")");

  int i = 0;
  foreach (string word in wordHistogram.Keys)
  {

    cloudBuilder.AppendLine("data.setValue(" + i.ToString()
    + ",0,'" + word + "');");
    cloudBuilder.AppendLine("data.setValue(" + i.ToString()
    + ",1," + wordHistogram[word] + ");");
    i++;
  }
  //Replacing the placeholder
  //If you can't put the file in C:\ drive. Put the file
  //anywhere else where you have access
  StreamReader sr = new StreamReader("C:\\TagCloudData.txt");
  string total = sr.ReadToEnd().Replace("!DATA!",
    cloudBuilder.ToString());
  sr.Close();
  //Writing the content to a temporary local file
  StreamWriter sw = new StreamWriter("C:\\Cloud.html");
  sw.Write(total);
  sw.Close();
  //Showing the generated cloud.
  System.Diagnostics.Process.Start("C:\\Cloud.html");

}
```

6. Compile and run the application. You will need to be connected to the internet while using this application as it uses the **Google Visualization API**.

What just happened?

As you execute the program, it will launch your default browser and will show the following tag cloud:

Apple Orange Strawberry Watermelon Guava Grape

Watermelon is the biggest tag, because it has the highest frequency assigned (150). A word histogram is nothing but a tabular view of a tag cloud. Every word has a weight. In the real world, the weight can be the frequency of occurrence in a text.

The declaration: `Dictionary<string, int> wordHistogram = new Dictionary<string, int>();` creates a dictionary, where the keys are of type string and the value is of type integer. This dictionary is used to store the histogram of the words. As you see, **Strawberry** has the lowest weight and **Watermelon** has the largest. So, they appear smallest and largest in the tag cloud respectively.

We are using the Google Visualization API for generating the tag cloud. So, we somehow need to replace the hardcoded values from the sample HTML file. That's being done in the method `ShowCloud()`.

All the keys can be obtained by the `Keys` property of the `Dictionary` class. It returns a `KeyCollection` object. `Dictionary`—similar to `SortedList` in the previous chapter—implements the `IDictionary` interface and thus, we can find the value associated with a key by indexing, using the key.

Thus, `wordHistogram[word]` will return the weight associated with the word in the dictionary `wordHistogram`.

Have a go hero

We have now created a console application to generate tag clouds from a single source. Can you extend the program, such that it can generate tag clouds from several text sources?

Hint: You can use a dictionary of dictionaries as follows:

```
Dictionary<string, Dictionary<string,int>>
```

The first string in the preceding dictionary is the type of key of the outer dictionary which represents the source file paths, and the inner dictionary stores the frequency of each word appearing in those files; or in other words histogram for those files.

Pop quiz

1. Which structure would you use when mapping country versus capital?
    a. `Dictionary<string,string>`
    b. `Dictionary<string,List<string>>`
2. Which structure would you use when mapping country versus state-wise per-capita income? Say, we represent per-capita income in decimal.
    a. `Dictionary<string,decimal>`
    b. `Dictionary<string, Dictionary<string,decimal>>`
    c. `Dictionary<string,List<decimal>>`
3. How would you refer to the stock price of MSFT in the month of June 2011, if they are stored like this in a dictionary:

```
Dictionary<string,Dictionary<string,double>> stockPrices =
           new Dictionary<string,Dictionary<string,double>>();

stockPrices.Add("MSFT",new Dictionary<string,double>());
stockPrices["MSFT"].Add("May2011",24.22);//Hypothetical stock
price.
stockPrices["MSFT"].Add("June2011",34.22);//Hypothetical stock
price.
```

Creating a bubble wrap popper game

Sometimes we all get bored and need an easy break from boredom. Bubble wrap popping is one of the most popular games. It doesn't require any brain power, but it is still a lot of fun. I have seen people popping virtual bubbles for several reasons. It acts very well as a stress buster too. My wife loves this game.

This is a paradise for any bubble popper. It launches with a screen full of bubbles. As you click on a bubble it emits a realistic bubble pop sound and changes the look of the pattern such that it looks as if the bubble you just clicked is punctured. So it looks somewhat similar to the following screenshot. I have minimized it:

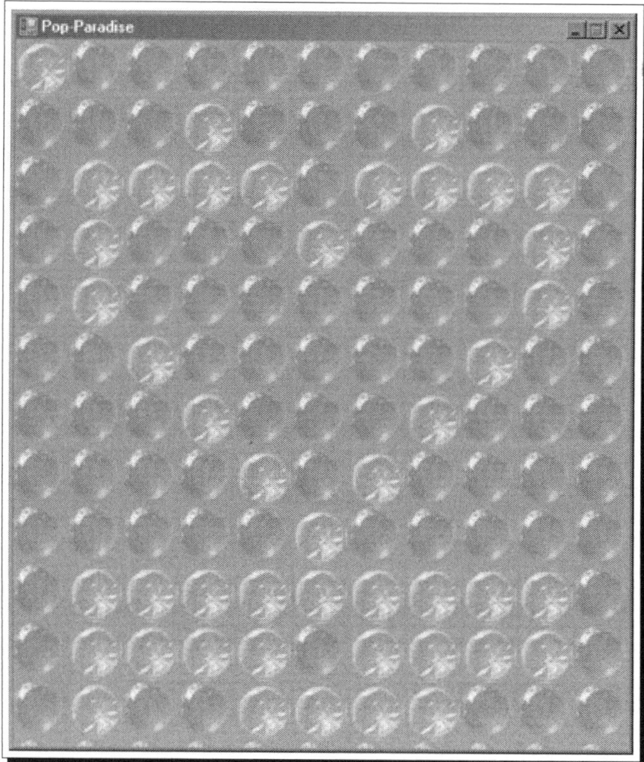

This is a simple game and we can make it using C# Dictionary. Let's get into action.

Time for action – creating the game console

Follow the given steps:

1. Create a Windows application.
2. Add the following code in `Form1.cs`:

```
Dictionary<string, bool> bubbleStatus =
  new Dictionary<string,bool>();

private void Form1_Load(object sender, EventArgs e)
{
```

```
//Lets find the width of the form
int totalWidth = this.Width;
//Lets find the height of the form
int totalHeight = this.Height;
//Lets see how many bubbles we can accommodate per row
int perRow = totalWidth / 45;
//Lets see how many bubbles we can accommodate per column
int perCol = totalHeight / 45;
//Bubbles will be images on picturebox controls
//This is the first bubble.
PictureBox pic = new PictureBox();
pic.Name = "pic0";
pic.Cursor = System.Windows.Forms.Cursors.Hand;
pic.Width = 45;
pic.Height = 45;
//Bubbles have to match the background image
//of the form for a realistic look
pic.BackgroundImage =
Image.FromFile("C:\\bubbleBackGround.jpg");
//Loading the normal bubble image
pic.ImageLocation = "C:\\bubble.jpg";
//Attaching a click event to handle the click.
//When user clicks a bubble it should play the pop sound
//and change the image to a popped bubble image to
//create a more realistic special effect
pic.Click += new EventHandler(pic_Click);
//adding the first bubble to the form's control
this.Controls.Add(pic);
//Remembering where we painted the first bubble on the form
Point lastLocation = pic.Location;
//Making a copy, we are going to need this
Point firstLocation = pic.Location ;
//Adding this bubble to the dictionary.
//Right now nobody popped it
//So the status is false.
bubbleStatus.Add(pic.Name, false);
for (int r = 1; r <= perCol; r++)
{
  firstLocation = pic.Location;
  for (int c = 1; c <= perRow; c++)
  {
```

```
//Creating bubbles on the fly
pic = new PictureBox();
pic.BackgroundImage =
Image.FromFile("C:\\bubbleBackGround.jpg");
pic.Name = "pic" + (r*10+c).ToString ();
pic.Cursor = System.Windows.Forms.Cursors.Hand;
pic.Width = 45;
pic.Height = 45;
pic.ImageLocation = "C:\\bubble.jpg";
pic.Click += new EventHandler(pic_Click);
//Checking if There is already a bubble
//in the dictionary with this ID
if (!bubbleStatus.ContainsKey(pic.Name))
bubbleStatus.Add(pic.Name, false);
else
{
  //Change the ID arbitrarily. It doesn't
  //have to be sequential
  //We are just going to need a way to
  //access the status
  //of a bubble given its ID
  pic.Name = pic.Name + c.ToString();
  //add this new bubble to the dictionary
  bubbleStatus.Add(pic.Name, false);
}
//Are we at the edge?
//If not we can still go on adding on the same column
if (c % perRow != 0)
pic.Location = new Point(lastLocation.X +
  pic.Width,lastLocation.Y);
else
//OOPs! we fell off the edge,
//we ran out of space to render any more
//bubbles in the current row. So lets go back to the second
//row where we started.
pic.Location =
new Point(firstLocation.X , firstLocation.Y + pic.Height);
//add the current bubble to the controls of the form
this.Controls.Add(pic);
```

```
        //Remember where you added this last bubble.
        lastLocation = pic.Location;
      }
    }

  }
  void pic_Click(object sender, EventArgs e)
  {
    PictureBox pic = (PictureBox)sender;
    if (bubbleStatus[pic.Name] == false)
    {
      //This bubble is Popped!!
      bubbleStatus[pic.Name] = true;
      //Play bubble wrap pop sound
      System.Media.SoundPlayer p =
      new System.Media.SoundPlayer("C:\\BubblePop.wav");
      p.Play();
      //Change the image to give an impression that it
      //actually popped.
      pic.ImageLocation = "C:\\bubblePopped.jpg";
    }
  }
```

3. Now compile and run the program.

What just happened?

You should get a screen full of bubbles ready to be popped, as shown in the preceding screenshot.

Look how easy it was!

See, every bubble can either be normal or already popped. So the status of a bubble in the game board is binary. Thus, it is best to describe their status using a Boolean field. Now, how do we identify one bubble from the other? Well, every bubble has to have an ID. As we don't know how many bubbles we shall have, depending on the screen size the number may vary, so generating the ID at runtime seems an obvious choice.

How did we decide we need a dictionary and not a list?

We could also have done it using a list. However, if we did it using a list, identifying which bubble has just popped would have been time consuming and difficult as we would have needed a sequential search. Dictionary, on the other hand, offers very fast access as it keeps the entries indexed by the key. In this case, `Key` is the `Name` of the picture boxes that show the bubble images.

The dictionary: `Dictionary<string, bool> bubbleStatus = new Dictionary<string, bool>();` stores the status of each bubble on the board. When a new bubble is created and gets its `Name`, then that is naturally not popped. At this point, the bubble is added to the dictionary as follows:

```
bubbleStatus.Add(pic.Name, false);
```

A `false` status means that the bubble has still not been popped. When the bubble is clicked, a check is made to see whether that bubble has already popped or not—by de-referencing the bubble status by its name—using the following code:

```
if (bubbleStatus[pic.Name] == false)
```

However, if this condition evaluates to be true, then the program changes the status of the bubble from `false` to `true` or conceptually from normal to popped if you assign the value `true` to the status using the following code snippet:

```
bubbleStatus[pic.Name] = true;
```

I thought it would be a good idea to see how the dictionary stores the elements in runtime, here is a snapshot of the middle of a game:

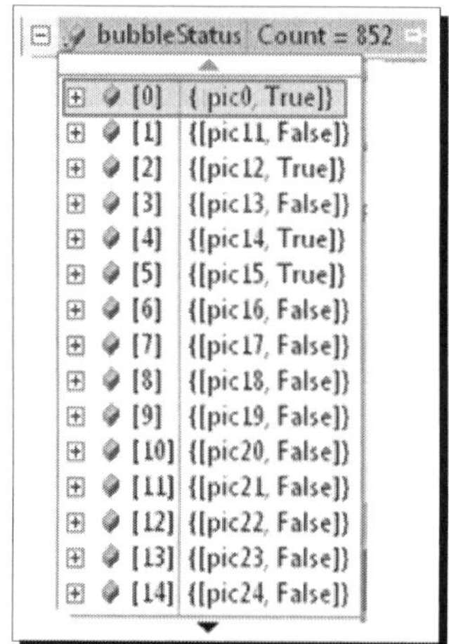

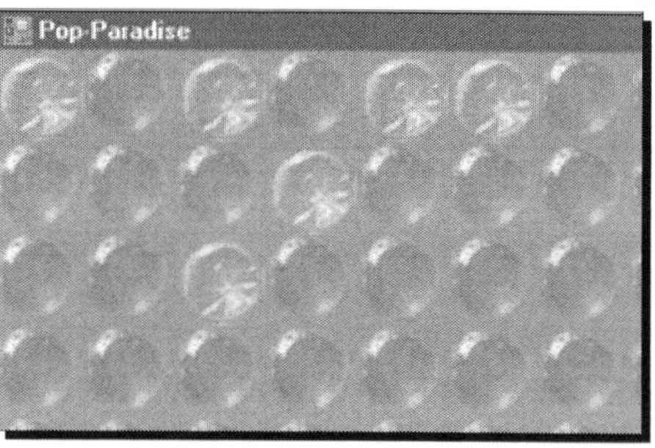

Check that the first, third, fifth, and sixth bubbles are popped. Check their status from the dictionary. The first entry is highlighted.

You can see the game in action at `http://sudipta.posterous.com/bubble-wrap-popper-in-c`.

Let's build a generic autocomplete service

We live in an interesting time and remembering everything exactly could be very challenging. For example, imagine yourself in the following scenarios:

- Coding in C# without intelligence support.
- Trying to find an Integrated Circuit (IC) from the local electronics store for your school project, but you can't remember the exact number of the IC.
- You work in a drugstore and a customer only knows first few letters of a drug. There are hundreds that start with those and you can't guess.
- You work for a travel website and customers are expecting intelligent drop-downs, where city names get completed as they type.

All these situations are example of autocomplete feature that completes the entry for the user. It is easy to create a generic structure using the generic C# dictionary that can support autocomplete.

The objective of the design is that it has to be user driven. Once written, we should be able to support the autocomplete facility for any custom list of values.

Time for action – creating a custom dictionary for autocomplete

Follow the given steps:

1. Create a class library project. Call it `MyDictionary`.
2. Rename `Class1.cs` to `MultiDictionary.cs`.
3. Modify the `MultiDictionary` class header as follows:

   ```
   public class MultiDictionary<Tkey,TValue> where Tkey : IComparable
   ```

4. Add the following variable and the constructor:

   ```
   Dictionary<Tkey, List<TValue>> innerDS;

   public MultiDictionary()
   {
     innerDS = new Dictionary<Tkey, List<TValue>>();
   }
   ```

5. Add the following method to add a single entry to the dictionary:

```
public void Add(Tkey key, TValue val)
{
  if (!innerDS.ContainsKey(key))
  {
    List<TValue> values = new List<TValue>();
    values.Add(val);
    innerDS.Add(key, values);
  }
  else
  {
    innerDS[key].Add(val);
  }
}
```

6. Add the following method:

```
/// <summary>
/// Find all the values for a given key
/// </summary>
/// <param name="key">The given key</param>
/// <returns>Values associated with this key</returns>
public IEnumerable<TValue> Values(Tkey key)
{
  List<TValue> values = new List<TValue>();
  innerDS.TryGetValue(key, out values);
  return values;
}
```

7. Add the reference of `MyDictionary` to this console application project and add the following lines to the `Program.cs`:

```
using MyDictionary;
```

And in the `Main()` method, add the following code:

```
static void Main(string[] args)
{
  MultiDictionary<string, string> authorBookMap =
    new MultiDictionary<string, string>();

  authorBookMap.Add("Sudipta", "Data Structure using C");
  authorBookMap.Add("Sudipta", ".NET Generics Beginners Guide");
  var booksBySudipta = authorBookMap.Values("Sudipta");
```

```
        foreach (string bookTitle in booksBySudipta)
        Console.WriteLine(bookTitle);

        Console.ReadLine();
    }
```

8. Compile and run the console application project.

What just happened?

As you execute the program, you will see the following output:

Data Structure using C

.NET Generics Beginners Guide

You might be thinking what's the point in discussing this in the autocomplete app? The reason is, for autocomplete we need to be able to map multiple entries to be associated with a single tag. In other words, we should be able to have duplicate keys in the structure.

Till now, we have used dictionaries to map one variable with another single variable. That's one-to-one mapping to be precise. However, for autocomplete, we need a one-to-many mapping capability. So, we should be able to map each key of the dictionary with a list of values. That's exactly what I did in this class `MultiDictionary`.

Pictorially `MultiDictionary` will look similar to the following diagram:

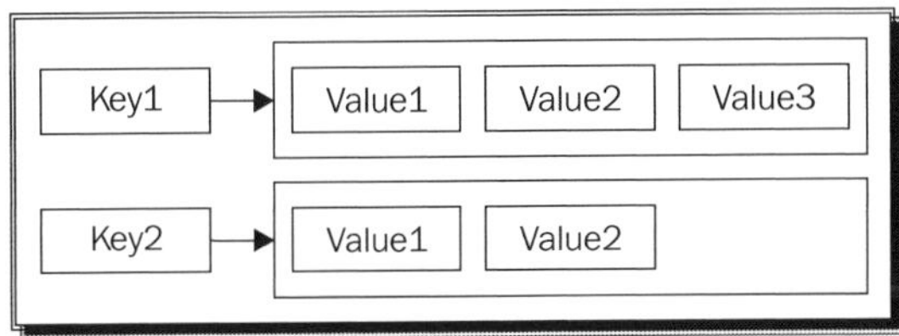

In the `Add()` method of the `MultiDictionary` class, it checks whether the `Key` is already present. If it is already present, we just add the value to the associated list of that `Key`. However, if it is not present, we create a blank list, add the new value to that list and then associate that list with the given key. However, the consumers of `MultiDictionary` get an impression that they can have duplicate keys.

Let's create an application showing how `MultiDictionary` can be used to offer an autocomplete feature.

Time for action – creating a class for autocomplete

Follow the given steps:

1. Stay in the class library project where we created the `MultiDictionary` project. Add a class called `AutoComplete.cs`.

2. Mark the class as public and add `using System.IO;` in the `using` directive list:

```
public class AutoComplete
```

3. Add the following variables and the constructor:

```
List<string> values = new List<string>();
MultiDictionary<string, string> autoCompleteMap;
string sourceFile;
int minimumLength;
public AutoComplete(string file, int min)
{
  autoCompleteMap = new MultiDictionary<string, string>();
  sourceFile = file;
  minimumLength = min;

  StreamReader reader = new StreamReader(sourceFile);
  string line = string.Empty;
  while ((line = reader.ReadLine()) != null)
  {
    if (line.Length > minimumLength)
    autoCompleteMap.Add(line.Substring(0, minimumLength), line);
  }

  reader.Close();
}
```

4. Add the following method:

```
public List<string> GetSuggestions(string initial)
{
  if (initial.Length == minimumLength)
  {
    values.Clear();
    List<string> vals = autoCompleteMap.Values(initial).ToList();
    values.AddRange(vals);
  }
```

```
  if (initial.Length > minimumLength)
  {
    List<string> currentItems = new List<string>();
    foreach (object s in values)
    currentItems.Add(s.ToString());
    values.Clear();
    foreach (string k in currentItems)
    if (k.StartsWith(initial))
    values.Add(k);
  }
  return values;
}
```

5. Now, create a Windows application to test this. Add a textbox (`textBox1`) as follows:

6. Now, add these two variables and add a reference to `MyDictionary`, and add the following `using` directive also:

```
using MyDictionary;

ListBox suggestionBox = new ListBox();
AutoComplete suggester;
```

7. Add code for the `form_Load` event as follows:

```
private void Form1_Load(object sender, EventArgs e)
{
  suggestionBox.Font = textBox1.Font;
  suggestionBox.DoubleClick+=new EventHandler
    (suggestionBox_DoubleClick);
```

```
    suggestionBox.KeyDown += new
      KeyEventHandler(suggestionBox_KeyDown);
    suggester = new AutoComplete("UK_Cities.txt", 2);
}
```

8. Add the following event:

```
private void textBox1_TextChanged(object sender, EventArgs e)
{
  if (textBox1.Text.Length < 2)
  {
    suggestionBox.Visible = false;
    suggestionBox.Items.Clear();
  }
  else
  {
    try
    {
      List<string> values = suggester.
        GetSuggestions(textBox1.Text);
      suggestionBox.Items.Clear();
      foreach (string value in values)
      suggestionBox.Items.Add(value);
      ShowListBox();
    }
    catch (Exception ex)
    {
      return;//Don't do anything.
    }
  }
}
```

9. Add the following method:

```
private void ShowListBox()
{
  suggestionBox.Location =
  new Point(textBox1.Location.X, textBox1.Location.Y +
    textBox1.Height);

  suggestionBox.Width = textBox1.Width;
  suggestionBox.Height = 10 * textBox1.Height;

  suggestionBox.Visible = true;
```

```
    this.Controls.Add(suggestionBox);
    suggestionBox.BringToFront();
  }
```

10. Add the following events:

```
void suggestionBox_KeyDown(object sender, KeyEventArgs e)
{
  if (e.KeyData == Keys.Enter)
  {
    textBox1.Text = suggestionBox.Text;
    suggestionBox.Visible = false;
  }
}

private void suggestionBox_DoubleClick(object sender, EventArgs e)
{
  textBox1.Text = suggestionBox.Text;
  suggestionBox.Visible = false;
}

private void textBox1_KeyDown(object sender, KeyEventArgs e)
{
  if (e.KeyData == Keys.Down)
  {
    suggestionBox.Focus();
    if (suggestionBox.Visible)
    suggestionBox.SelectedIndex = 0;
  }
}
```

11. Compile and run the program.

What just happened?

As you execute the program, you will see the following output:

As you start typing, after two characters you shall received autocomplete suggestions, as shown in the following screenshot:

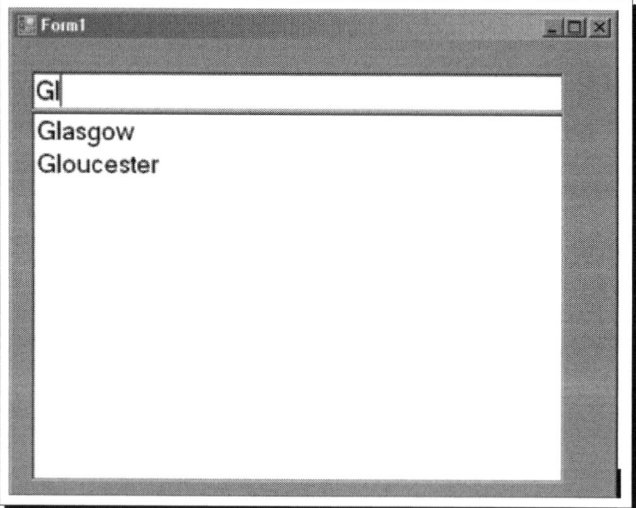

You can find a video of this output in my blog at: `http://sudipta.posterous.com/auto-complete-feature-demo-video-written-in-c#`.

The code described in steps 9 and 10 is for making the autocomplete feature more useful. As you press the down arrow key, it will set the focus on the listbox so that you can scroll for the right one in the suggestions. If you press *Enter* while one entry in the listbox is highlighted, that entry will be copied to the textbox and the same will happen if you double-click any item in the listbox. These make the program more real-world ready.

The heart and soul of this program is the following code snippet:

```
suggester = new AutoComplete("UK_Cities.txt", 2);
```

This creates an `AutoComplete` object. This tells the program that it must populate the entries from the file `Uk_Cities.txt` and it should offer suggestions as soon as the first two characters are typed in the textbox.

In the constructor of the `AutoComplete` class, the following code snippet:

```
autoCompleteMap.Add(line.Substring(0, minimumLength), line);
```

stores the words in a `MultiDictionary` where `Keys` of the `MultiDictionary` are prefixes of length `minimumLength`. One entry in this `MultiDictionary` is as follows:

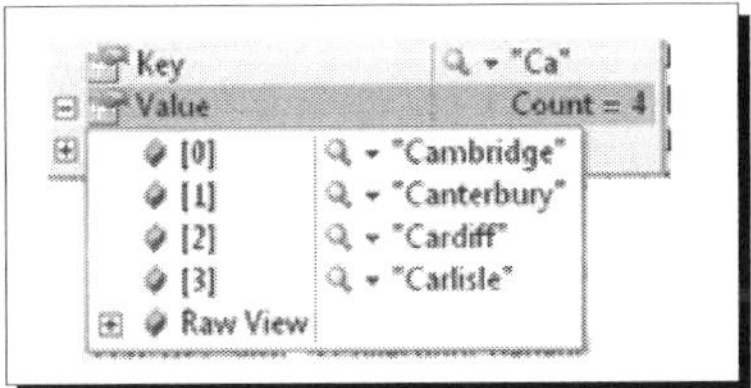

The most interesting method is the `GetSuggestion()` method as it calculates the list of suggestions with every changing few initial letters. If the length of the initial text is more than the minimum length for offering a suggestion, then the already suggested strings are filtered depending on whether it starts with the same pattern as the input string.

For example, as soon as you type **Gl** in the box, you will see **Glasgow** and **Gloucester** in the list as they both start with **Gl**. However, if you keep typing, then the input string of **Gla** will only match **Glasgow** and show that in the suggestion box.

While we deal with dictionaries, we should try to avoid the biggest possible error that might crash a program at runtime. Let's see how.

The most common pitfall. Don't fall there!

The most common pitfall is what is known as a **hole problem**. It means you are trying to access the value for a key from a dictionary which doesn't exist. This throws a `KeyNotFoundException`. In order to avoid this, you can use the `TryGetValue()` method that first checks whether the key is present and then tries to de-reference that.

Here is a typical use:

```
Dictionary<string, int> histogram = new Dictionary<string, int>();
histogram.Add("a", 1);
histogram.Add("b", 2);

//The following call will throw KeyNotFoundException
int x = histogram["c"];int y;
//The following call will set y to default value for int, which is 0
histogram.TryGetValue("c", out y);
```

Let's play some piano

The piano is one of the closest analogies of a C# Dictionary (at least conceptually) in the real world. Every key of the piano is associated with a particular note. In this example, we shall create a table-top piano with 12 keys (**A**, **B**, **C**, **D**, **E**, **F**, **G**, **B#**, **C#**, **E#**, **F#**, **G#**) as shown in the following screenshot:

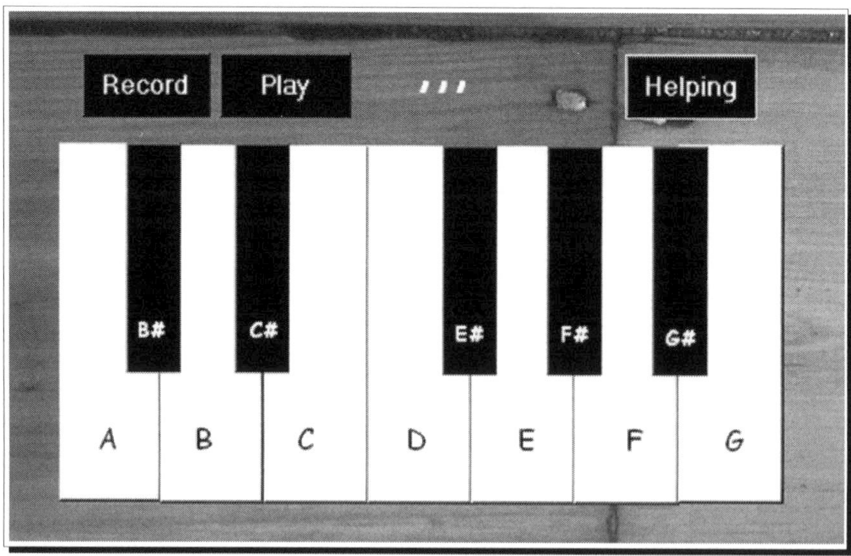

This would have the following functionalities:

- Users should be able to play it by clicking on the keys
- Users should be able to play it by pressing keys on the keyboard
- Users should be able to customize the key settings to their preference
- It should be able to record a note and play it back
- It should show labels for each key on demand (as shown in the preceding screenshot)

The preceding screenshot might look very fancy, but it is composed with only winform buttons and labels. I have skipped the details for laying out the controls and their event handlers. However, you can find all that from the website including the background image and the `.wav` files used.

Time for action – creating the keys of the piano

Follow the given steps:

1. Create a Windows form. Place the controls as shown in this video: `http://sudipta.posterous.com/private/eweuvoFJwb`. Eventually, your layout should look like the one shown in the preceding screenshot. As it is a complex layout, I have created the video to help you.

2. Add the following variables to `Form1.cs`:

   ```
   bool startRecording = false;
   ```

   This will be set to `true` when the app starts recording keystrokes.

3. Add the following field to the `Form1.cs`:

   ```
   string alphabet = "ABCDEFGHIJKLMNOPQRSTUVWXYZ";

   Dictionary<string, string> pianoNotes =
     new Dictionary<string, string>();

   Dictionary<string, char> keySettings =
     new Dictionary<string, char>();

   List<KeyValuePair<string, DateTime>> keyPressRecord =
     new List<KeyValuePair<string,DateTime>>();
   ```

4. Add the following methods:

```
/// <summary>
/// Plays the .WAV file associated with the pressed key
/// </summary>
/// <param name="pianoKey">The piano key that is pressed</param>

private void PlayPiano(string pianoKey)
{
  try
  {
    System.Media.SoundPlayer p = new System.Media.SoundPlayer
      (pianoNotes[pianoKey]);
    p.Play();
  }
  catch (KeyNotFoundException ex)
  {
    return;
  }
}

/// <summary>
/// This method fills the key settings
/// with recommended values by yours truly!
/// Every time the program starts these values will be loaded.
/// So even if the users make any customization, for now, that
/// will not be sticky.
/// </summary>

private void FactoryReset()
{
  keySettings.Add("A", 'A');
  keySettings.Add("B", 'B');
  keySettings.Add("C", 'C');
  keySettings.Add("D", 'D');
  keySettings.Add("E", 'E');
  keySettings.Add("F", 'F');
  keySettings.Add("G", 'G');
  keySettings.Add("B#", 'Q');
  keySettings.Add("C#", 'W');
  keySettings.Add("E#", 'R');
  keySettings.Add("F#", 'T');
  keySettings.Add("G#", 'H');
```

```
}

/// <summary>
/// Populates the drop down boxes with the recommended keys
/// </summary>

private void PopulateKeys()
{
  cmbA.Text =
          alphabet[alphabet.IndexOf(keySettings["A"])].ToString();
  cmbB.Text =
          alphabet[alphabet.IndexOf(keySettings["B"])].ToString();
  cmbC.Text =
          alphabet[alphabet.IndexOf(keySettings["C"])].ToString();
  cmbD.Text =
          alphabet[alphabet.IndexOf(keySettings["D"])].ToString();
  cmbE.Text =
          alphabet[alphabet.IndexOf(keySettings["E"])].ToString();
  cmbF.Text =
          alphabet[alphabet.IndexOf(keySettings["F"])].ToString();
  cmbG.Text =
          alphabet[alphabet.IndexOf(keySettings["G"])].ToString();
  cmbBSharp.Text =
         alphabet[alphabet.IndexOf(keySettings["B#"])].ToString();
  cmbCSharp.Text =
         alphabet[alphabet.IndexOf(keySettings["C#"])].ToString();
  cmbESharp.Text =
         alphabet[alphabet.IndexOf(keySettings["E#"])].ToString();
  cmbFSharp.Text =
         alphabet[alphabet.IndexOf(keySettings["F#"])].ToString();
  cmbGSharp.Text =
         alphabet[alphabet.IndexOf(keySettings["G#"])].ToString();
}
```

5. Add the following code in `Form_Load`:

```
private void Form1_Load(object sender, EventArgs e)
{
  //Associating the .WAV files with the keystrokes
  pianoNotes.Add("A", "A.wav");
  pianoNotes.Add("B", "B.wav");
  pianoNotes.Add("B#", "B#.wav");
  pianoNotes.Add("C", "C.wav");
  pianoNotes.Add("C#", "C#.wav");
  pianoNotes.Add("D", "D.wav");
  pianoNotes.Add("E", "E.wav");
```

```
    pianoNotes.Add("E#", "E#.wav");
    pianoNotes.Add("F", "F.wav");
    pianoNotes.Add("F#", "F#.wav");
    pianoNotes.Add("G", "G.wav");
    pianoNotes.Add("G#", "G#.wav");
    FactoryReset();
    PopulateKeys();
  }
```

6. Add event handlers for all the buttons (representing piano keys) as follows:

```
private void btnA_Click(object sender, EventArgs e)
{
  //Showing what key is pressed.
  lblKeyStroke.Text = "A";
  PlayPiano("A");
  //If user intended to start recording,
  //let's remember this key stroke.
  if (startRecording)
  keyPressRecord.Add (new KeyValuePair<string,
    DateTime>("A", DateTime.Now));
}
```

7. The helper button's name is `btnShowLables` and add the following event handler for that:

```
private void btnShowLables_Click(object sender, EventArgs e)
{
  if (btnShowLables.Text == "Help")
  {
    keyLabelA.Visible = true;
    keyLabelB.Visible = true;
    keyLabelC.Visible = true;
    keyLabelD.Visible = true;
    keyLabelE.Visible = true;
    keyLabelF.Visible = true;
    keyLabelG.Visible = true;
    keyLabelBSharp.Visible = true;
    keyLabelCSharp.Visible = true;
    keyLabelESharp.Visible = true;
    keyLableFSharp.Visible = true;
    keyLabelGSharp.Visible = true;
    grpKeySettings.Visible = true;
    btnShowLables.Text = "Helping";
  }
```

```
        else
        {
          keyLabelA.Visible = false;
          keyLabelB.Visible = false;
          keyLabelC.Visible = false;
          keyLabelD.Visible = false;
          keyLabelE.Visible = false;
          keyLabelF.Visible = false;
          keyLabelG.Visible = false;
          keyLabelBSharp.Visible = false;
          keyLabelCSharp.Visible = false;
          keyLabelESharp.Visible = false;
          keyLableFSharp.Visible = false;
          keyLabelGSharp.Visible = false;
          grpKeySettings.Visible = false ;
          btnShowLables.Text = "Help";
        }
      }
```

What just happened?

Once you compile and run the application, it will show the piano interface. You can click on each key to play.

Now, let's see what our code can do so far.

These two dictionaries: `Dictionary<string, string> pianoNotes = new Dictionary<string, string>();` and `Dictionary<string, char> keySettings = new Dictionary<string, char>();` are the heart and soul of this application.

The first one, `pianoNotes`, associates a piano key to a given `.wav` file. So, as you click on that button, that associated media file (`.wav`) could be played.

The second one, maps the keyboard keys to the piano keys. For example, there is no key on the keyboard to directly show "C#". So the key *W* is mapped to "C#". All these are being done in the `FactoryReset()` method.

As soon as you click on any button, the `PlayPiano()` method plays the associated media file. This is done using key-based indexing of Dictionaries. For example, if you click on `btnA` then `pianoNotes[pianoKey]` will return the value of the key *A* in the dictionary `pianoNotes`, which is `A.wav`.

Now, suppose you want to play the "C#" note. Which keyboard key should you click on? The answer is you should click `btnW` or press *W* on the keyboard; which is the associated keyboard key for piano key "C#".

This type of single unique key and value association is known as **one-to-one mapping**. And the type of dictionary we created for autocomplete is called **one-to-many mapping**.

How are we recording the key strokes?

Well, we are using `List<KeyValuePair<string, DateTime>> keyPressRecord = new List<KeyValuePair<string,DateTime>>();` for that. As the same piano note can be played many times during a session, we can't use a dictionary to record keystrokes, because the dictionary can't have duplicate keys. So, the solution is a list of `KeyValuePair<TKey,TValue>` class objects that allows us to store `KeyValuePair` with the same key. The value type is `DateTime`, because we need to remember exactly when which key was pressed, if we need to play it back. The duration between each such key press will be determined by finding the difference between the values of consecutive DateTime items.

When I played and recorded my keystrokes, for a while it was stored in the list of key-value pairs as follows:

keyPressRecord	Count = 14
[0]	{[A, 6/20/2010 11:29:32 PM]}
[1]	{[B, 6/20/2010 11:29:36 PM]}
[2]	{[C, 6/20/2010 11:29:38 PM]}
[3]	{[D, 6/20/2010 11:29:38 PM]}
[4]	{[B, 6/20/2010 11:29:39 PM]}
[5]	{[C, 6/20/2010 11:29:40 PM]}
[6]	{[D, 6/20/2010 11:29:40 PM]}
[7]	{[B, 6/20/2010 11:29:40 PM]}
[8]	{[C#, 6/20/2010 11:29:41 PM]}
[9]	{[A, 6/20/2010 11:29:44 PM]}
[10]	{[B, 6/20/2010 11:29:45 PM]}
[11]	{[C, 6/20/2010 11:29:45 PM]}
[12]	{[E, 6/20/2010 11:29:46 PM]}
[13]	{[F#, 6/20/2010 11:29:46 PM]}
Raw View	

So you see, I waited two seconds after I hit the first key *A*. So while playing it back, we must play the second note (which is *B* in this case) after two seconds of playing the first note.

Let's see how we can do that!

Time for action – switching on recording and playing recorded keystrokes

Follow the given steps:

1. Add the following method in `Form1.cs`:

```
/// <summary>
/// Switch on recording.
/// </summary>
private void btnRecord_Click(object sender, EventArgs e)
{
  if (btnRecord.Text.Equals("Record"))
  {
    //let's remember this key stroke.
    keyPressRecord.Clear();
    //We need to start recording.
    startRecording = true;
    btnRecord.Text = "Stop";
  }
  else
  {
    startRecording = false ;
    btnRecord.Text = "Record";
  }
}
```

2. Add the following method and event in `Form1.cs`:

```
private void SleepInBetween(TimeSpan span)
{
  System.Threading.Thread.Sleep(span.Minutes);
  System.Threading.Thread.Sleep(span.Seconds);
  System.Threading.Thread.Sleep(span.Milliseconds);
}

/// <summary>
/// Plays the recorded keystrokes
/// </summary>

private void btnPlay_Click(object sender, EventArgs e)
{
  try
  {
```

```
        int i;
        TimeSpan span;
        for (i = 0; i < keyPressRecord.Count - 1; i++)
        {
          PlayPiano(keyPressRecord[i].Key);
          span = keyPressRecord[i + 1].Value
          .Subtract(keyPressRecord[i].Value);
          //Lets wait till the timespan between
          //these two key-strokes are spent.
          SleepInBetween(span);
        }
        span = keyPressRecord[i].Value.Subtract
          (keyPressRecord[i - 1].Value);
        SleepInBetween(span);
        PlayPiano(keyPressRecord[i].Key);
      }
      catch (Exception ex)
      {
        //Let's go back
        return;
      }
    }
```

How it works?

We are iterating over the recorded keystrokes using this loop: `for (i = 0; i < keyPressRecord.Count - 1; i++)`.`keyPressRecord[i].Key` gives the *ith* key pressed by the user from the start.

`keyPressRecord[i + 1].Value.Subtract(keyPressRecord[i].Value);` returns the time difference between the two consecutive recorded keystrokes. The program needs to sleep during this time. Once we reach out of this loop, we need to play the last recorded keystroke. You can access the `key` and `value` of a `KeyValuePair` by public property `Key` and `Value`.

You can see the piano being played at `http://sudipta.posterous.com/my-table-top-piano-12-keys`.

C# Dictionaries can help detect cancer. Let's see how!

Now that you are aware of the `KeyValuePair`, let's see another interesting situation where this structure can be used.

Pattern recognition is an emerging science. **K Nearest Neighbor** (popularly known as KNN) is a supervised learning algorithm that can be used in binary classification problems very efficiently.

A binary classification problem is just what it states. It is a classification problem. Typically, classification of several entries are previously known and depending on that a new entry has to be classified in either of the two categories. Thus it is called binary.

Suppose we have records of several patients who are diagnosed with either malignant (class 'M' cancerous) or benign (class 'B' not cancerous) cases. Now, we gather details from the tests for a new patient. Depending on what we know previously from past patient records, can we classify the new patient's case as either a malignant case or a benign case? That's where binary classification helps in real life.

KNN uses a voting mechanism to solve this problem. It considers test results as a vector. If two vectors, representing two patient's test records, are near then they are probably suffering from the same type of case (either benign or malignant). Now this mechanism can lead to confusing results sometimes, if only the nearest vector is considered. So, K nearest vectors are considered. Thus the name KNN.

In this example, we shall see how C# Dictionary-based data structures can be used to solve this problem.

Time for action – creating the KNN API

Follow the given steps:

1. Create a class library project.
2. Add a class to the project. Call it `Entry`. Add the following code:

```
public class Entry
{
  public string Id
  {
    get;
    set;
  }
  public string Tag
  {
    get;
    set;
```

```
    }
    public List<double> ParamValues
    {
      get;
      set;
    }
  }
```

3. Add another class to this project. Call it `KNN`.

4. Add the following variable and the constructor:

```
private List<KeyValuePair<string, List<double>>> map ;
public KNN()
{
  map = new List<KeyValuePair<string, List<double>>>();
}
```

5. Add the following methods:

```
/// <summary>
/// Adds a patient record to the list
/// </summary>
/// <param name="entry"></param>
public void Add(Entry entry)
{
  map.Add(new KeyValuePair<string,List<double>>(entry.Tag,
    entry.ParamValues));
}
/// <summary>
/// Adds an entry to the list
/// </summary>
/// <param name="tag">Class of the new entry</param>
/// <param name="entries">Patient Records</param>

public void Add(string tag, List<double> entries)
{
  map.Add(new KeyValuePair<string, List<double>>(tag, entries));
}
/// <summary>
/// Calculates the Euclidean Distance between two entries
/// </summary>
/// <param name="index1">Index of the first entry in the
/// list</param>
```

```
/// <param name="index2">Index of the second entry in the
/// list</param>/// <returns>
///  To know more about Euclidean Distance please refer
///  http://en.wikipedia.org/wiki/Euclidean_distance
///  </returns>
private double distance(int index1,int index2)
{
  double sum = 0;
  for (int i = 0; i < map[index1].Value.Count; i++)
  {
    sum += Math.Pow(Math.Round(map[index1].Value[i] -
      map[index2].Value[i],2),2);
  }
  return Math.Round(Math.Sqrt(sum),2);
}
```

6. Add the following method:

```
/// <summary>
/// Predicts the suspected class of the input data
/// </summary>
/// <param name="entries">Values. In this case value of several
/// parameters</param>
/// <param name="class1">The first of the binary classes this data
/// set can belong to. In this example, either "B" or "M"
/// </param>
/// <param name="class2">The second of the binary classes this
/// data set can belong to. In this example either "B" or "M"
/// </param>
/// <param name="k">Number of nearest neighbor for we need to
/// consider to conclude a class.</param>
/// <remarks>For more information visit http://en.wikipedia.org/
/// wiki/K-nearest_neighbor_algorithm</remarks>
public string Predict(List<double> entries, string class1, string
  class2, int k)
{
  //Dictionary to keep the entries indexed and sorted by their
  //distance from the new values
  SortedDictionary<double, string> distanceMap =
    new SortedDictionary<double, string>();
  int count = 0;

  this.Add("X", entries);//Right now it is unknown
```

```
    int lastIndex = map.Count - 1;
    int firstIndex = 0; //Lets start counting at 0
    double minDistance = distance(firstIndex, lastIndex);
    for (int i = firstIndex + 1; i < lastIndex - 1; i++)
    {
      double currentDistance = distance(i, lastIndex);
      if(!distanceMap.ContainsKey(currentDistance))
      distanceMap.Add( currentDistance,map[i].Key);
    }

    map.RemoveAt(map.Count - 1);//lets remove the last entry
    Dictionary<double, string> kVals =
      new Dictionary<double, string>();

    foreach (double key in distanceMap.Keys)
    {
      if (count == k)
      break;
      kVals.Add(key, distanceMap[key]);

    }
    //Finding Class of the new entry "class1"
    int class1Count = 0;
    int class2Count = 0;
    foreach (double key in kVals.Keys)
    {
      if (kVals[key] == class1)
      class1Count++;
      else
      class2Count++;
    }
    return class1Count > class2Count ? class1 : class2;
  }
```

What just happened?

You can compile the project but can't run it yet. It doesn't have any data. We shall get to that in a while. Let's see what we created.

The class `Entry` represents a particular patient's record. Records from different tests are obtained and we are using numeric record values.

The class `KNN` implements the `KNN` algorithm. The inner data structure of the `KNN` class is: `List<KeyValuePair<string, List<double>>>`.

Let's see why. We have a list of patient records, where the patients might be suffering from either of the two cases and there could be multiple patients suffering from the same class of disease. So a plain dictionary is ruled out as it can't support duplicate keys. We can't use a `MultiDictionary`—described earlier in the chapter—because we would need integer indexing. So, we need a key-value pair list where the `key` is the class of disease and the `value` is the list of values of different test results.

So pictorially, we are using the structure shown in the following screenshot:

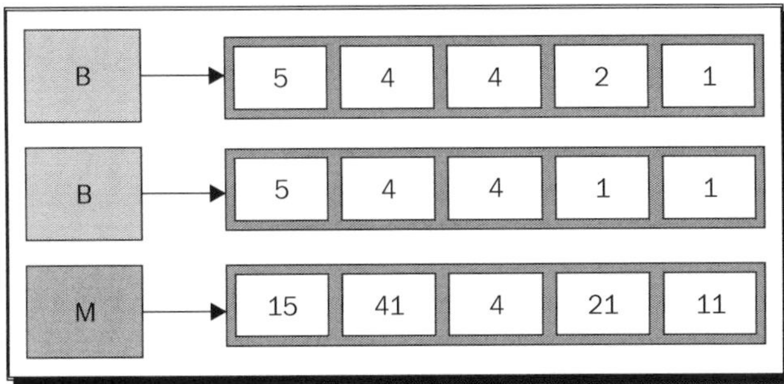

The `Predict()` method is doing all the magic. It predicts the possible class of the new patient entry. It uses a sorted dictionary to keep a list of entries in the ascending order of their distance from the new entry:

```
SortedDictionary<double, string> distanceMap = new
                                  SortedDictionary<double, string>();
```

This dictionary keeps the class tags and the distance of the patient's record data entries from the newly-added unidentified one, ordered by the distance because tags will be duplicate, however, distance can't be in most instances. And if they are, we don't need to add that entry to the dictionary as it actually is a duplicate entry.

So the entries in this dictionary will look similar to the following:

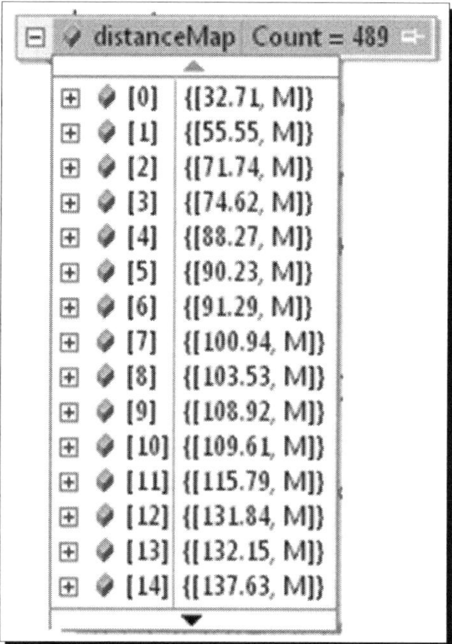

The index on the left is the value for `k`. So the first entry `k=1` is the closest to an entry which is of type **M**.

Once we have this dictionary in the `Predict()` method, we need to consider only the first `k` entries of the `SortedDictionary distanceMap`. If the number of entries among these first `k` elements having tag value `class1` is more than that of entries having tag value `class2`, then the new unidentified entry will be marked as `class1` else it will be marked as `class2`. That's how the voting works.

Time for action – getting the patient records

Follow the given steps:

1. Download patient records from the following website:

   `http://archive.ics.uci.edu/ml/machine-learning-databases/breast-cancer-wisconsin/wdbc.data`.

   If you are interested to know what are these values check out: `http://archive.ics.uci.edu/ml/machine-learning-databases/breast-cancer-wisconsin/wdbc.names`.

2. Copy about one-third of the entries to another file and delete them from this one. Save the new file as `wdbctest.txt` and the left over entries in the original file as `wdbc.txt`. You can get these files from the book website.

Time for action – creating the helper class to read a delimited file

Follow the given step:

1. Stay in the class library project and add a class called `TextReader.cs`:

```
public class TextReadHelper
{
  private string fileName;//Delimited source file that has
  // patient records
  private int tagIndex; //Index of the class of disease this
  // patient is suffering
  private int idIndex;//Index of the ID of the patient in
  // the delimited file
  string delim; //delimiter
  public TextReadHelper(string fileName,int tagIndex,
    int idIndex,string  delim)
  {
    //id,tag,values
    //tag,values
    this.fileName = fileName;
    this.tagIndex = tagIndex;
    this.idIndex = idIndex;
    this.delim = delim;
  }
  /// <summary>
  /// Returns the list of patient records
  /// </summary>
  public List<Entry> GetEntries()
  {
    //Include System.IO for this line of code
    StreamReader sr = new StreamReader(fileName);
    string line = string.Empty;
    List<Entry> entries = new List<Entry>();
    while ((line = sr.ReadLine()) != null)
    {
      string[] tokens = line.Split(new string[]
        {delim}, StringSplitOptions.RemoveEmptyEntries);
      Entry current = new Entry();
```

```
            if(idIndex!=-1)
            current.Id = tokens[idIndex];
            current.Tag = tokens[tagIndex];
            current.ParamValues = new List<double>();
            for (int i = 2; i < tokens.Length; i++)
            current.ParamValues.Add(Convert.ToDouble(tokens[i]));
            entries.Add(current);
          }
          sr.Close();
          return entries;
        }
      }
```

What just happened?

We wanted to read records of patient data from delimited notepad files. So, we needed a mechanism to be able to read these files and convert them to a list of `Entry` objects, which represents patient data.

With this, we are now ready to put it all together.

Time for action – let's see how to use the predictor

1. Create a console application and add a reference of the class library we built earlier.
2. Add the following `using` directive at the beginning:

```
using ClassLibrary1;
```

3. Add the following code in the `Main()` method of the console application:

```
static void Main(string[] args)
{
  TextReadHelper helper =
    new TextReadHelper("C:\\wdata.txt",1,0,",");
  KNN knnHelper = new KNN();
  List<Entry> entries = helper.GetEntries();

  foreach (Entry current in entries)
  knnHelper.Add(current);

  int k = 3;
```

```
    string tag = knnHelper.Predict(new List<double>()
      {21.56, 22.39, 142, 1479, 0.111, 0.1159, 0.2439, 0.1389,
      0.1726, 0.05623, 1.176, 1.256, 7.673, 158.7, 0.0103, 0.02891,
      0.05198, 0.02454,0.01114, 0.004239, 25.45, 26.4, 166.1, 2027,
      0.141, 0.2113, 0.4107, 0.2216, 0.206,0.07115 },"M", "B", k);

    Console.WriteLine("Suspected diagnoses  " + tag);
    Console.ReadLine();
  }
```

4. Compile and run this console application.

What just happened?

As you execute the program, it will print the following output:

`Suspected diagnoses  M`

The call to the `Predict()` method takes only a new patient's test data record, saves the patient ID and `tag`. `k` is set to 3. So in this case, we are considering three nearest neighbors for reaching a conclusion about the possible disease class the new patient is suffering from.

I thought it would be a good idea to see the final dictionary of distance mapped entries. So, here it is for the call we made from `Main()`:

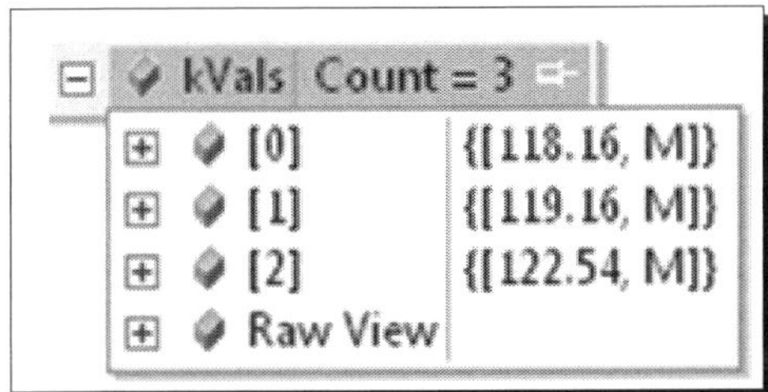

Tuples are great for many occasions including games

Tuples are a new inclusion in the .NET 4.0 framework and they are a perfect fit for many situations, some of them are as follows:

- To represent a database table row in the code.
- To replace all those dummy classes that have no methods and are just acting as placeholders for several types of objects.

- To bring association between more than a couple of types. Have you ever found yourself using Dictionary of Dictionaries? Then you shall find Tuples really useful.

Tuples can be used to refactor a nested branching statement. In this example, we shall create a number rearranging game that I used to play in my childhood.

Time for action – putting it all together

Follow the given steps:

1. Create a Windows application. Call it `TilO`.
2. Add nine button controls. Also add one `label` control and one `pictureBox` control, as shown in the following screenshot. Add large borders to buttons ("10"), make them flat, and name them as follows:

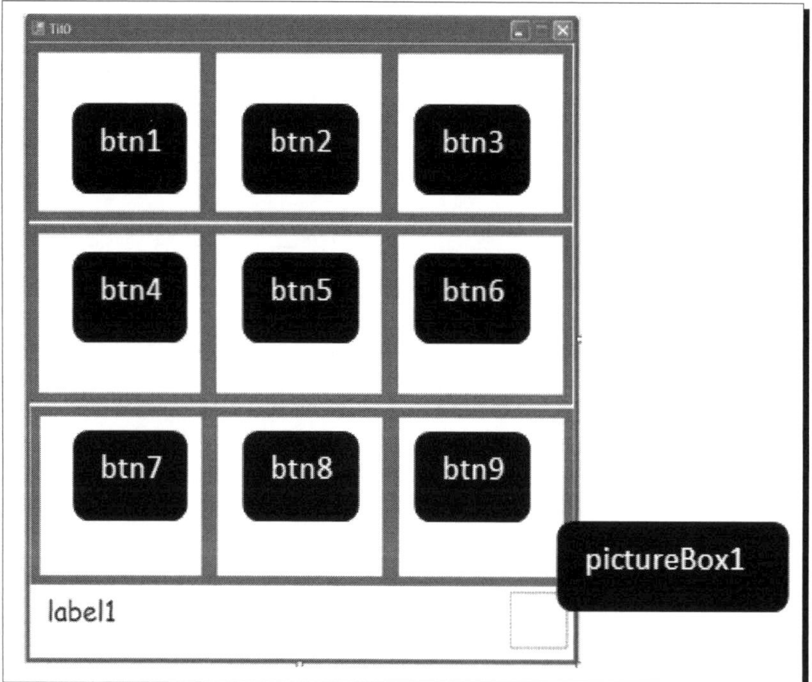

3. Add the following variables in the `Form1.cs`:

```
bool mute = false;
int totalMoves = 0;
```

```
List<Tuple<int, int, int>> board =
  new List<Tuple<int, int, int>>();
Dictionary<int, Button> buttons = new Dictionary<int, Button>();
```

4. Add the following methods to draw the `board` properly. You can customize the colors:

```
private void DrawBoard()
{
  int emptyIsAt = board.First(t => t.Item3 == 0).Item1;
  DrawEmpty(emptyIsAt);

  //Draw Rest
  for (int i = 0; i < board.Count; i++)
  {
    if (board[i].Item3 != 0)
    {
      DrawOthers(board[i].Item1, board[i].Item3);
    }
  }
}

private void DrawOthers(int index,int number)
{
  buttons[index].Text = number.ToString();
  buttons[index].BackColor = Color.White;
}

private void DrawEmpty(int index)
{
  buttons[index].BackColor = Color.Black;
  buttons[index].Text = string.Empty;
}
```

5. Add the following methods to check whether the tiles the players want to swap can actually move or not. If so, the second method `DoMove()` handles the movement:

```
private bool CanMove(int first, int second)
{
  if (first != 0 && second != 0)
  return false;
  int firstIndex = board.First(tuple => tuple.Item3 ==
    first).Item1;
  int secondIndex = board.First(tuple => tuple.Item3 ==
    second).Item1;
```

```
    int absDiff = Math.Abs(firstIndex - secondIndex);
    //Handle Edge cases
    if (absDiff == 1 && Math.Min(firstIndex, secondIndex) % 3 == 0)
    return false;
    if (absDiff == 1 || absDiff == 3)
    return true;
    else
    return false;

  }

  private void DoMove(string moveCommand, bool silent)
  {
    string[] moveThese = moveCommand.Split(new char[] { '=' },
      StringSplitOptions.RemoveEmptyEntries);

    //If some player just clicks the Empty box then it will
    //generate
    //an invalid command "0". And in this time moveThese will be
    //of length 1.
    if (moveThese.Length == 2)
    {
      int first = Convert.ToInt16(moveThese[0]);
      int second = Convert.ToInt16(moveThese[1]);
      bool CanTheseBeMoved = CanMove(first, second);
      if (CanTheseBeMoved)
      {
        //Move
        int firstIndex = board.First(t => t.Item3 == first).Item1;
        int secondIndex = board.First(t => t.Item3 == second).Item1;
        int expectedFirst = board.First(t => t.Item3 ==
          first).Item2;
        int expectedSecond = board.First(t => t.Item3 ==
          second).Item2;
        Tuple<int, int, int> newFirstTuple =
          new Tuple<int, int, int>(firstIndex,
          expectedFirst, second);

        Tuple<int, int, int> newSecondTuple =
          new Tuple<int, int, int>(secondIndex,
          expectedSecond, first);

        board.RemoveAt(firstIndex - 1);
```

```
        board.Insert(firstIndex - 1, newFirstTuple);

        board.RemoveAt(secondIndex - 1);
        board.Insert(secondIndex - 1, newSecondTuple);

        if (!mute)
        {
          System.Media.SoundPlayer player = new
          System.Media.SoundPlayer("Blip.wav");
          player.Play();
        }
        totalMoves++;
        lblMoves.Text = String.Format("You have made {0}
          moves so far.", totalMoves);
      }
      else
      {

        if (!silent && !mute)
        {
          System.Media.SoundPlayer player = new
          System.Media.SoundPlayer("Error.wav");
          player.Play();
        }
      }
    }
  }
```

6. Add the following methods to initialize `board` and `buttons`:

```
private void InitializeStartUpBoard()
{
  board.Add(new Tuple<int, int, int>(1, 1, 8));
  board.Add(new Tuple<int, int, int>(2, 2, 7));
  board.Add(new Tuple<int, int, int>(3, 3, 6));
  board.Add(new Tuple<int, int, int>(4, 4, 5));
  board.Add(new Tuple<int, int, int>(5, 5, 4));
  board.Add(new Tuple<int, int, int>(6, 6, 3));
  board.Add(new Tuple<int, int, int>(7, 7, 2));
  board.Add(new Tuple<int, int, int>(8, 8, 1));
  board.Add(new Tuple<int, int, int>(9, 0, 0));
}

private void InitializeNumberButtonMap()
{
```

```
    buttons.Add(1, btn1);
    buttons.Add(2, btn2);
    buttons.Add(3, btn3);
    buttons.Add(4, btn4);
    buttons.Add(5, btn5);
    buttons.Add(6, btn6);
    buttons.Add(7, btn7);
    buttons.Add(8, btn8);
    buttons.Add(9, btn9);
}
```

7. Add these event handlers to handle the events of `button Click` and volume control `pictureBox Click`:

```
void but_Click(object sender, EventArgs e)
{
    Button button = (Button)sender;
    DoMove(String.Format("{0}=0", button.Text), false);
    DrawBoard();
    GameOverYet();
}

//This is for volume toggle. You can skip it.
private void pictureBox1_Click(object sender, EventArgs e)
{
    if (mute)
    pictureBox1.ImageLocation = @"Volume_img.jpg";
    else
    pictureBox1.ImageLocation = @"Mute_img.JPG";
    //Switch the state
    mute = !mute;
}
```

8. Add the following code to randomize the board. Getting the same initial board every time is not what we want:

```
private void RandomizeBoard()
{
    //generate random move commands and move them whenever
    possible
    //finally return the modified board
    string randomMoveCommand = string.Empty;
    int total = new Random().Next(100);
    for (int i = 0; i < total; i++)
    {
        try
```

```
        {
          randomMoveCommand = new Random().Next(9).ToString() + "=0";
          System.Threading.Thread.Sleep(10);
          DoMove(randomMoveCommand, true);
        }
        catch
        {
          //This randomly generated move is illegal. Don't
            worry, just go.
          continue;
        }
      }

    }
```

9. Add the following code for the `Form1_Load` event:

```
private void Form1_Load(object sender, EventArgs e)
{
  //Attach the event handler for al the buttons
  this.Controls.OfType<Button>().ToList()
  ForEach(but => but.Click+=new EventHandler(but_Click));

  //Show the Volume Control image
  pictureBox1.ImageLocation = @"Volume_img.JPG";

  buttons.Clear();
  board.Clear();
  InitializeNumberButtonMap();
  InitializeStartUpBoard();
  RandomizeBoard();
  lblMoves.Text = "How many moves do you think ?";
  //When we were randomizing the board, there were some moves
  //(probably)
  //But we want to give the player a fresh start.
  //So set the total Moves count to Zero.
  //totalMoves = 0;
  //Draw the initial Board
  DrawBoard();
}
```

10. Add the following method:

```
private void GameOverYet()
{
  if (board.Where(tuple => tuple.Item2 != tuple.Item3).Count()
    == 0)
  {
    MessageBox.Show("Game Over! Congratulations!");
  }
}
```

What just happened?

As you execute the program, you will see something similar to the following screenshot:

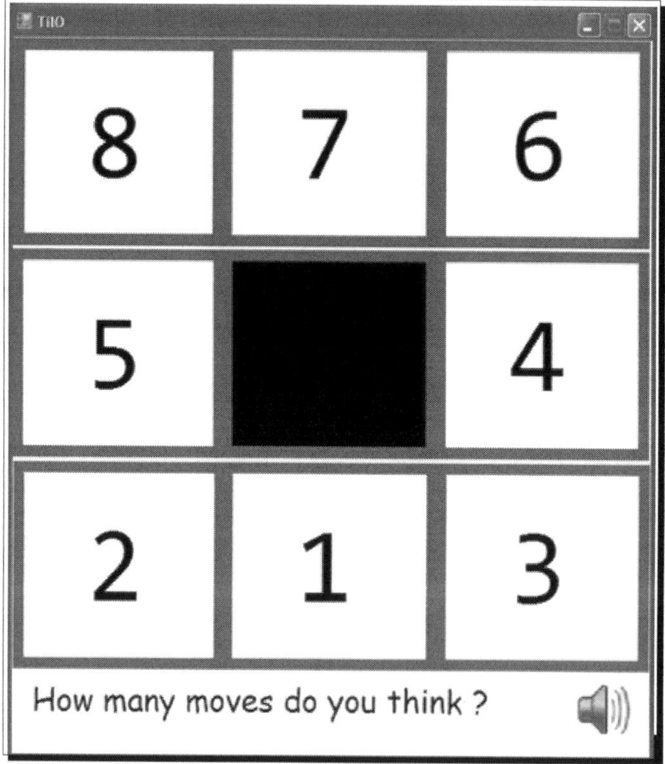

If you click on any of the numbered tiles, if it is adjacent to the black empty tile, it will swap its position with the empty tile. For example, in this case 5, 7, 4, and 1 are only eligible to swap their positions. As a tile moves, it will emit a sound. If you don't want sound, click on the speaker icon at the bottom-right.

You can take a look at the completed game demo video at my blog: `http://sudipta.posterous.com/number-re-arrange-game-an-application-of-tupl`.

Why have we used Tuples?

The board at any time can be represented as a list of three different integers attached together:

1. The index of the tile
2. The expected value of the tile in order for the game to end
3. The actual value of the tile in that index right now

Tips!

Tuples are a great way of representing database tables. There are eight overloaded versions of Tuple constructors. You can use one of them or use the static `Create()` method of the `Tuple` class. The last parameter for the last overload is another Tuple itself. So, you can plug in another Tuple if you need more than seven parameters.

For example, the board we have now and our goal (to finish the game) board are as follows:

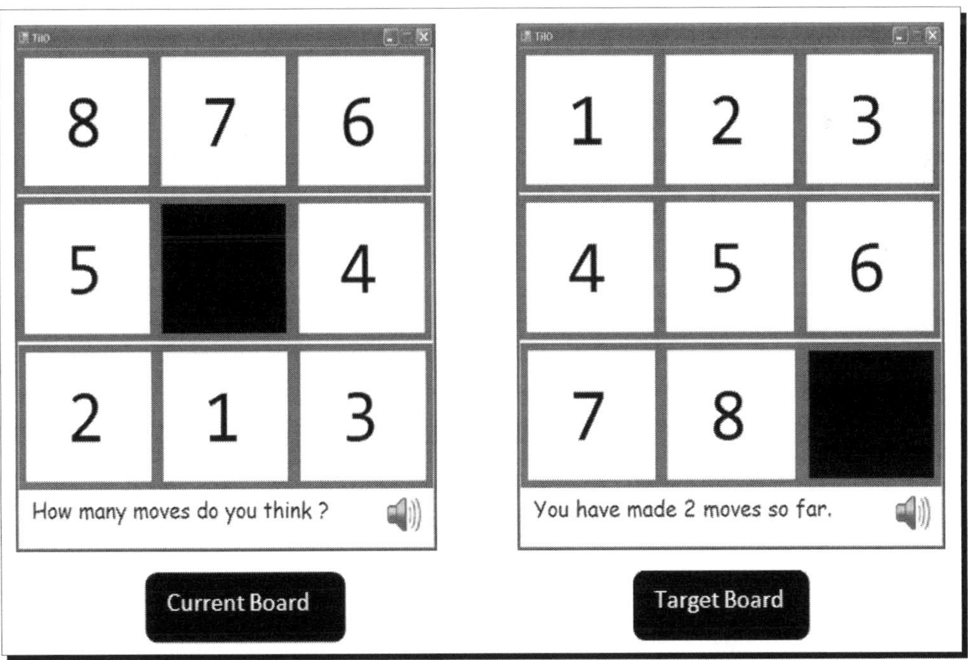

If we had to represent this without Tuples, we would have had to create a dump placeholder class with three values and create a list of such class objects. But the construct: List<Tuple<int, int, int>> board = new List<Tuple<int, int, int>>(); helps remove that special need. A list of Tuples represents the game board in this case. The first item of the Tuple is the index of the tile, the second is the expected numeric value on that tile, the third is the actual numeric value on that tile right now.

The InitializeStartUpBoard() method initializes the board with some default values. The next RandomizeBoard() method randomizes the board using some randomly generated moves. Some of these random moves might/will fail and that's ok.

Here is how the board looks after initialization is complete and randomization is yet to start:

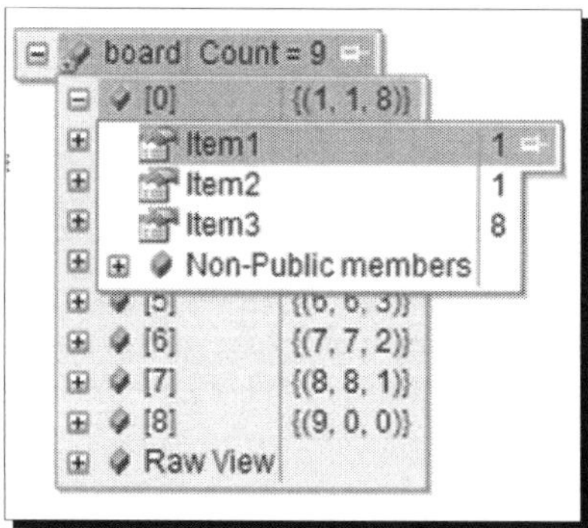

One disadvantage some people find using Tuples is that they reduce the readability of the code, because we can't name the items.

The method DoMove() moves two tiles visually. Actually, it swaps those two Tuples with changed entries. The following code:

```
int firstIndex = board.First(t => t.Item3 == first).Item1;
```

finds the index of the first integer in the command passed. So, if the command passed is 3=0 then first is 3 and firstIndex will store the index of tile with text 3 in the board.

First() is an extension method. We shall discuss this in detail in the next chapter, but for now just use it as it makes the code much cleaner.

The following lines:

```
Tuple<int, int, int> newFirstTuple = new Tuple<int, int,
  int>(firstIndex, expectedFirst, second);
```

```
Tuple<int, int, int> newSecondTuple = new Tuple<int, int,
  int>(secondIndex, expectedSecond, first);
```

create two Tuples with swapped actual values. Now, the older Tuples are deleted and replaced with these new Tuples in their positions by the following lines:

```
board.RemoveAt(firstIndex - 1); //removes the old tuple
board.Insert(firstIndex - 1, newFirstTuple); //Add the new tuple

board.RemoveAt(secondIndex - 1);
board.Insert(secondIndex - 1, newSecondTuple);
```

Inserting at the correct position is very important because the `DoMove()` method relies on it.

How did we figure out whether the game is over or not?

The game will be over if `Item2` and `Item3` for each Tuple on the board become the same. Because `Item2` is the expected value of the tile and `Item3` is the current value, if there is no such tile that has a mismatch between `Item2` and `Item3`, then we can conclude that the game is over.

`board.Where(tuple => tuple.Item2 != tuple.Item3)` returns all those Tuples as an `IEnumerable<Tuple<int,int,int>>` where `Item2` and `Item3` are not the same. If the count of such entries is `0` then we can conclude that the game is over.

Have a go hero

Now that you know list-based containers and dictionaries, can you add a recording feature to the number rearrange game. This should enable players to record their moves from the initial board positions. Being able to save and retrieve a saved game would be great. Remember that there can be several players starting from the same board.

Hint: You might want to use this structure to store and replay games for users:

```
List<Tuple<string, List<Tuple<int, int, int>>, List<string>>> games
```

The first `string` in the `Tuple` will represent the name of the player, the inner `Tuple` one will represent the game board and the last `List` of `string` will represent the moves the player used to solve the puzzle or wherever he/she saved the game last.

Tuples have been around for a long time in functional programming languages. Recently, Microsoft research created a new programming language called F#, which has great support for Tuples. Although it is not related to Generics, it is a great thing to know how C# is borrowing from other languages and growing.

Summary

We learned a lot in this chapter about .NET Generics dictionary-based containers.

Specifically, we covered:

- Dictionary<TKey,TValue>
- SortedDictionary<TKey,TValue>
- KeyValuePair<TKey,TValue>
- Tuples
- How to design dictionaries to support one-to-many mapping

We also discussed how to create a custom generic dictionary using the inbuilt generic containers. Now that we've learned about all the lists and dictionary-based containers, we're ready to learn more about how to query them better using LINQ. That's the topic of the next chapter.

4

LINQ to Objects

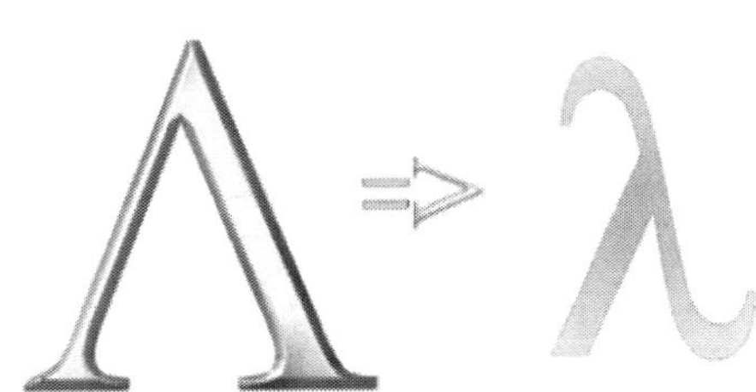

Unity in diversity

In the last two chapters, we have learned about lists and dictionaries. These are two very important data structures which .NET Generics has to offer. The ability to query these in an efficient manner is a very important factor for the all-over efficiency of an app.

Imperative programming languages enforce the how part of the program more than the what part. Let me explain that a little bit. Suppose you want to sort a list of `student` *objects. In an imperative style, you are bound to use a looping construct. So the what part is to sort the elements and the how part is the instructions that you write as part of the program, to achieve sorting.*

However, we are living in a very exciting time where a purist programming approach is fast becoming a thing of the past. Computing power is more popular than ever. Programming languages are going through a change. Declarative syntax that allows programmers to concentrate on the what part more than the how part is the new trend. This allows compiler developers to tune the compiler to emit optimized machine code for any given declarative syntax. This will eventually increase the performance of the application.

.NET 3.5 came up a step ahead with the introduction of **Language Integrated Query** *(***LINQ***). This allows programmers to query in-memory objects and databases (in fact any data source) alike, while it does the required optimization in the background.*

In this chapter, we shall learn:

- How to put your own method for existing classes using Extension methods
- How to use Functors
- How to use Actions
- Lambda expressions
- LINQ Standard Query Operators (LSQO)

Some of the LSQO for joining have been left out deliberately as they are not very useful for LINQ to Objects in general. A couple of other operators such as `Aggregate` and `Average` are also left out as they are not very applicable to LINQ to Objects in general; they find specific usage while dealing with numeric data types.

After reading this chapter, you should be able to appreciate how LINQ drastically removes the complexity for querying in-memory collections and the usage of looping constructs and its side effects. There is a lot more in LINQ to Objects than we can discuss in this chapter. We shall concentrate more on the LSQO as we need them to be able to query-out generic collections in a better optimized way.

What makes LINQ?

LINQ is not a technology in itself, instead it is made up using different building blocks. These are the things that make LINQ.

Extension methods

.NET Generics follows a good design philosophy. This API is open for extension, but closed for modification. Think about the .NET string API. You can't change the source code for any member method. However, if you want you can always put a new method that can behave as if it was built-in.

The technology that allows us to do this legal stretching (if you will) is known as the Extension method. Here are a few very important details about Extension methods:

- Every Extension method must be in a static class.
- Every Extension method must be static.

- Every Extension method must take at least one parameter, passed as this `Type <parameter name>`.

  One example is `this string name`.

- The argument declared with `this` has to be the first one in the parameter list. Every other parameter (which is optional, if any) should follow.
- This gives a feel that this newly introduced method is like one of those inbuilt ones. If we want to inject a method for all concrete types of an interface, the Extension method declared on the interface is the only option.

Time for action – creating an Extension method

Let's say that you have a `List` of strings and you want to find out how many match a given regular expression pattern. This is a very common activity:

1. Create a class library project. Call it `StringEx`. We are trying to extend `string` class functionalities, so I named it `StringEx`.
2. Rename the generated class as `StringExtenstions.cs`.
3. Mark the class as static:

   ```
   public static class StringExtensions
   ```

4. Add the following *using directive* to the header of the class:

   ```
   using System.Text.RegularExpressions;
   ```

5. Add the following code snippet as the method body:

   ```
   public static bool IsMatching(this string input, string pattern)
   {
     return Regex.IsMatch(input,
     pattern,RegexOptions.CultureInvariant);
   }
   ```

What just happened?

We just created an Extension method called `IsMatching()` for the `string` class. The first argument of the method is the calling object. `pattern` is the regular expression against which we want to validate the input string. We want to compare the strings ignoring the culture.

So, while calling `IsMatching()`, we shall just have to pass the `pattern` and not the string.

Time for action – consuming our new Extension method

Now, let's see how we can consume this method:

1. Stay in the project you created. Add a console application. Call it `StringExTest`.
2. Add a reference of `StringEx` class library to this project:

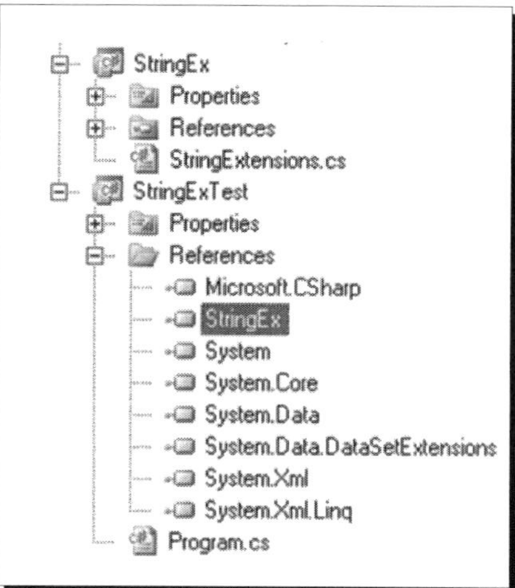

3. Add the following *using directive* in `Program.cs`:

```
using StringEx;
```

4. Add the following string variable in the `Main()` method. This validates Swedish zip codes:

```
string pattern = @"^(s-|S-){0,1}[0-9]{3}\s?[0-9]{2}$";
```

5. Add a few test input strings in a `List` of strings:

```
List<string> testInputs = new List<string>()
  {"12345", "425611", "932 68", "S-621 46", "5367", "31 545" };
```

Iterate through all these test inputs to find out whether they match the given regular expression pattern or not:

```
foreach (string testInput in testInputs)
{
  if (testInput.IsMatching(pattern))
  Console.WriteLine(testInput + " is a valid Swedish ZIP code");
```

```
        else
        Console.WriteLine(testInput +
          " is NOT a valid Swedish ZIP code");
      }
```

When run, this program should generate the following output:

```
12345 is a valid Swedish ZIP code
425611 is NOT a valid Swedish ZIP code
932 68 is a valid Swedish ZIP code
S-621 46 is a valid Swedish ZIP code
5367 is NOT a valid Swedish ZIP code
31 545 is NOT a valid Swedish ZIP code
```

What just happened?

As this `IsMatching()` method is described as an Extension method in `StringEx`; and `StringEx` is referenced in this `StringExTest` project, `IsMatching()` will be available for invocation on any string object in the `StringExTest` project.

Any Extension method appears with a downward arrow, as shown in the following screenshot. Also the compiler shows the intelligence support (if it is selected) mentioning that this is an Extension method:

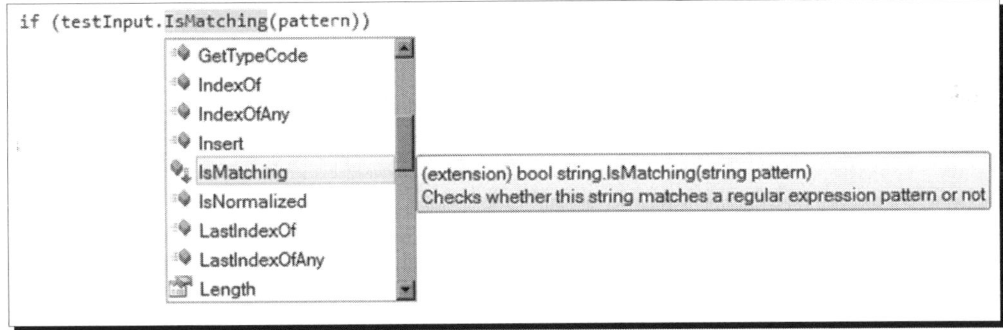

Notice that while calling the Extension method, we do not need to pass the string argument. `testInput` is the string object on which we call this Extension method.

The keyword `this` in the parameter list did the trick.

It is possible to define the Extension method for any type of .NET class. So all you have to do is add a static class and add the static Extension methods to the class. You can find an API for string processing written using the Extension method at `http://www.codeplex.com/StringDefs`. I created this for different kinds of string processing needs. This will give you an idea about how Extension methods can be written for several purposes.

For using LINQ to Objects, we shall need `System.Linq` namespace. The standard query operators of LINQ are based on the Extension methods that extend any type that implements `IEnumerable<T>`.

Check out these guidelines for when not to use Extension methods

Although an Extension method might seem to solve your problem, too much usage of the Extension method is probably an indication that you should re-think your design a little bit. Remember; they are meant to extend the functionality of an existing type. So, if the functionality you want to achieve can't be done using already existing methods, you are better off creating your own type by inheriting the type you wanted to extend.

Object initializers

Assume that you have a class called `Student` and you want to initialize `student` objects using different variables at different times. Sometimes, you will only have name and age, while at other times you might also have the course they are enrolled in as part of the input. These situations call for a set of parameterized constructors in the `Student` class.

Otherwise, we can have a blank constructor and public properties for the `Student` class attributes. In this situation, the code to assign a `student` object might look similar to the following:

```
Student sam = new Student();
sam.FirstName = "Sam";
sam.LastName = "Hood";

Student dorothy = new Student();
dorothy.Gender = "F";
dorothy.LastName = "Hudson";
```

This type of object initialization spans over multiple code lines and, at times, is difficult to read and keep up. Thus, C# 3.0 came up with a feature called **object initializers** that allows programmers to construct and assign an object in a single line. Any public field or property can be assigned in the initialization statement by assigning that property name to a value. Multiple assignments can be made by the comma-separated assignment list. The C# compiler calls the default constructor behind the scene and assigns each public field or property as if they were previously declared and assigned one after another. So, the previous two initializations will be changed to the following:

```
Student sam = new Student()
{
   FirstName = "Sam";
   LastName = "Hood";
};
```

```
Student dorothy = new Student()
{
   Gender = "F";
   LastName = "Hudson";
};
```

Although this technical advancement might, at first, look like syntactical sugar, while writing LINQ queries, we shall find ourselves using this feature quite often to construct object instances as part of the result set by setting property values on the fly.

Collection initializers

Taking the object initializers a step ahead, the ability to add elements to the collections at the time of creating them is added. This is called a **collection initializer**. The only constraint is that the collection has to implement the `IEnumerable` interface and provide an appropriate `Add()` method implementation that will be used to add the elements.

The good thing is that collection initializers can use object initialization technique to create objects on the fly while adding them to the collection. Here are some examples:

```
List<string> names = new List<string>() { "Anders", "David", "James",
  "Jeff", "Joe", "Erik" };

List<int> numbers = new List<int>() {56, 12, 134, 113, 41, 1, 0};

List<Student> myStudents = new List<Student>()
{
  new Student(){Name = "Sam", Course = "C#"},
  new Student(){Name = "Dorothy", Course  = "VB.NET"}
};
```

Implicitly typed local variables

C# 3.5 introduced a new way to declare variables using the `var` keyword. This type of a new variable is inferred from the initialization expression. These types of variables are strongly typed.

Here are a few examples:

```
var shirtSize = "L";
var shoeSize = 10;
var age = 29;
var coursesTaken = new List<string>() { "C#", "C++", "Java", "Ruby" };
Console.WriteLine(shirtSize + " " + shirtSize.GetType().Name);
Console.WriteLine(shoeSize + " " + shoeSize.GetType().Name);
Console.WriteLine(age + " " + age.GetType().Name);
Console.WriteLine(coursesTaken + " " + coursesTaken.GetType().Name);
```

And here is the output for the preceding snippet:

```
L String
10 Int32
29 Int32
System.Collections.Generic.List`1[System.String] List`1
```

Although declaring a variable in this way may seem to have little value, it is a necessary feature for declaring some types that can't be declared in any other way; for example, anonymous types.

Anonymous types

Anonymous types are compile-time generated types where the public properties are inferred from the object initialization expression at compile time. These types serve the purpose of temporary storage. This saves us from building specific classes for any operation.

Anonymous types are declared using the `var` keyword as an implicit variable and their type is inferred from the expression used to initialize.

Anonymous types are declared by omitting the type after the `new` keyword. Here are a few examples:

```
var item = new { Name = "Sam", Age = 30 };
var car = new { Make = "Honda", Price = 30000 };
```

These types are used in queries where collections are built using a subset of properties from an existing type also known as **projections**. We shall see how these help in LINQ in a short while.

Lambda expressions

Lambda expressions are built on an anonymous method. These are basically delegates in a very brief syntax. Most of the time these expressions are passed as an argument to the LINQ Extension methods. This type of expression can be compound and can span multiple lines while used in LINQ Extension methods also known as LINQ Standard Query Operators or LSQO in short.

Lambda expressions use the operator `=>` to separate parameters from expressions.

Before the Lambda expression came into existence, we had to write query using delegates as follows:

```
Students.Find(delegate(Student s) {return s.Course == "C#";});
```

Using the Lambda expression, the query will be as follows:

```
Students.Find(s => s.Course == "C#");
```

The highlighted part in the second code line is the Lambda expression. One way to visualize this is to think about mathematical sets. Assume `=>` stands for rule of membership. So the preceding line is basically trying to find all the `students` where course is `C#` and `s` denotes a temporary variable of the data source being queried; in this case the `Students` collection.

This is a very important concept for understanding and using LINQ.

Functors

Functors are basically space holders for Lambda expressions. It is a parameterized type in C#. There are 17 overloaded constructors to declare different types of Functors. These are created by the `Func<>` keyword as follows:

```
Func<bool> boolMethod = new Func<bool> (
                          Func<bool>.Func(bool () target)
```

Notice the tooltip. It is expecting a method name that accepts no parameter but returns a Boolean value. So `boolMethod` can hold any method that matches that signature.

So if we have a method as shown in the following snippet:

```
private static bool IsTime()
{
  return DateTime.Today.Day == 8 && DateTime.Today.Month == 7;
}
```

the Functor can be created using the method name as an argument to the constructor, as follows:

```
Func<bool> boolMethod = new Func<bool>(Program.IsTime);
```

The last parameter to a Functor is the output and the rest all are input. So the following Functor constructor expects a method that accepts an integer and returns a bool:

```
Func<int,bool> intCheck = new Func<int,bool>(
                    Func<int,bool>.Func(bool (int) target)
```

These types of Functors that take some argument and return a Boolean variable (in most cases due to some operation on the input argument) are also known as **Predicates**.

You can also use Lambda expression syntax to declare Functors as follows:

```
//Declaring the Functor that takes an integer and checks if it is odd
//When the Functor takes only one input it is not needed to wrap the
//input by parenthesis. Highlighted part is the Lambda expression
//So you see, Lambda expressions can be used directly where the
//argument type is of Func<>
Func<int, bool> isEven = x => x % 2 == 0;

//Invoking the Functor
bool result = isEven.Invoke(8);
```

Most of the LSQO accept Functors as **selector functions**. A selector function is a function that operates on each of the element in a collection. The outcome of these operations decide which values will be projected in the resulted collection. This will be more clear as we discuss all the LSQO in a while.

Predicates

Predicates are essentially `Func<int, bool>`. You can use Lambda expressions to initialize them like Functors as follows:

```
Predicate<int> isEven = new Predicate<int>(c => c % 2 == 0);
```

Here is how you can call this Functor:

```
int[] nums = Enumerable.Range(1, 10).ToArray();
foreach (int i in nums)
  if(isEven(i))
  Console.WriteLine(i.ToString() + " " +  " is even " );
```

The Lambda expression is hidden. It is advisable to use `Func<>` for LINQ-related operations as it matches the signatures of the LSQO. Predicates was introduced with `System.Collections.Generic` in .NET Framework 2.0 and `Func<>` was introduced in .NET 3.5.

Although they behave similarly, there are a couple of key differences between a Predicate and a Functor:

1. Predicate always returns a Boolean value whereas Functors can be programmed to return a custom type:

   ```
   public delegate bool Predicate<T>(T obj);
   public delegate TResult Func<TResult>();
   ```

2. Predicates can't take more than one parameter while Functors can be programmed to take a maximum of four input parameters:

   ```
   public delegate TResult Func<T1, T2, T3, T4, TResult>
   (T1 arg1, T2 arg2, T3 arg3, T4 arg4);
   ```

Actions

This is a built-in delegate, introduced in .NET Framework 4.0. There are several overloaded versions to handle different styles of delegates.

Here is an example:

```
Action<string> sayHello = new Action<string>
  (c=>Console.WriteLine("Hello " + c));

List<string> names = new List<string>()
  { "Sam", "Dave", "Jeff", "Erik"};
names.ForEach(sayHello);
```

`ForEach()` is a method in the `List<T>` class that takes an argument of the type `Action<T>`. The preceding snippet prints the following output:

```
Hello Sam
Hello Dave
Hello Jeff
Hello Erik
```

Putting it all together, LINQ Standard Query Operators

There are several operators (which are basically Extension methods) based on the `IEnumerable<T>` type. These can be broadly classified as follows:

- Restriction operators
- Projection operators
- Partitioning operators
- Ordering operators
- Grouping operators
- Set operators
- Conversion operators
- Element operators
- Generation operators
- Quantifiers
- Aggregate operators
- Join operators
- Merge operators

All these will be discussed except the Aggregate operators and Join operators as they come in more handy while using the query syntax and while dealing with numeric data types and LINQ to SQL respectively. But we shall be more focused towards LINQ to Objects in this chapter.

We shall use LINQPad for running our LINQ snippets, as described next in this chapter. **Source Collection** is the collection on which the operator is invoked. Every time we refer to Source Collection please assume this definition.

Time for action – getting the LINQPad

Follow the given steps:

1. Download LINQPad from `www.linqpad.net/`.
2. Download the executable for .NET Framework 4.0 from the website:

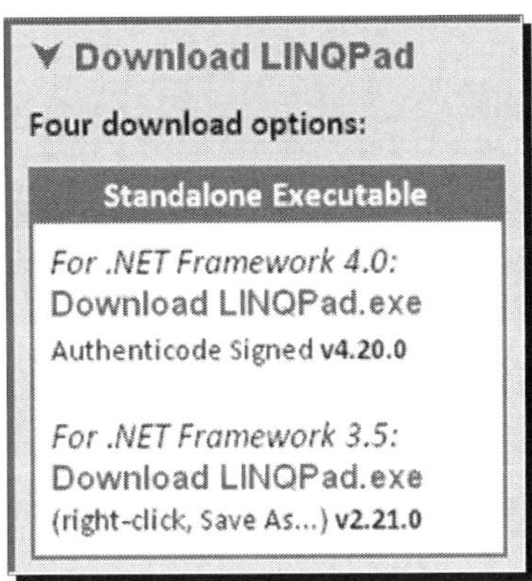

3. Start LINQPad.

   LINQPad is capable of running C# Expressions, Statements, and complete C# Programs.

4. Type the following query in the query area in the tab space to the right, as shown in the following screenshot. Select **C# Statement(s)** from the drop-down, as shown in the following screenshot. The query comprises complete C# Statements. A C# Expression is a partial C# Statement:

```
"I You Love".Split(' ').OrderBy(c => c).ToList().
ForEach(c=>Console.Write(c+" ")); Console.Write("Linq");
```

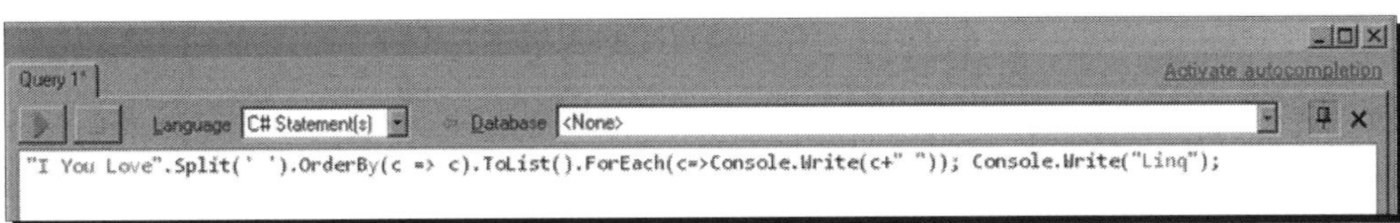

5. Press the green play button on the top left-hand corner.

6. See the result at the bottom:

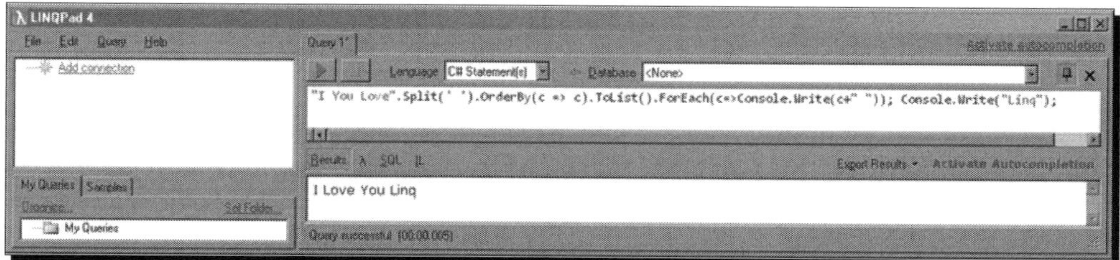

You did expect to see something that is shown in the screenshot. Didn't you?

One important method of LINQPad is `Dump()`. It's a very useful function because it shows the data type of the query results. You can use `Dump()` to see the result without explicitly channeling the data to the console output.

Here is how you can use it:

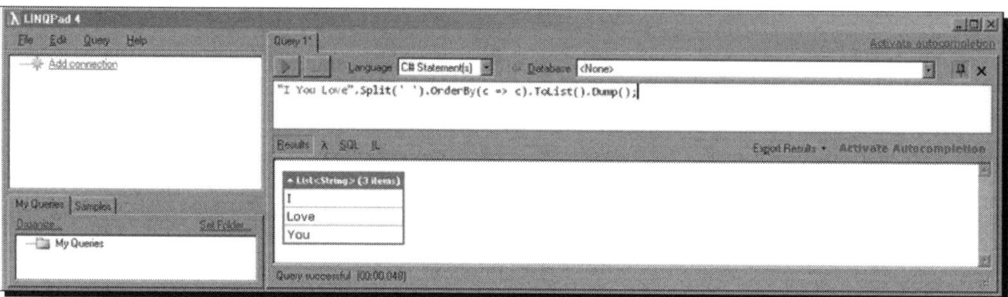

Basically, you terminate any query with `Dump()` and it will give you the result type.

The other version of `Dump()` takes an argument. This argument will be used as a header of the result as follows:

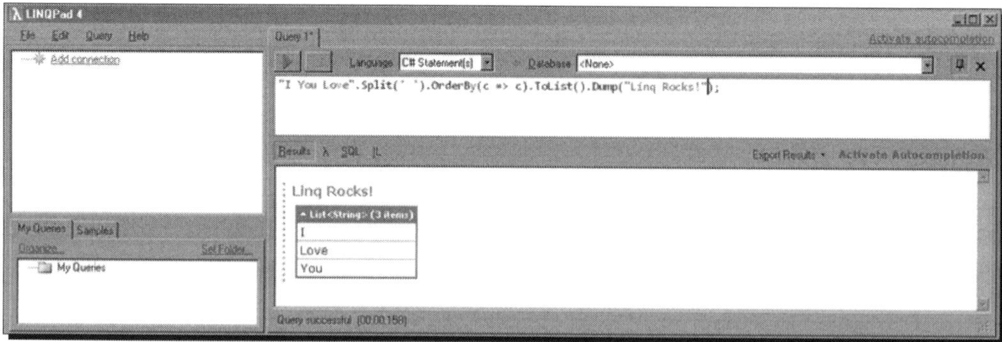

Restriction operators

In this section, we will discuss the following Restriction operators:

Where()

This query operator allows the user to filter their data source for some condition passed as a predicate. With .NET 3.5+ this can be a Lambda expression.

There are two overloads of this operator:

▲ 1 of 2 ▼ (extension) IEnumerable<T> IEnumerable<T>.Where(**Func<T,bool> predicate**)
Filters a sequence of values based on a predicate.
predicate: *A function to test each element for a condition.*

This one takes a predicate that accepts an element of type **T** and returns a bool applying some logic on the element passed. So, if we are operating this operator on an array of strings, then this version of `Where()` would expect a `Func<string, bool>`.

Both overloaded versions return an `IEnumerable<T>` instance so that we can pass the result obtained as input to another LSQO.

Time for action – finding all names with *am*

Here is the first problem:

Say we have a `List` of names and we want to find all those names where "am" occurs:

1. Copy the following code snippet on LINQPad:

```
string[] names = { "Sam", "Pamela", "Dave", "Pascal", "Erik" };
List<string> filteredNames =
  names.Where(c => c.Contains("am")).ToList().Dump(
  "Names with pattern *am*");
```

2. Run the snippet. Make sure **C# Statement(s)** is selected in the **Language** drop-down, otherwise it will not work. Once successfully run, you should expect the output shown in the following screenshot:

Names with pattern *am*

List<String> (2 items)

Sam
Pamela

What just happened?

The first version of Where() takes a Func<T, bool> (T is the type of source collection). In this case, T is a string. So in this case, it will expect a Func<string, bool>. As described earlier, Functors can be expressed as Lambda expressions. This leads to much shorter code.

The highlighted part in the query is the Lambda expression that takes the form of a Func<string, bool>. c represents an element in the source being queried (in this case, names). Where() loops through the entire source and outputs those to the returned IEnumerable<T> instance. As we want to store the result in a List of strings, I have used the ToList() Extension method to convert the results from IEnumerable<string> to List<string>.

filteredNames will have **"Sam"** and **"Pamela"**, as shown in the following screenshot:

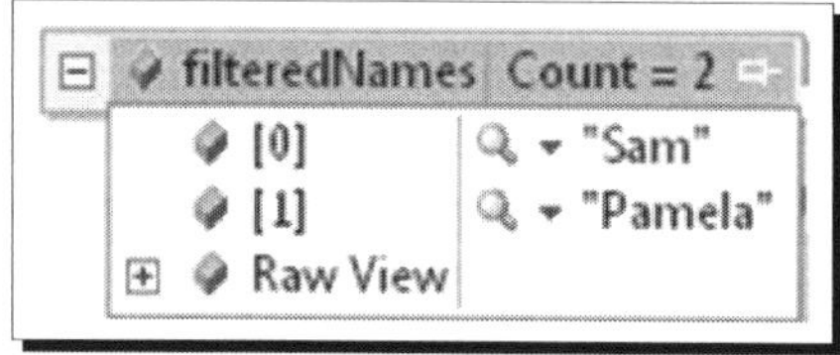

Here are some examples that might interest you!

Time for action – finding all vowels

Here is the second problem:

Finding all the vowels in a string:

1. Copy the following code snippet as a query in LINQPad:

```
List<char> vowels = "Packt Publishing".ToLower().Where(c =>
  "aeiou".Contains(c)).ToList();
vowels.Dump();
```

2. Run the query. You will get the following output:

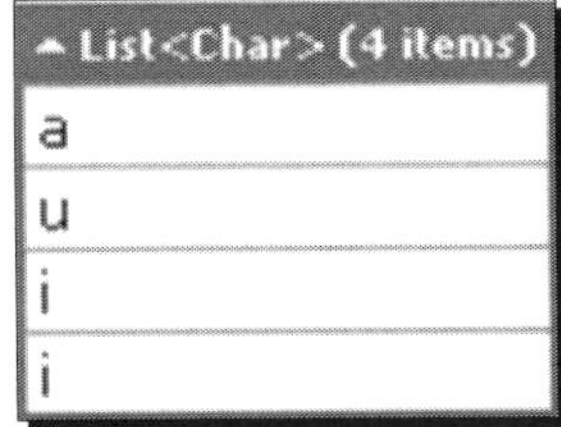

What just happened?

The Lambda expression `c => "aeiou".Contains(c)` matches only that character that is a vowel from the source. As the string is a character array, the `Where()` in this case is operating on `IEnumerable<char>`.

In the end, `ToList()` converts the `IEnumerable<char>` back to a `List`.

Time for action – finding all running processes matching a Regex

Here is the third problem:

Finding all processes where process names match a regular expression pattern:

1. Copy the following code snippet as a query in LINQPad:

```
//Finding all processes that match the directions
string pattern = "win+";
var myProcesses = Process.GetProcesses().Where(p =>
  Regex.IsMatch(p.ProcessName,pattern));

//Iterating over the result to print records
foreach (Process proc in myProcesses)
  Console.WriteLine(proc.ProcessName + " " + proc.MachineName);
```

2. Run the query. You will get the following output:

```
winlogon .
```

What just happened?

Process.GetProcesses() returns an array of System.Diagnostics.Process and thus, it is an IEnumerable<Process> so Where() can operate on this. LSQO is being written as an Extension method of the IEnumerable<T> interface which can operate on any collection that implements this interface. System.Array() implements IEnumerable(), which is also inherited by IEnumerable<T>. This is because of the **Liskov Substitution Principle**.

Note, implicit variable declaration is used to store the result of the query. However, later on, a strongly typed variable is used in the loop to iterate over the result. This is proof that var actually enforces strong typing implicitly.

Time for action – playing with the indexed version of Where()

The second overloaded version lets you use the index of a particular element in the source collection in the query:

▲ 2 of 2 ▼ (extension) IEnumerable<T> IEnumerable<T>.Where(**Func<T,int,bool> predicate**)
Filters a sequence of values based on a predicate. Each element's index is used in the logic of the predicate function.
predicate: *A function to test each source element for a condition; the second parameter of the function represents the index of the source element.*

So in this case, the Lambda expression will expect two input parameters. The item and its index. Then it will return a bool depending on the parameters.

This can be particularly handy when you want to exclude certain elements from the source collection; while processing:

1. Copy the following code snippet to LINQPad:

```
//This will find all the names in the array "names".
//where length of the name is less than or equal to the index of
//the element + 1

string[] names  = { "Sam", "Pamela", "Dave", "Pascal", "Erik" };
var nameList = names.Where((c, index) => c.Length  <= index + 1);
nameList.Dump();
```

2. Run the query. You will get the following output:

▲ IEnumerable<String> (1 item)
Erik

What just happened?

In the Lambda expression `(c,index) => c.Length <= index + 1`, `c` denotes any variable in the array `names`, while `index` denotes the index of that particular element in the array `names`. So, for example, if the current element being scanned is "Dave" then the index will be 2 (the array index starts from zero).

`c.Length` means the length of the current element. So `c.Length <= index + 1` will return `true` if the length of the current element being scanned is less than or equal to the expression index plus unity.

Now, if we scan from the first element, the results will be as follows:

c	index	c.Length	c.Length <= index + 1
Sam	0	3	false
Pamela	1	6	false
Dave	2	4	false
Pascal	3	6	false
Erik	4	4	true

As only "Erik" matches the Lambda expression, it gets added to the returned `IEnumerable<string>`.

You can do pretty much anything depending on the index of the element.

Time for action – learn how to go about creating a Where() clause

Suppose there is a `Student` class and we want to find only those students who have enrolled for the C# course:

1. We want to find all students whose `Course` is `C#`. Write the Lambda expression for that:

```
s => s.Course.Equals("C#")
```

2. Pass this Lambda expression to the `Where()` clause (sometimes, LSQO are referred to as clauses) as follows:

```
Students.Where(s => s.Course.Equals("C#") );
```

3. Receive the result of this operation in an implicit variable, as shown next:

```
var cSharpStudents = Students.Where(s => s.Course.Equals("C#") );
```

What just happened?

We have a List of Student objects and we wanted to find all the students that have opted for C#. Assuming Course is a public property of the Student object, s.Course gives the course of the current student on the collection, while we keep moving along the collection.

s => s.Course.Equals("C#") is the expression that evaluates to true when the course of the current student is C# and that Student object gets added to the List of IEnumerable<Student>, which is returned after the operation is complete.

We used the var keyword to use implicit typing while receiving this IEnumerable<Student> instance. Later in this chapter, you will learn some conversion operators, so that we can project the result on a concrete collection.

The following screenshot shows how we can visualize Where():

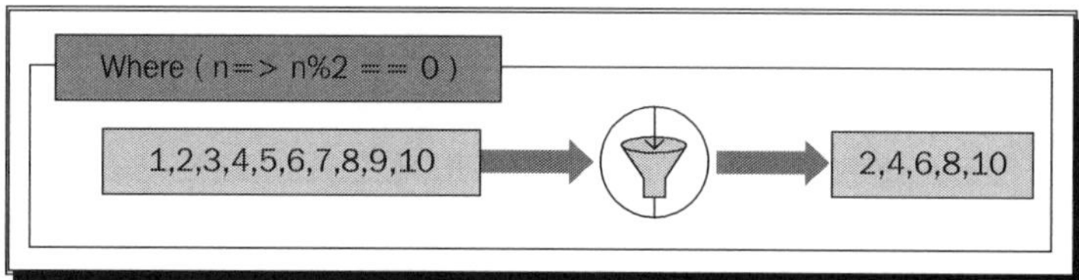

Pop quiz – doing the thing

1. Let's see if you have learned Where(). Fill in the following blanks:

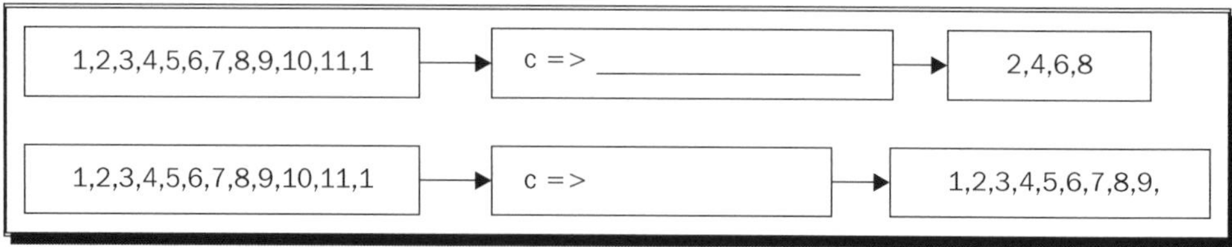

Projection operators

In this section, we will discuss the following Projection operators:

Select()

This operator allows you to project the elements in the result collection in a customized manner. Like `Where()` this also comes in two overloaded versions. The first version takes a Lambda expression that describes how the projection has to be made. The other version allows us to consider the index of the element:

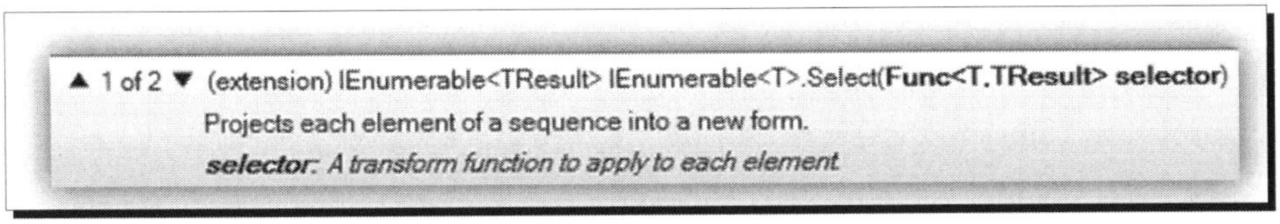

▲ 1 of 2 ▼ (extension) IEnumerable<TResult> IEnumerable<T>.Select(**Func<T,TResult> selector**)
Projects each element of a sequence into a new form.
selector: *A transform function to apply to each element*

Time for action – let's say "Hello" to your buddies

Here is the first problem:

Say we have a `List` of names and we want to print "Hello" in front of all the names:

1. Copy the following code snippet as a query to the LINQPad:

```
List<string> nameList1 = new List<string> (){ "Anders", "David",
  "James", "Jeff", "Joe", "Erik" };
nameList1.Select(c => "Hello! " + c).ToList().ForEach(c =>
  Console.WriteLine(c));
```

2. Run the query.

The preceding code snippet will give the following output:

```
Hello! Anders
Hello! David
Hello! James
Hello! Jeff
Hello! Joe
Hello! Erik
```

What just happened?

The Lambda expression `c => "Hello!" + c` is basically creating a projection of the elements of `nameList1 List` and the result will be an instance of IEnumerable<string> with all the elements of `nameList1` and a "Hello!" in front of them.

`ToList()` is a conversion operator, which we shall learn later in this chapter. This converts the generated IEnumerable<string> to a List<string>. I used this conversion because I wanted to use the `ForEach()` method of the List<T> class that accepts an action.

Now that we have the `List` of processed strings, we need to tell the computer how we want it to be printed. The last Lambda expression `c => Console.WriteLine(c)` does just that. This means taking a string from the `List` and printing it to the console, one per line.

Making use of the overloaded indexed version of Select()

Here we will see how to make use of the overloaded indexed version of `Select()`.

Time for action – radio "Lucky Caller" announcement

Suppose you are writing a program for a radio station where you need to find every third name in the array and say "Hi! <Name> You are the Lucky 3*rd* Caller". So you see in this case, the index of the element currently being projected is of importance. A little change in the Lambda expression used in the previous example, is all it will take to make this happen:

1. Copy the following code snippet as a query to LINQPad:

```
List<int> First100LuckyCallerIndices = new List<int>();
//First lucky third caller's index in the array will be 2.
First100LuckyCallerIndices.Add(2);
for (int i = 0; i < 100; i++)
First100LuckyCallerIndices.
  Add(First100LuckyCallerIndices.Last() + 3);
List<string> nameList1 = new List<string>() { "Anders", "David",
  "James", "Jeff", "Joe", "Erik", "A", "B", "C", "D", "E" };
var query = nameList1.Select((c, index) => new { Name = c, Prize =
  First100LuckyCallerIndices.Contains(index) });
foreach (var person in query)
{
  if (person.Prize)
  {
    Console.WriteLine(
    "Hello! {0} You are the Lucky 3rd Caller.", person.Name);
  }
}
```

2. Run the query.

The previous code snippet will generate the following output:

```
Hello! Anders You are the Lucky 3rd Caller.
Hello! Jeff You are the Lucky 3rd Caller.
```

What just happened?

This query makes use of the anonymous type. The Lambda expression: `nameList1.Select((c,index) => new {Name = c, Prize = index % 3 == 0})` uses the index of the current element. Instead of projecting the current string or some concatenated string, this time we want to project an anonymous type. The properties of this type get populated by the current element and its index.

The name of this anonymous object is assigned as the current element by the code `Name = c`, while whether this person has won a prize or not depends on the index of the current element.

`Prize = index % 3 == 0` means if the index of the current element is a multiple of 3 then the attribute `Prize` for the anonymous object gets set to `true`, otherwise it gets set to `false`.

So the query `Select((c,index) => new {Name = c, Prize = index % 3 == 0});` returns an instance of `IEnumerable<string>` that has the names of the lucky winners.

So once we have it, we iterate over the instance to print the results.

Have a go hero – can you tell me what's going on here?

Can you predict what will be the result of the following query?

```
nameList1.Select((c,index)=>  new {Name = c, Prize = index % 3 == 0})
  .Select(c=>c.Prize==true?"Hello! " + c.Name +
    " You are the Lucky 3rd Caller":"no")
  .ToList()
  .Where(c=>c.StartsWith("Hello!"))
  .ToList()
  .ForEach(c=>Console.WriteLine(c));
```

Hint: In order to understand it, you can break the query into parts and put them in LINQPad and execute them step-by-step.

SelectMany()

This operator projects each element of a sequence to an `IEnumerable<T>` instance and flattens the resulting sequences into one sequence.

This lets us query the data of the source collection using a normal key selector or an indexed version, where we can use the index of the elements in the source collection to be a deciding factor in their inclusion in the result.

Time for action – flattening a dictionary

Suppose, we have a dictionary such that each key has a list of values attached to them. Now, we want to project all the elements in a single collection:

1. Copy the following code snippet as a query to LINQPad:

```
Dictionary<string, List<string>> map = new Dictionary<string,
  List<string>>();

map.Add("UK", new List<string>() { "Bermingham", "Bradford",
  "Liverpool" });
map.Add("USA", new List<string>() { "NYC", "New Jersey", "Boston",
  "Buffalo" });

var cities = map.SelectMany(c => c.Value).ToList();
cities.Dump("All Cities");
```

2. Run the query. You should see the following output:

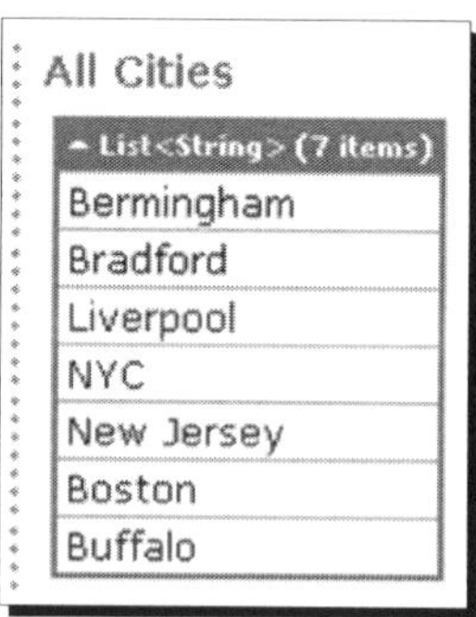

What just happened?

In this example, we use the first version of the SelectMany() method that has the following signature:

▲ 1 of 4 ▼ (extension) IEnumerable<TResult> IEnumerable<T>.SelectMany(**Func<T,IEnumerable<TResult>> selector**)
Projects each element of a sequence to an System.Collections.Generic.IEnumerable<T> and flattens the resulting sequences into one sequence.
selector: *A transform function to apply to each element*

Note that it accepts a Functor that accepts a string and returns an instance of IEnumerable<T>.

In this case, the Lambda expression c => c.Value means that each key returns the list of values associated with that key.

The second overloaded version allows us to use the index of the current element in the source collection in the Lambda expression.

Later in this chapter, you will see some other applications of this operator.

Partitioning operators

In this section, we will discuss the following Partitioning operators:

Take()

Suppose we are only interested in the first few values of a collection and we don't want to consider the rest for now. In this situation, in the absence of LINQ, we had to create a blank collection and iterate over the original one to populate the other empty collection.

With the introduction of LSQO, Take() all that is going to be history. Take() takes an integer parameter and returns IEnumerable<T> (where the source collection is of type T) containing as many elements as you want starting from the first element in the source collection.

The method signature is as shown in the following screenshot:

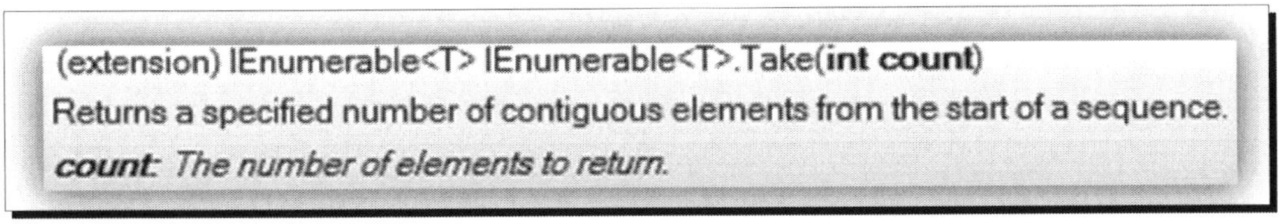

(extension) IEnumerable<T> IEnumerable<T>.Take(**int count**)
Returns a specified number of contiguous elements from the start of a sequence.
count: *The number of elements to return.*

Time for action – leaving the first few elements

Follow the given steps:

1. Copy the following code snippet as a query to LINQPad:

```
int[] numbers = { 1, 2, 3, 4, 5, 6, 7, 8, 9, 10, 11, 12,13 };
var first4 = numbers.Take(4);
first4.Dump();
```

2. Run the query. You will get the following output:

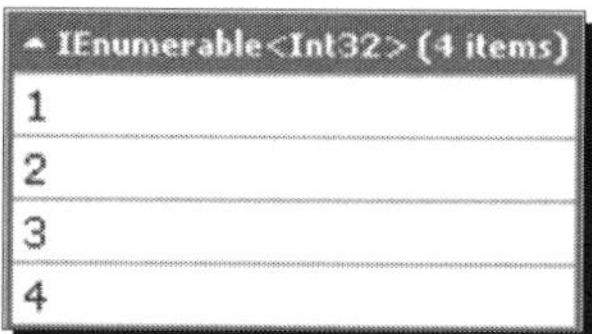

What just happened?

Numbers is an `int` array, `int` in C# is an alias for `System.Int32` type in CTS. Thus, the query `numbers.Take(4);` returns an `IEnumerable<System.Int32>` that has first four elements.

One good thing about `Take()` is that it doesn't throw an exception if the argument number is out of range (say negative, or more than the number of elements in the collection).

If a negative index is passed, `Take()` returns the entire collection. The following is a visual representation of this operator:

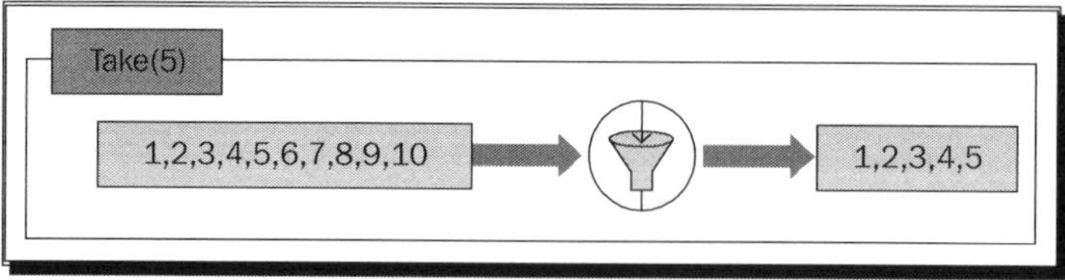

TakeWhile()

Suppose you have to pick elements from a collection as long as those elements meet a certain criterion. We have already learned about `Take()` that lets you pick from the start of the collection. In order to allow conditional picking, `TakeWhile()` was introduced. This operator takes a Lambda expression that describes the condition.

There are two overloaded versions of the method. The first one takes a Functor, as shown in the following screenshot:

▲ 1 of 2 ▼ (extension) IEnumerable<T> IEnumerable<T>.TakeWhile(**Func<T,bool> predicate**)
Returns elements from a sequence as long as a specified condition is true.
predicate: *A function to test each element for a condition.*

Time for action – picking conditionally

Here is the first problem:

Say we have a `List` of names and we want to create another `List` picking names from this `List` as long as the names start with "S". Here is how we can do that using `TakeWhile()`:

1. Copy the following code snippet as a query to LINQPad:

```
string[] names  = { "Sam", "Samuel", "Dave", "Pascal", "Erik",
  "Sid" };
var sNames = names.TakeWhile(c => c.StartsWith("S"));
sNames.Dump("S* Names");
```

2. Run the query. You should get the following output:

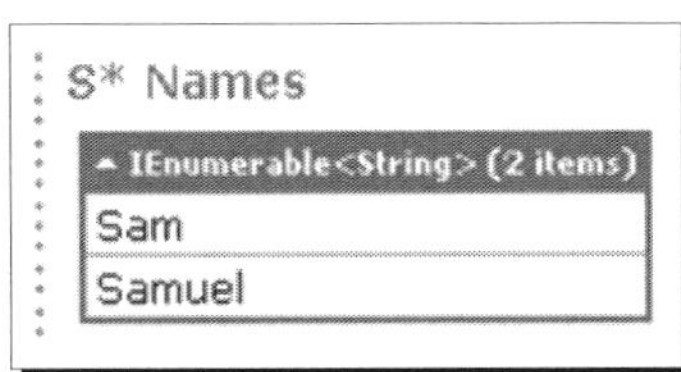

What just happened?

If you are thinking, why "Sid" didn't make it to the `List` of the matching names, you are not alone. I thought so too initially. However, you must understand that `TakeWhile()` operates on the collection as it is, without any modification or sorting. So it processes the elements as they appear in the `List`.

`TakeWhile()` picks elements from the start of the collection as long as the given condition expressed as the argument Lambda expression is `true`.

"Sam" and "Samuel" are two names that match the condition and the next name "Dave" does not match the expression and thus scanning stops there. Did you get the *While* of `TakeWhile()` now? This essentially means *Take as long as the condition is satisfied.*

So, if the expression was `c => c.StartsWith("D")`, it would have returned an empty `IEnumerable<string>` as shown in the following screenshot:

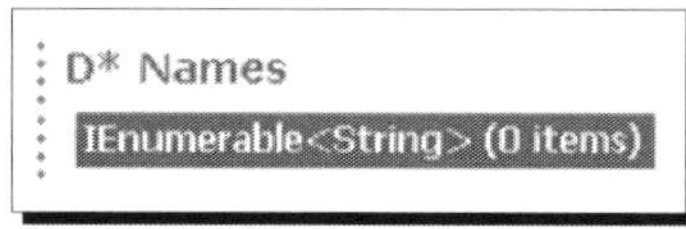

The following is a visual representation of the `TakeWhile()` operator:

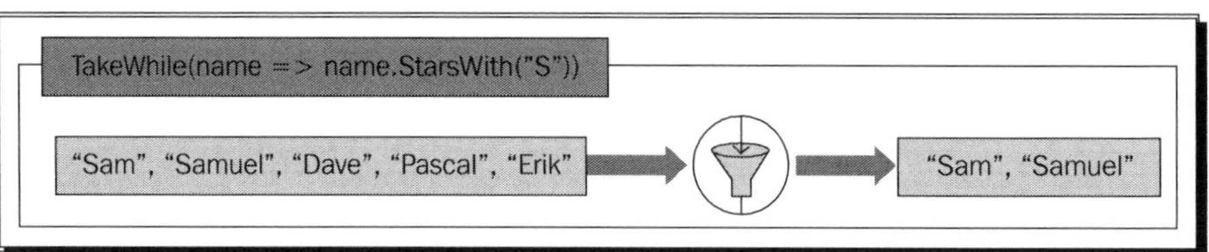

Like `Where()`, `TakeWhile()` queries can also be indexed using the second version of the method.

▲ 2 of 2 ▼ (extension) IEnumerable<T> IEnumerable<T>.TakeWhile(**Func<T,int,bool> predicate**)
Returns elements from a sequence as long as a specified condition is true. The element's index is used in the logic of the predicate function.
predicate: *A function to test each source element for a condition; the second parameter of the function represents the index of the source element.*

Say we want to check whether every second name starts with "S" or not:

```
var sNames = names.TakeWhile((c,index) => index%2==0 &&
  c.StartsWith("S"));
```

Like `Take()`, `TakeWhile()` doesn't throw any exception when the number is out of bounds. Notice that `TakeWhile()` doesn't take an explicit number of items to pick. It just stops scanning as soon as the condition is dissatisfied.

Skip()

This operator allows you to skip the first *n* number of items from the source collection while processing. This is the exact opposite of `Take()`, conceptually.

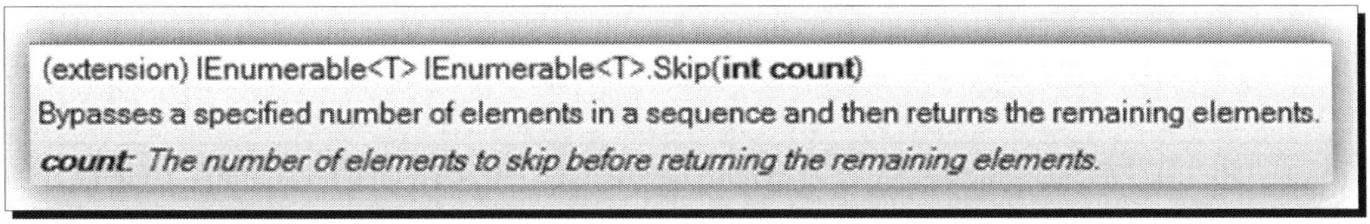

(extension) IEnumerable<T> IEnumerable<T>.Skip(**int count**)
Bypasses a specified number of elements in a sequence and then returns the remaining elements.
***count**: The number of elements to skip before returning the remaining elements.*

The previous screenshot shows an example of the `Skip()` operator.

Time for action – skipping save looping

Here is the first problem:

Say we have a `List` of names, and we want to create another `List` leaving the first few names:

1. Copy the following code snippet as a query to LINQPad:

```
string[] names = { "Sam", "Samuel", "Samu", "Remo", "Arnold",
  "Terry" };
var skippedList = names.Skip(3);//Leaving the first 3.
foreach (var v in skippedList)
  Console.WriteLine(v);
```

2. Run the query. You will see the following output:

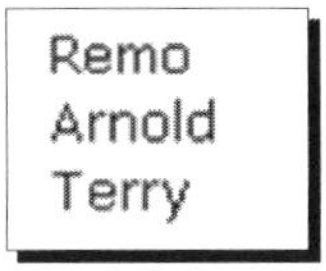

```
Remo
Arnold
Terry
```

What just happened?

`Skip()` creates an `IEnumerable<T>` instance that will have only the chosen few elements. In this case, we wanted to skip the first three elements. If you want to conditionally skip elements, then you would need `SkipWhile()`. That's next!

However, if you want to filter the entire collection, your best bet is `Where()`. This works without sorting.

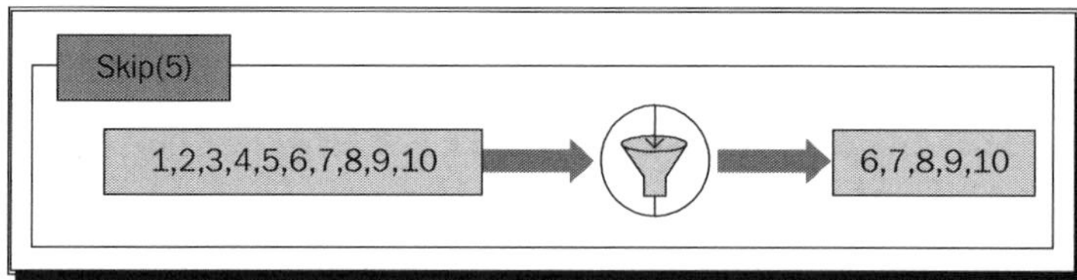

Similar to `Take()`, it doesn't throw any exception when the number passed is out of bounds of the source collection. It returns an empty `IEnumerable<T>` when the source collection is of type `T`. Interestingly, if a negative argument is passed to `Skip()`, it doesn't skip anything and returns the entire source collection.

SkipWhile()

This is a conditional skip from the source collection. The elements from the source collection do not get added to the projected output as long as the given condition holds good:

▲ 1 of 2 ▼ (extension) IEnumerable<T> IEnumerable<T>.SkipWhile(**Func<T,bool> predicate**)
Bypasses elements in a sequence as long as a specified condition is true and then returns the remaining elements.
predicate: *A function to test each element for a condition.*

Say we have a `List` of integers and we don't want to get anything that is less than 10. Following is the code:

```
int[] numbers = { 1, 2, 3, 4, 5, 6, 7, 8, 9, 10, 11, 12,20 };
int[] nums = numbers.ToArray();
var skippedList = nums.SkipWhile(c=>c<10);//Leaving everything less
  //than ten
foreach (var v in skippedList)
  Console.WriteLine(v);
```

This code snippet will output as follows:

```
11
12
20
```

Like `TakeWhile()`, `SkipWhile()` also has an indexed version that lets us use the index of the element in the query.

Ordering operators

In this section, we will discuss the following Ordering operators:

Reverse()

This operator reverses the given sequence. This will return `IEnumerable<T>` when we operate on source collections of type `T`, as follows:

Time for action – reversing word-by-word

Follow the given steps:

1. Copy the following code snippet as a query to LINQPad:

   ```
   string sentence = ".NET Generics is a great API";
   sentence.Split('').
   Reverse().ToList().ForEach(c=>Console.Write(c+""));
   ```

2. Execute the query. You will get the following result:

   ```
   API great a is Generics .NET
   ```

What just happened?

`sentence.Split(' ')` generates a `string[]`, and `Reverse()` returns an `IEnumerable<string>` with a reversed order of the words. Now I can convert this back to a `List<string>` to use the `ForEach()` method as it was used earlier.

Time for action – checking whether a given string is a palindrome or not

Palindromes are fascinating and it is more fun to find them. Here we shall write a program to demonstrate how we can find whether a string is a palindrome or not, using the operators we have learned so far:

1. Copy the following code snippet as a query to LINQPad:

```
string sentence = "A Man, A Plan, A Canal, Panama";
//Listing the characters of the original input string.
var original = sentence
.ToLower()
.Replace(" ",string.Empty)
.Split(',')
.SelectMany(c=>c.ToCharArray());
//Storing the reversed one.
var reversed = original.Reverse();
//Checking if the original character sequence matches with the
//reveresed one.
string verdict = original.SequenceEqual(reversed)
? "This is a Palindrome"
: "This is not a Palindrome";
Console.Write(verdict);
```

2. Run the query. You will see the following output:

```
This is a Palindrome
```

What just happened?

In this case, we are cleaning all the whitespaces. Then the cleaned string is tokenized by a comma (,) and this gives us a `List` of strings.

This is where `SelectMany()` steps in, to create an `IEnumerable<char>` from all the characters of the strings, of the string array generated out of `Split(',')` call.

So, the `original` now has the list of all the characters of all the words in the sentence.

Using `original.Reverse();`, we create an `IEnumerable<char>` that has all the characters in reverse order.

The next line compares these two character sequences using the operator: `SequenceEqual()`. If both the character streams are the same, the verdict will be set to `"This is a Palindrome"`.

There are several long palindromic sentences. You can find a long list at `http://www.cs.arizona.edu/icon/oddsends/palinsen.htm`.

OrderBy()

This operator allows us to sort the elements of the source collection depending on some parameter, if the type of the collection already implements `IComparable`. It also allows us to sort elements of a collection of user defined objects (denoted by `T`) by letting us pass an instance of `IComparer<T>` to it.

The following are some examples:

Sorting an array of strings alphabetically

Here we will see how to sort an array of strings alphabetically.

Time for action – sorting names alphabetically

Follow the given steps:

1. Copy the following code snippet as a query to LINQPad:

```
string[] names = { "Sam", "Pamela", "Dave", "Anders", "Erik" };
names.Dump("Before Alphabetical Sorting");
names = names.OrderBy(c => c).ToArray();
names.Dump("Alphabetically Sorted");
```

2. Run the query. You will see the `names` sorted, as shown in the following screenshot:

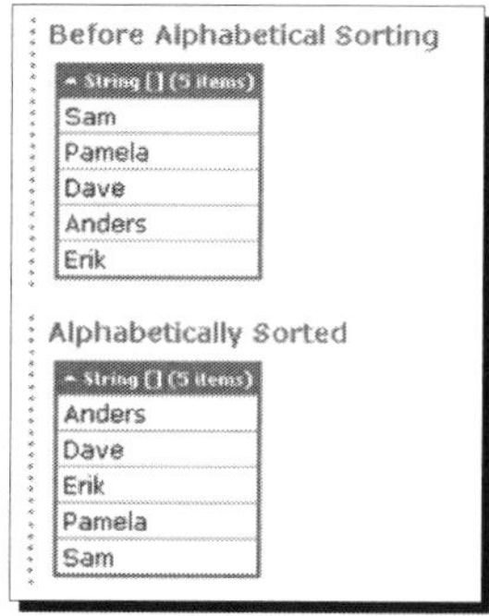

What just happened?

The following query uses a funny looking Lambda expression, which can be quite confusing at the first glance:

```
c => c
```

Which essentially means sort by the string itself.

Now, if you want to sort the elements by their length, here is how to make the change:

```
string[] names = { "Sam", "Pamela", "Dave", "Anders", "Erik" };
names.Dump("Before Sorting");
names = names.OrderBy(c => c.Length).ToArray();
names.Dump("Sorted by Length");
```

And the results will be as follows:

Time for action – sorting 2D points by their co-ordinates

Let's say we have an array of points in 2D and we want to sort them as per their X co-ordinates. Here is how to do it:

1. Copy the following code snippet as a query to LINQPad:

```
System.Drawing.PointF[] points =
{
  new System.Drawing.PointF(0, -1),
  new System.Drawing.PointF(-1, 1),
  new System.Drawing.PointF(3, 3)
};

var sortedPoints = points.Select(c=>new {X = c.X, Y =
  c.Y}).OrderBy(c => c.X).ToList();

sortedPoints.Dump("Sorted Points");
```

2. Run the query. You should see the following output:

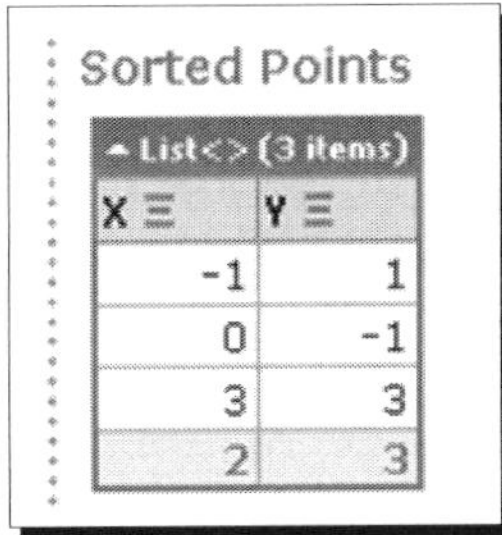

What just happened?

We have a `List` of points in 2D and we wanted to sort them by their X co-ordinates. We created an anonymous type out of these points and projected them to an `IEnumerable<>` by `Select()`.

Next, `OrderBy()` comes and sorts this `List` by their X co-ordinates. This sorting intent has been described by the Lambda expression `c => c.X`.

At the end, we converted the result to a `List` of the anonymous type. Notice that the header of the table in the output, shown in the preceding screenshot, doesn't have any data type, as the result is of anonymous type.

Have a go hero – sorting Student objects

Suppose, we have a `List` of some user-defined `Student` objects as follows:

```
Student[] someStudents =
{
  new Student(){Age = 20, Course = "C#", Name = "Sam" },
  new Student(){Age = 19, Course = "Ruby", Name = "Bobby" },
  new Student(){Age = 18, Course = "F#", Name = "Shakira" }
};
//Sorting the students by their age.
```

Can you sort these students by their age using the LINQ `OrderBy()` operator?

OrderByDescending()

This operator does just the reverse of the `OrderBy()`, as the name suggests. `OrderBy()` sorts elements in ascending order, while this operator sorts everything in descending order.

ThenBy()

After the source collection is sorted, if you want to sort it again by some other parameter, you shall have to use `ThenBy()`. This sorts the elements in ascending order like `OrderBy()`. However, if you want to sort elements in descending order, you shall have to use `ThenByDescending()`.

Say we have a `List` called `fruits`. We shall first sort the `List` by the length of the fruit name and then sort the `List` alphabetically. The following snippet shows how we can do it:

Time for action – sorting a list of fruits

Follow the given steps:

1. Copy the following code snippet as a query to LINQPad:

```
string[] fruits = { "grape", "passionfruit", "banana", "apple",
  "orange", "raspberry", "mango", "blueberry" };

//Sort the strings first by their length.
var sortedFruits =  fruits.OrderBy(fruit => fruit.Length);
sortedFruits.Dump("Sorted Fruits by Length");
```

2. Run the query. You should get the following output:

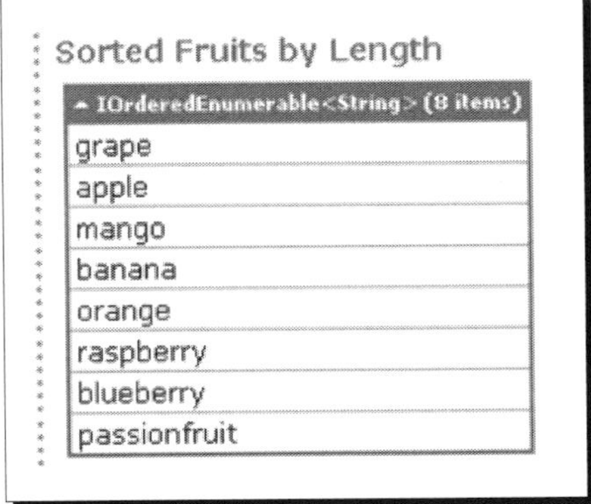

So you see the fruit names are sorted in ascending order of their length.

Now, let's see what happens if we sort the elements alphabetically, maintaining this primary sorting as per their length.

3. Change the query and paste the following query in LINQPad:

```
string[] fruits = {"grape", "passionfruit", "banana", "apple",
  "orange", "raspberry", "mango", "blueberry" };

//Sort the strings first by their length and then alphabetically.
//preserving the first order.
var sortedFruits =  fruits.OrderBy(fruit =>
  fruit.Length).ThenBy(fruit => fruit);
sortedFruits.Dump(
  "Sorted Fruits by Length and then Alphabetically");
```

4. Run the query. You will get the following output:

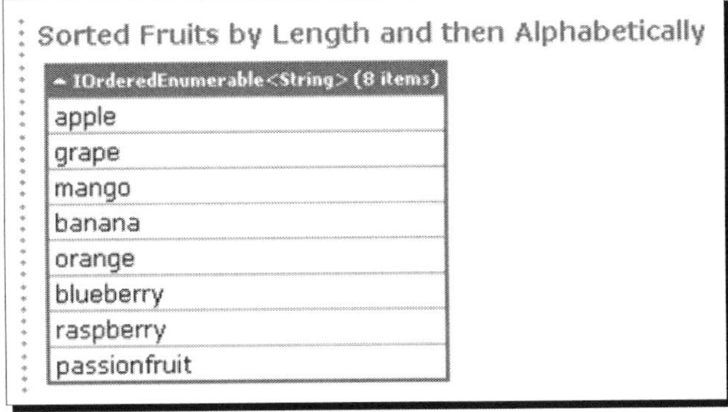

What's the difference between a sequence of OrderBy().OrderBy() and OrderBy().ThenBy()?

`ThenBy()` preserves the previous ordering of data, while a cascaded `OrderBy()` will only have the last one's order preserved.

ThenByDescending()

It's the same as `ThenBy()`, while `ThenBy()` is the cousin of `OrderBy()` and sorts in ascending order, `ThenByDescending()` partners with `OrderByDescending()`.

Grouping operator

In this section, we will discuss the following Grouping operators:

GroupBy()

Using this operator, we can easily group the elements of the source collection. This operator returns an `IEnumerable<IGrouping<TKey, TValue>>`.

Time for action – indexing an array of strings

The following is the first problem:

Group names by the first two characters. This can be used in indexing algorithms:

1. Copy the following code snippet as a query to LINQPad:

```
string[] names = { "Sam", "Samuel", "Samu", "Ravi", "Ratna",
  "Barsha" };
var groups  = names.GroupBy(c => c.Substring(0, 2));
groups.Dump();
foreach (var gr in groups)
{
  Console.WriteLine(gr.Key);
  foreach (var p in gr)
  Console.WriteLine("---- " + p);
}
```

2. Run the query. You shall get the following output:

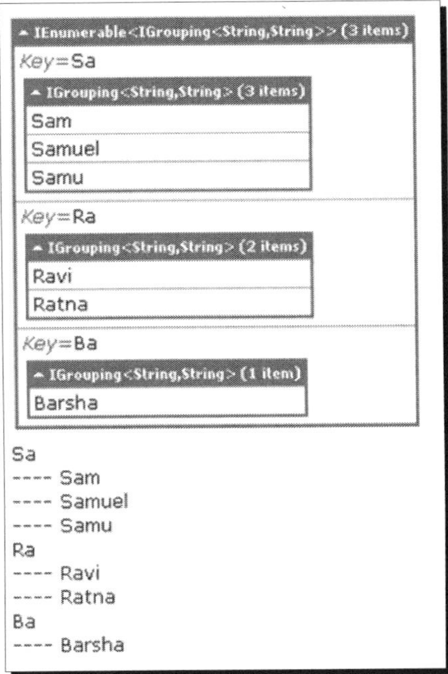

What just happened?

`GroupBy()` returns an instance of `IEnumerable<IGrouping<Tkey, TValue>>`.

Assume this is a dictionary of dictionaries. `TKey` is the key of the entries and `TValue` is the value of the entries. So, in this case, each key will be associated with an `IGrouping<string, string>`.

The first part of the output (that is the table) is generated by the `Dump()` command. Here you can see how the data structure is organized within.

The second part is generated manually by iterating the group. Each group entry has a read-only property called `Key`, and this looping construct used is typically how you can extract data from a group (`IGrouping<TKey, TValue>`).

We have successfully created the index. Now you might ask the question, how do we get items for the particular `Key`, such as dictionaries?

Here is how to do it. Suppose I want to find out all the entries for the `Key` "Sa" from the preceding group. The syntax will be as follows:

```
groups.Where(c=>c.Key=="Sa").ToList().Dump();
```

Add the preceding line after the previous query in LINQPad and you should get the following output:

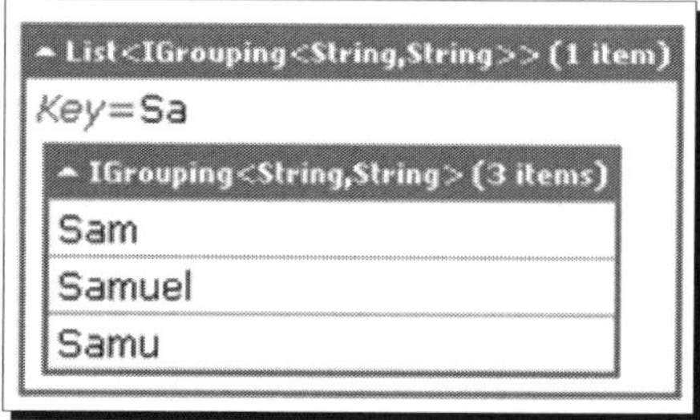

Time for action – grouping by length

We can change the indexing key to anything we like. For example, say we want to group names as per their length. Only the Lambda expression will need the following change, everything else will remain the same. However, to give the output a better view, I changed the way the group key is printed:

1. Copy the following code snippet as a query to LINQPad:

```
string[] names = {"Sam", "Samuel", "Samu", "Ravi", "Ratna",
  "Barsha"};
var groups  = names.GroupBy(c => c.Length);
foreach (var gr in groups)
{
  Console.WriteLine("Words of Length {0}", gr.Key);
  foreach (var p in gr)
  Console.WriteLine("----" + p);
}
```

2. Run the query. You should get the following output:

```
Words of Length 3
---- Sam
Words of Length 6
---- Samuel
---- Barsha
Words of Length 4
---- Samu
---- Ravi
Words of Length 5
---- Ratna
```

This operator can also be used to project elements of the collection using a specified generic result selector method. That way, we can only project the elements we need.

The following is an example:

1. Copy the following code snippet as a query to LINQPad:

```
//Some junk license plate numbers
string[] licensePlateNumbers = {"MO 123 X#4552", "MO 923 AS#",
  "MAN HATTON", "MADONNA", "MARINE" };
var plateGroup = licensePlateNumbers.GroupBy
  (//Key selector lambda expression
c => c.Substring(0, 2),
//Result selector lambda expression
(c, values) => values.Count()>2?values.Skip(2):values
);
foreach (var pg in plateGroup)
{
  Console.WriteLine(pg.ElementAt(0).Substring(0, 2));
  foreach (var g in pg)
  {
    Console.WriteLine("----- " + g);
  }
}
```

2. Run the query and you will get the following output:

```
MO
----- MO 123 X#4552
----- MO 923 AS#
MA
----- MARINE
```

What just happened?

In this example, we have used an overloaded version of the method. It takes two Lambda expressions. The first one is the key selector, which will determine the keys of the elements added in the group. The second one is called the result selector, which is a function to create a result value from each group.

Let's see, what it means:

```
//Key selector lambda expression
c => c.Substring(0, 2)
```

This means we need to take only the first two characters of the string as the key of the group:

```
//Result selector lambda expression
(c, values) => values.Count()>2?values.Skip(2):values
```

This means if the strings matching the key are more than two, then skip the first two elements and put the rest as the result.

Now, note that there are three license plate numbers starting with "MA". That's why the first two are skipped from the result. However, plates starting with "MO" were only two in number, thus, they appear as it is in the result.

Try removing the second Lambda and you should get the following output:

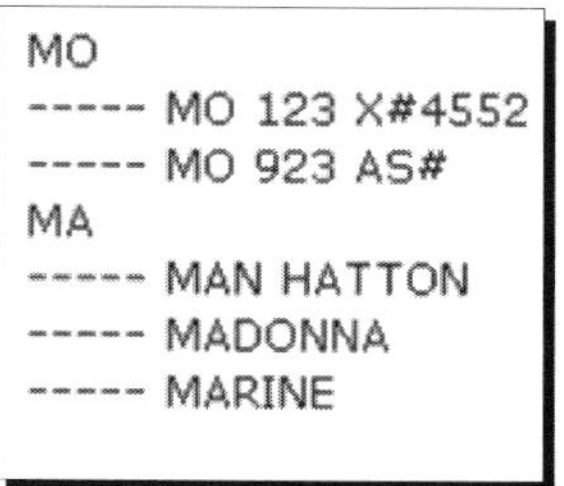

Set operators

In this section, we will discuss the following Set operators:

Intersect()

This is a Set operator. This returns the intersection (or the common elements) of two collections. There are two overloaded versions of this method. The first one takes a collection of type `IComparable`, so explicit `IEqualityComparer` is not needed.

▲ 1 of 2 ▼ (extension) IEnumerable<T> IEnumerable<T>.Intersect(**IEnumerable<T> second**)
Produces the set intersection of two sequences by using the default equality comparer to compare values.
second: *An System.Collections.Generic.IEnumerable<T> whose distinct elements that also appear in the first sequence will be returned.*

Say we have two string lists and we want to find out what the common elements in them, are here is how we can do that using `Intersect()` on `List<T>`.

Time for action – finding common names from two names' lists

Follow the given steps:

1. Copy the following code snippet as a query to LINQPad:

```
List<string> nameList1 = new List<string>()
  {"Anders", "David", "James", "Jeff", "Joe", "Erik"};
List<string> nameList2 = new List<string>()
  {"Erik","David","Derik"};
var commonNames = nameList1.Intersect(nameList2);
foreach (var name in commonNames)
Console.WriteLine(name);
```

2. Run the query. You will see the following output:

```
David
Erik
```

What just happened?

`Intersect()` returns an `IEnumerable<T>`, including only the elements that appear in both the collections. `Intersect()` has two overloaded versions. One works with the primitive data type and the other requires an explicit `IEqualityComparer` to know how to compare the elements of the collection.

The order in which the results appear in the result collection, depends on the sequence of calling.

Note that the sequence of appearance of the objects, in the intersected `List`, is that of the first collection or the collection on which this operator is invoked.

So, if you change the invoking object to the second collection, we shall get a different order:

1. Copy the following code snippet as a query to LINQPad:

```
List<string> nameList1 = new List<string>()
  {"Anders", "David", "James", "Jeff", "Joe", "Erik"};
List<string> nameList2 = new List<string>()
  {"Erik","David","Derik"};
var commonNames = nameList2.Intersect(nameList1);
foreach (var name in commonNames)
Console.WriteLine(name);
```

2. Run the query. You will see the following output:

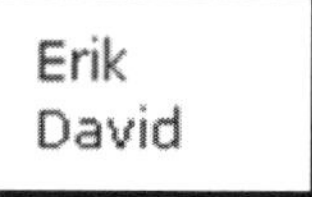

This happened because "Erik" appears before "David" in the invoking collection.

However, if you must enforce alphabetical order, use `OrderBy(c=>c)` on the result obtained.

See this action in the following diagram:

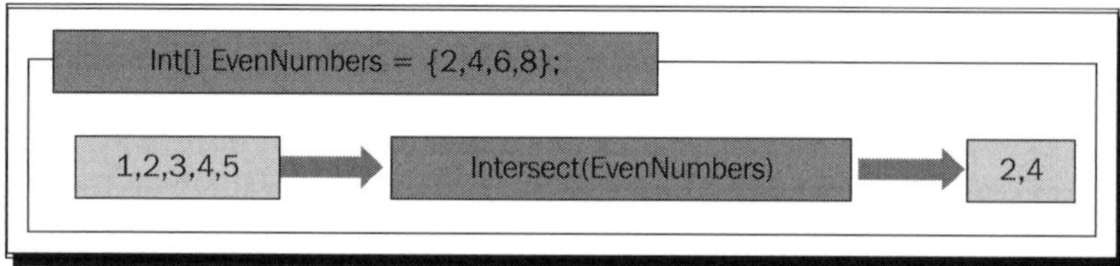

The other version, however, needs to know how to compare objects in the collection. So, an `IEqualityComparer` needs to be passed explicitly.

Union()

This operator provides what a set union is for any collection that implements `IEnumerable<T>`. This, unlike `Concat()`, removes the duplicates.

`Union()`, like `Intersect()`, has two overloaded versions. The first one deals with the collections of type that implements `IComparable`.

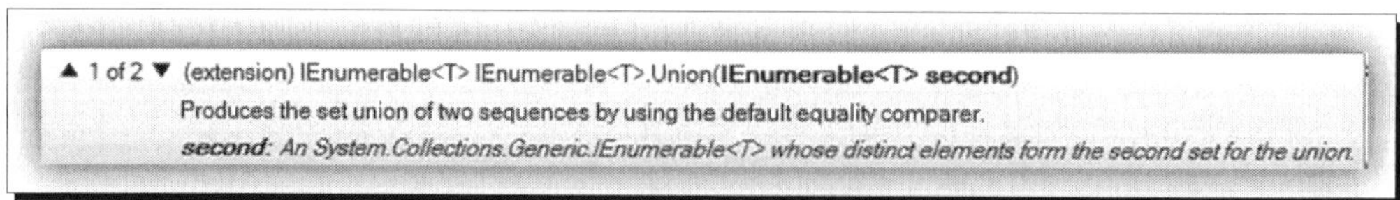

The other one needs an explicit `IEqualityComparer` for comparing objects in the collection.

▲ 2 of 2 ▼ (extension) IEnumerable<T> IEnumerable<T>.Union(IEnumerable<T> second, **IEqualityComparer<T> comparer**)
Produces the set union of two sequences by using a specified System.Collections.Generic.IEqualityComparer<T>.
comparer: *The System.Collections.Generic.IEqualityComparer<T> to compare values.*

The following diagram shows how `Union()` works:

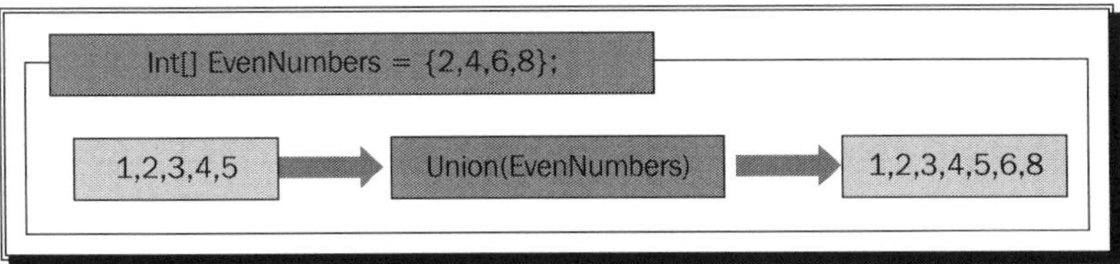

Time for action – finding all names from the list, removing duplicates

Follow the given steps:

1. Copy the following code snippet as a query to LINQPad. Using the previous example, the change is highlighted:

```
List<string> nameList1 = new List<string>()
  {"Anders", "David", "James", "Jeff", "Joe", "Erik"};
List<string> nameList2 = new List<string>()
  {"Erik","David","Derik"};
var commonNames = nameList1.Union(nameList2);
foreach (var name in commonNames)
Console.WriteLine(name);
```

2. Run the query. You should see the following output:

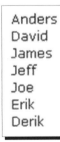

```
Anders
David
James
Jeff
Joe
Erik
Derik
```

What just happened?

Union() returns a list of all the strings in both the collections, removing duplicates. Like Itersect(), it also has an overloaded version that needs an IEqualityComparer instance to compare elements of the collection.

As "Erik" and "David" appear in both the lists, they are added only once.

Concat()

There is another query operator called Concat(). If you want to include the duplicate items, you should use this operator.

Time for action – pulling it all together including duplicates

Follow the given steps:

1. Just change the preceding query by replacing Union() with Concat().
2. Run the query and you should see the following output:

```
Anders
David
James
Jeff
Joe
Erik
Erik
David
Derik
```

However, you can still get the same result as Union() if you apply a Distinct() operator on this result. Distinct() removes the duplicates from a collection.

Except()

This operator returns the mutually exclusive elements of two collections. This operator extracts the elements present in one collection and not in the other one. Like Union() and Intersection(), Except() also has two overloaded versions. The first one takes an instance IEnumerable<T>, where T implements IComparable. While the other version does need an IEqualityComparer interface:

▲ 1 of 2 ▼ (extension) IEnumerable<T> IEnumerable<T>.Except(**IEnumerable<T> second**)
Produces the set difference of two sequences by using the default equality comparer to compare values.
second: *An System.Collections.Generic.IEnumerable<T> whose elements that also occur in the first sequence will cause those elements to be removed from the returned sequence.*

The following diagram shows how `Except()` works:

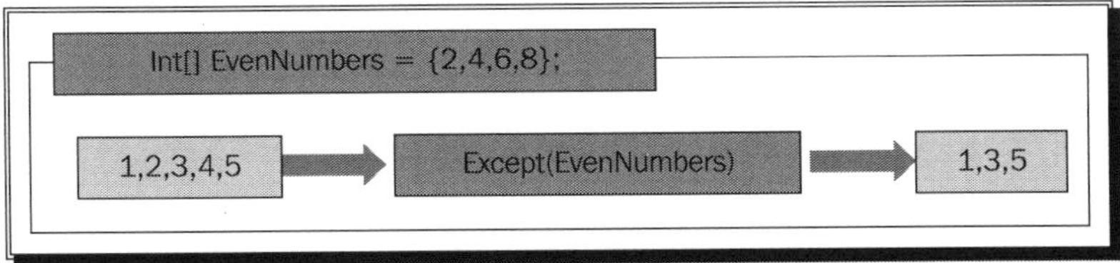

Time for action – finding all names that appear mutually exclusively

Follow the given steps:

1. Copy the following code snippet as a query to LINQPad:

```
List<string> nameList1 = new List<string> ()
  {"Anders", "David", "James", "Jeff", "Joe", "Erik"};
List<string> nameList2 = new List<string>()
  {"Erik", "David", "Derik"};

//This will store the names that appear in nameList2 but not in
//nameList1.
var exclusiveNames = nameList2.Except(nameList1);
foreach (var v in exclusiveNames)
Console.WriteLine(v);
```

2. Run the query. You should get the following output:

```
Derik
```

What just happened?

The name "Derik" is present only in `nameList2` and not in `nameList1`, so it is returned. However, the sequence matters! Suppose, we want to find out what is in collection A and not in collection B, then the call will be made to `Except()` such as `A.Except(B)` and vice-versa.

So, we change the invoking collection to `nameList1` as follows:

```
var exclusiveNames = nameList1.Except(nameList2);
```

The output will be as shown in the following screenshot:

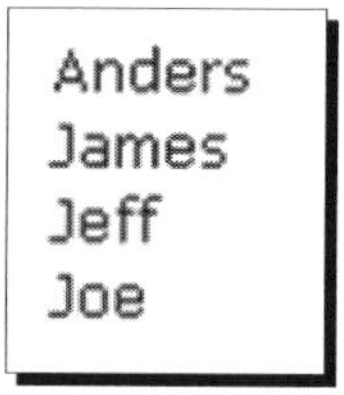

```
Anders
James
Jeff
Joe
```

Like its cousins `Intersect()` and `Union()`, `Except()` also comes with a different version, where you can pass an `EqualityComparer<T>` instance that will tell it how to compare the elements of the source collection.

Distinct()

This removes any duplicate from the given source collection. This method has two versions. If the type of the collection has implementation of `IComparable` then the method doesn't need any explicit `IEqualityComparer` to compare objects in the source collection.

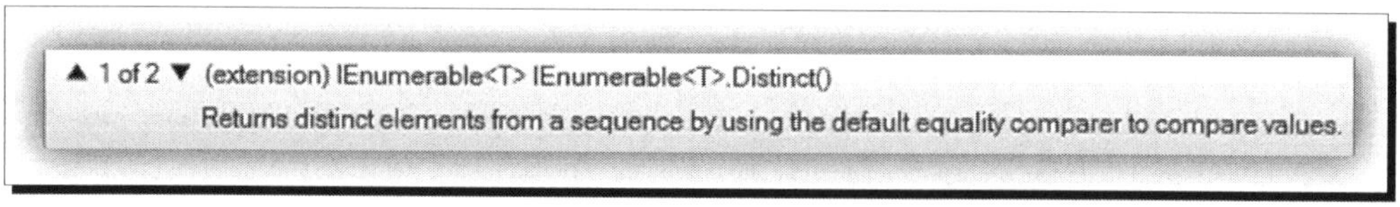

▲ 1 of 2 ▼ (extension) IEnumerable<T> IEnumerable<T>.Distinct()
Returns distinct elements from a sequence by using the default equality comparer to compare values.

Assume that you are writing software for a radio station, where songs are played on demand. Lot of people send the same song ID as a request. The radio jokey wants to make sure he/she plays the song only once. In such a queue, removing duplicates is needed. `Distinct()` does this quite gracefully.

Time for action – removing duplicate song IDs from the list

Follow the given steps: .

1. Copy the following code snippet as a query to LINQPad:

```
string[] songIds = {"Song#1", "Song#2", "Song#2", "Song#2",
  "Song#3", "Song#1"};
//This will work as strings implement IComparable
var uniqueSongIds = songIds.Distinct();
//Iterating through the list of unique song IDs
foreach (var songId in uniqueSongIds)
Console.WriteLine(songId);
```

2. Run the query. You should see the following output:

```
Song#1
Song#2
Song#3
```

Assume, `Distinct()` as a filter that removes duplicate items and returns a collection with only unique items:

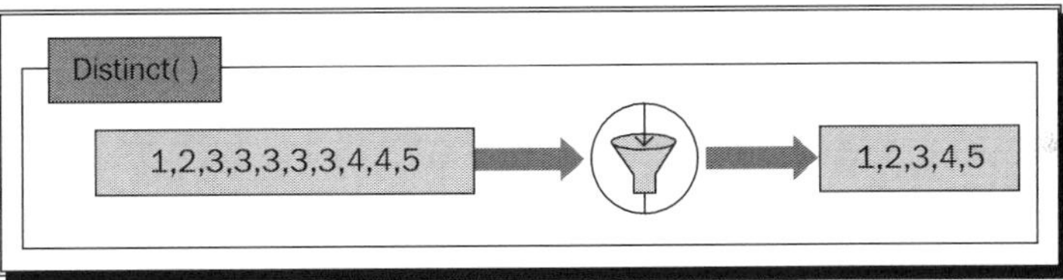

However, if that's not the case, an `IEqualityComparer` is passed, which will be needed to compare objects of the source collection.

▲ 2 of 2 ▼ (extension) IEnumerable<T> IEnumerable<T>.Distinct(**IEqualityComparer<T> comparer**)
Returns distinct elements from a sequence by using a specified System.Collections.Generic.IEqualityComparer<T> to compare values.
comparer: *An System.Collections.Generic.IEqualityComparer<T> to compare values.*

In order to use this second version, we shall have to write a custom comparer first by implementing `IEqualityComparer<T>` for the `Student` class.

Assume we already have a `Student` class with the public property `ID`:

```
public class StudentComparer : IEqualityComparer<Student>
{
  #region IEqualityComparer<Student> Members
  bool IEqualityComparer<Student>.Equals(Student x, Student y)
  {
    //Check whether the compared objects reference the same data.
    if (Object.ReferenceEquals(x, y))
    return true;
    //Check whether any of the compared objects is null.
    if (Object.ReferenceEquals(x, null) ||
      Object.ReferenceEquals(y, null))
    return false;
    //If two students have same ID
    //they are same
    return x.ID == y.ID;
  }

  int IEqualityComparer<Student>.GetHashCode(Student obj)
  {
    return obj.GetHashCode();
  }
  #endregion
}
```

After we have this in place, we can use this to call the second version of `Distinct()` as follows:

```
List<Student> uniqueStudents = someStudents.Distinct(new
  StudentComparer()).ToList();
```

Conversion operators

In this section, we will discuss the following Conversion operators:

ToArray()

This method converts the IEnumerable<T> to Array<T>. This is used if you want to project your data as an array of the result set. This calls for immediate execution of the query:

(extension) T[] IEnumerable<T>.ToArray()
Creates an array from a System.Collections.Generic.IEnumerable<T>.

The main objective is to generate a strongly typed array, instead of using the var keyword (which is also strongly typed). If the source collection is empty, it doesn't complain and returns an empty array.

Here is an example:

Time for action – making sure it works!

Follow the given steps:

1. Copy the following code snippet as a query to LINQPad:

```
string[] firstNames = {"Samuel", "Jenny", "Joyace", "Sam"};
string[] matchingFirstNames =
        firstNames.Where(name=>name.StartsWith("Sa")).ToArray();
matchingFirstNames.Dump("Name Array");
```

2. Run the query. It will result in the following output:

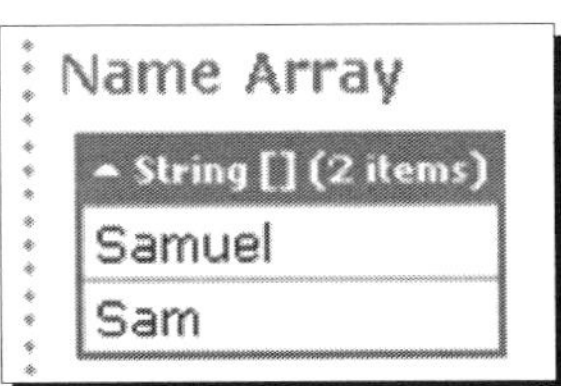

What just happened?

firstNames.Where(name=>name.StartsWith("Sa")) returns an IEnumerable<string>, and ToArray() converts it to a string[].

Thus, the result header shows the type of the returned result as a string[].

ToList()

This one is similar to ToArray(). However, this one returns a List<T>

(extension) List<T> IEnumerable<T>.ToList()
Creates a System.Collections.Generic.List<T> from an System.Collections.Generic.IEnumerable<T>.

Time for action – making a list out of IEnumerable<T>

Follow the given steps:

1. Copy the following code snippet as a query to LINQPad:

```
string[] firstNames = { "Samuel", "Jenny", "Joyace", "Sam" };
List<string> matchingFirstNames =
  firstNames.Where(name=>name.StartsWith("Sa")).ToList();
matchingFirstNames.Dump("Name List");
```

2. Run the query. You should get the following output:

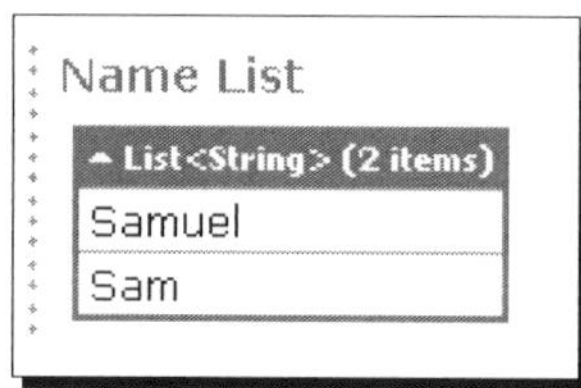

What just happened?

This proves that ToList<T>() essentially converts the results to a List<T>. This operator can come in particularly handy when we need to use the ForEach() method of List<T> for running some action on each element of the collection. However I don't recommend heavy usage of these conversion operators as these affect query performance.

ToDictionary()

This operator lets us create a `Dictionary` out of the source collection by letting us tag each element of the collection. All the elements in the source collection will be keys of the dictionary. As a dictionary can't have duplicate keys, it will throw an exception complaining about a duplicate key being added.

Time for action – tagging names

Follow the given steps:

1. Copy the following code snippet as a query to LINQPad:

```
List<string> boys = new List<string> {"Anders", "Anders",
  "David", "James", "Jeff", "Joe", "Erik"};

List<string> girls = new List<string> {"Anna", "Anzena",
  "Dorothy", "Jenny", "Josephine", "Julee"};

List<string> nameList1 = new List<string>() {"Anders", "Anna",
  "Joe", "Jenny", "Anzena", "Josephine", "Erik"};

Dictionary<string, string> nameMap = nameList1.ToDictionary(c =>
  c,c=>boys.Contains(c)?"boy":"girl");

nameMap.Keys.Dump("All Members");
nameMap.Keys.Where(c => nameMap[c] == "boy").Dump("Boys");
nameMap.Keys.Where(c => nameMap[c] == "girl").Dump("Girls");
```

2. Run the query. You will see the following output:

What just happened?

The Lambda expression `c => c,c=>boys contains(c)?"boy":"girl"` means that if `c` is in the `List` of boys names (`boys`) then return `boy` as the value for this key else return `girl` in the resultant `Dictionary`.

The first `Dump()` command `nameMap.Keys.Dump("All Members");` prints all the names.

The second `Dump()` command `nameMap.Keys.Where(c => nameMap[c] == "boy").Dump("Boys");` first does a filtering over the `Dictionary` to find the boys names and then only prints them.

The third command `nameMap.Keys.Where(c => nameMap[c] == "girl").Dump("Girls");` does the same thing for `girls`.

ToLookup()

This returns a one-to-many lookup table from the given source collection as per the provided `keySelector()` method. There are four different overloaded versions of this method. It also lets us select the elements of the source collection that we want to use in the conversion.

The following is an example that uses the first version, which just takes a Lambda expression as the `keySelector()`:

▲ 1 of 4 ▼ (extension) ILookup<TKey,T> IEnumerable<T>.ToLookup(**Func<T,TKey> keySelector**)
Creates a System.Linq.Lookup<TKey,TElement> from an System.Collections.Generic.IEnumerable<T> according to a specified key selector function.
***keySelector**: A function to extract a key from each element*

Time for action – one-to-many mapping

Here is the first problem:

Suppose, we have a `List` of names and we want to index them as per the first two letters of these names:

1. Copy the following code snippet as a query to LINQPad:

```
string[] firstNames = { "Samuel", "Jenny", "Joyace", "Sam" };
var map = firstNames.ToLookup(c => c.Length);
foreach (var m in map)
{
  Console.WriteLine(m.Key);
  foreach (var n in m)
  {
    Console.WriteLine("--" + n);
  }
}
```

2. Run the query and you should get the following output:

```
6
--Samuel
--Joyace
5
--Jenny
3
--Sam
```

What just happened?

`ToLookup()` creates what you can imagine as a one-to-many `Dictionary`.

The Lambda expression `c => c.Length` describes the key to be used for the `Lookup` table.

So, in this case, the key for the table is the length of the words.

Element operators

In this section, we will discuss the following Element operators:

First()

This operator gets the first element of the source collection. In case the source collection has only one element, it brings that one. If there is no matching element, it throws an Exception

Time for action – finding the first element that satisfies a condition

Follow the given steps:

1. Copy the following code snippet as a query to LINQPad:

```
string[] names = {"Sam", "Danny", "Jeff", "Erik",
  "Anders","Derik"};
string firstName = names.First();
string firstNameConditional = names.First(c => c.Length == 5);

firstName.Dump("First Name");
firstNameConditional.Dump("First Name with length 5");
```

2. Run the query. The following output will be generated:

```
First Name
Sam

First Name with length 5
Danny
```

What just happened?

There are two overloaded versions of the method. The first one doesn't take an input and returns the first element of the collection. The second version takes a predicate in the form of a Lambda expression and returns the first matching element.

So, in this case, the first element is returned when `First()` is used, on the other hand the second call returns the first name of length `5` matching the Lambda expression.

Please note that there is no sorting involved. So don't expect the first element after sorting. `First()` picks elements as they are laid out.

If there is no element in the source collection, it throws `InvalidOperationException` like `Single()`. That's why there is `FirstOrDefault` like `SingleOrDefault`.

How First() is different from Single()?

`First()` checks whether there is more than one element present in the collection. `Single()` does the same thing. However, `First(Func<T, bool>)` does not complain if there is more than one element in the collection, matching the given Lambda expression. However, `Single()` throws an exception if there is more than one element in the sequence, matching the Lambda expression pattern.

FirstOrDefault()

`FirstOrDefault()` is the same as `First()`. It doesn't throw an exception if there is no element, rather it fills the blank with the default value.

The following is an example:

Time for action – getting acquainted with FirstOrDefault()

Follow the given steps:

1. Copy the following code snippet as a query to LINQPad:

```
string[] names = {};
string defaultName = names.FirstOrDefault();
defaultName.Dump();
```

2. Run this query. You will see the following output:

null

What just happened?

As there is no element in the array `names`, `FirstOrDefault()` puts the default value for the string (which is null) in the variable `defaultName`.

Last()

It's the same as `First()`; however, it returns the last element instead. It throws an exception if there is no element. If you want to push the default value when the collection is empty, use `LastOrDefault()` instead, which works in exactly the same way as `FirstOrDefault()`.

LastOrDefault()

It's the same as `FirstOrDefault()`. It doesn't throw an exception if there is no element, rather it fills the blank with the default value.

SequenceEquals()

This operator checks whether two given instances of `IEnumerable<T>` are the same or not by comparing the elements by the default comparer. Otherwise, if the type doesn't have a default comparer implementation, then the overloaded version allows you to pass in a `IEqualityComparer`.

Here is an example, where `SequenceEquals` and `Reverse` are used together to find whether a sequence of strings is palindromic in nature or not.

Time for action – checking whether a sequence is palindromic

Follow the given steps:

1. Change the language to **C# Program** in the **Language** box of LINQPad.
2. Paste the following query in LINQPad:

```
static bool IsPalindromic(string sentence)
{
  List<string> wordsInOrder = sentence.Split(' ').ToList();
  List<string> wordsInReverseOrder =
    sentence.Split(' ').Reverse().ToList();
  return wordsInOrder.SequenceEqual(wordsInReverseOrder);
}
void Main()
{
```

```
    string response = IsPalindromic("Veni, vidi, vici") ?
      "\"Veni, vidi, vici\" Is Palindromic":"\"Veni, vidi, vici\"
      Is Not Palindromic";
    response.Dump();

    response = IsPalindromic("Nada Ney Nada") ? "\"Nada, Ney, Nada\"
      Is Palindromic":"\"Nada, Ney, Nada\" Is Not Palindromic";
    response.Dump();
}
```

3. Run the query. This should generate the following output:

```
"Veni, vidi, vici" Is Not Palindromic
"Nada, Ney, Nada" Is Palindromic
```

What just happened?

In the `IsPalindromic()` method, the original sentence is split into words and then these words are stored in a collection. Next, this collection of words is reversed and stored into another `List`.

Then these two collections are checked for equality. Like other standard operators `SequenceEqual()` has another overloaded version that takes an `EqualityComparer`, which tells it how to compare items of the collection that don't already implement `IComparable<>`.

ElementAt()

This operator returns the element at the index that is passed. This operates on a zero-based indexing as in an array. Using this Extension method, you can peek through any data structure that implements the `IEnumerable<T>` interface, a `Stack` for instance.

However, use this judiciously as there is no other way than a linear search to get to the element at index *i* in an unsorted source collection. If you are needing this method quite often, you are better off reviewing your existing design.

Time for action – understanding ElementAt()

Follow the given steps:

1. Copy the following as a query to LINQPad:

```
Stack<string> tags = new Stack<string>();
tags.Push("<html>");
tags.Push("<body>");

List<string> tagList = new List<string>();
tagList.Add("<html>");
tagList.Add("<body>");

Queue<string> queue = new Queue<string>();
queue.Enqueue("<html>");
queue.Enqueue("<body>");

LinkedList<string> linkedTags = new LinkedList<string>();
linkedTags.AddLast("<html>");
linkedTags.AddLast("<body>");

string lastStackTag = tags.ElementAt(tags.Count - 1);
string lastListTag = tagList.ElementAt(tagList.Count - 1);
string lastQueueTag = queue.ElementAt(queue.Count - 1);
string lastLinkedListTag = linkedTags.ElementAt(linkedTags.Count -
                                                 1);

lastStackTag.Dump("Last Stack<T> Element");
lastListTag.Dump("Last List<T> Element");
lastQueueTag.Dump("Last Queue<T> Element");
lastLinkedListTag.Dump("Last LinkedList<T> Element");
```

2. Run the query and you should see the following output:

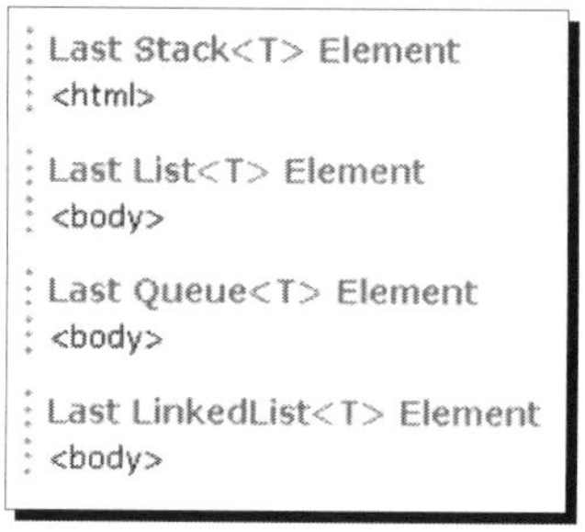

Last Stack<T> Element
<html>

Last List<T> Element
<body>

Last Queue<T> Element
<body>

Last LinkedList<T> Element
<body>

What just happened?

Internally, the elements are stored differently for different data structures. Thus, for `Stack<>` the last element stored at `lastStackTag` comes as **<html>** instead of **<body>**, as you would expect for a `List<>`. All the list-based containers, however, store the element in the same way.

ElementAtOrDefault()

It's the same as `ElementAt()`. However, this one won't complain if there isn't an element in the location at index *i*, unlike `ElementAt()` that will throw an exception if it doesn't find an element at the index mentioned.

So, if there is no element in the source collection at the given index, this method returns the default value of that data type.

The following is an example:

```
Stack<string> codeStack  = new Stack<string> ();
codeStack.Push("PC001");
string secondCode = codeStack.ElementAtOrDefault(1);
```

The value of `ElementAt()` and `ElementAtOrDefault()` is not very evident on the collections that primitively support zero-based indexing; such as list and array.

However, it can be pretty useful for other containers such as stack, which doesn't offer a peek at elements. `ElementAtOrDefault()` saves you from extensive usage of exception handling techniques.

DefaultIfEmpty()

This is kind of misnamed. It should instead be called `SetDefaultIfEmpty()`, because it allows you to set a default value as the sole value of an `IEnumerable<T>` instance; unlike `ElementAtOrDefault()` that forces you to choose the .NET CTS default value for that particular data type.

This can be particularly handy when working with external resources such as web services. Assume you are writing a weather monitoring application and if the service hasn't responded back within a predefined time span, you would want one of your variables—that you and your team have agreed upon—to be set to a default value.

Time for action – check out DefaultIfEmpty()

Follow the given steps:

1. Copy the following as a query to LINQPad:

```
public static List<double> GetLastWeekHumidity()
{
  //Assume this is where we get the result from the Web Service
  List<double> humidityThisWeek = new List<double>();
  //Assume Web Service didn't return anything
  return humidityThisWeek.DefaultIfEmpty(80.0).ToList();
}
static void Main()
{
  List<double> humidity = GetLastWeekHumidity();
  humidity.Dump("Humidity");
}
```

2. Run the query. You should see the following output:

```
Humidity
▲ List<Double> (1 item)
80
```

What just happened?

`DefaultIfEmpty()` allows you to push only one default value in the source collection. In this case, `80.0` was pushed and `ToList()` converted the result to a `List<double>`.

Generation operators

In this section, we will discuss the following Generation operators:

Range()

Suppose we want a `List` of constantly increasing positive integers starting from a seed number. This can be done by a single loop. However, using `Range()` solves the problem very easily. `Range()` is a static method of the `Enumerable` class.

Say, for example, we want integers 1 to 10.

Here is how to create that using `Range()`.

Time for action – generating arithmetic progression ranges

Follow the given steps:

1. Copy the following as a query to LINQPad:

```
var naturalNumbers = Enumerable.Range(1, 10);
naturalNumbers.Dump("First 10 Natural Numbers");
```

2. Run the query and you should get the following output:

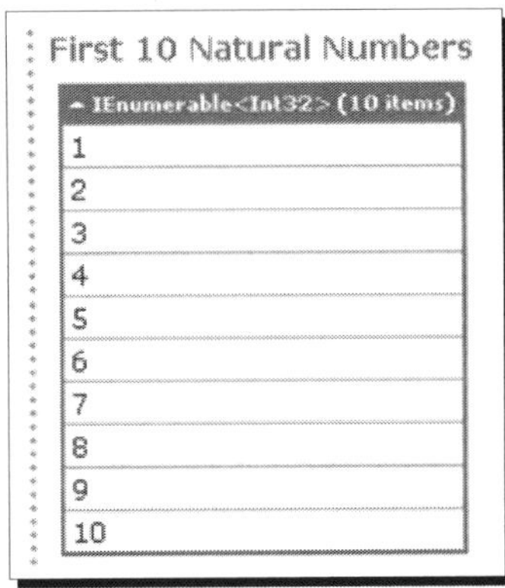

What just happened?

`Range()` returns an `IEnumerable<int>`. So, we can pass the result obtained from `Range()` as the input to other query operators.

Time for action – running a filter on a range

Assume that you want to find all the numbers in the previously-mentioned range that are multiples of 11. Here is how we can do that using `Range()` and `Where()`:

1. Copy the following as a query to LINQPad:

```
var multiplesOfEleven = Enumerable.Range(1, 100).Where(c => c % 11
  == 0);
multiplesOfEleven.Dump("Multiples of 11 from 1 to 100");
```

2. Run the query and you should get the following output:

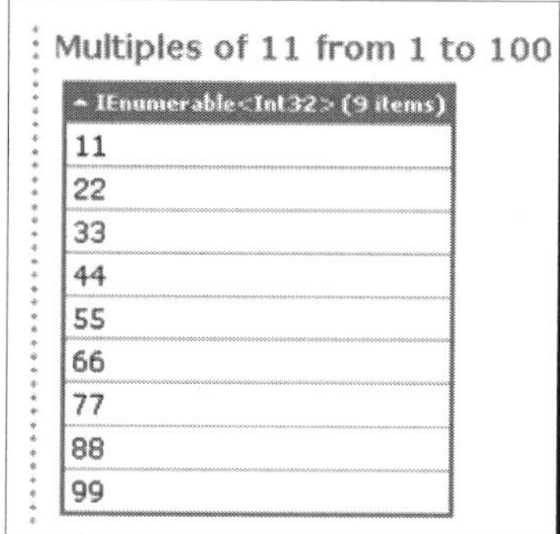

What just happened?

Range() returned an IEnumerable<int> instance and that was passed to Where() as an input. Thus, Where() operates to find the numbers divisible by 11 and returns only those as the final IEnumerable<Int32> instance.

Repeat()

This is also a static method declared in the Enumerable class. This makes it easy for us to create generic collections using repetitive values. All you need to mention is the object's value that you want to be repeated and how many times it should repeat, as follows:

Time for action – let's go round and round with Repeat()

Follow the given steps:

1. Copy the following as a query to LINQPad:

```
Enumerable.Repeat<string>("World is not enough", 5)
          .ToList()
          .ForEach(c => Console.Write(c+Environment.NewLine));
```

2. Run the query. This will display the following output:

```
World is not enough
World is not enough
World is not enough
World is not enough
World is not enough
```

What just happened?

The `Repeat()` method works on a string type in the current query and the string to be repeated is passed as `"World is not enough"` and it has to be repeated five times.

Then `ToList()` converted it to a `List<string>` and then `ForEach()` is used to print the result.

Quantifier operators

In this section, we will discuss the following Quantifier operators:

Single()

This is used to find out if there is only one element in the source collection that matches a given condition. There are two overloaded versions of this method.

The first one doesn't take any parameter and only checks whether there is more than one element present in the source. If there is more than one element, the invocation of this method throws `InvalidOperationException` and complains that the sequence contains more than one element. However, if the sequence contains only one element then this version returns that element:

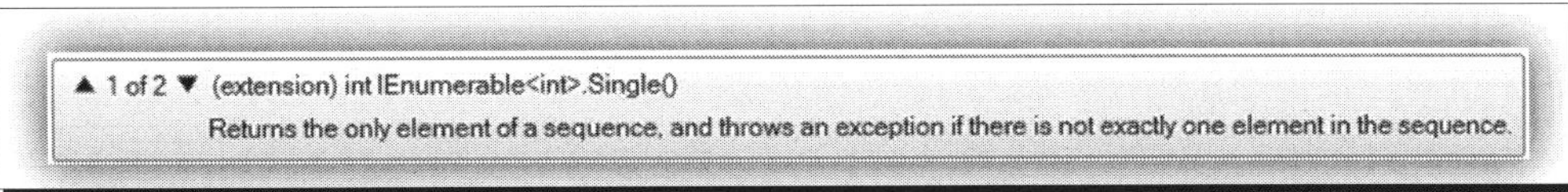

Here is an example that uses the second version of `Single()` taking a Lambda expression as the predicate:

▲ 2 of 2 ▼ (extension) int IEnumerable<int>.Single(**Func<int,bool> predicate**)
Returns the only element of a sequence that satisfies a specified condition, and throws an exception if more than one such element exists.
predicate: *A function to test an element for a condition.*

Time for action – checking whether there is only one item matching this pattern

Follow the given steps:

1. Copy the following as a query to LINQPad:

```
string[] names = { "Sam", "Danny", "Jeff", "Erik", "Anders" };
string onlyOne = names.Single(c => c.StartsWith("Dan"));
onlyOne.Dump("Only name with Dan*");
```

2. Run the query and you should get the following output:

```
Only name with Dan*
Danny
```

What just happened?

This will have `"Danny"` stored in `onlyOne` as that's the only name in the sequence `names` that starts with `"Dan"`. However, the following snippet will throw an exception as there is more than one element in the source collection:

```
try
{
  string w = names.Single();//This line will throw
  //InvalidOperationException
}
catch (Exception ex)
{
  throw;
}
```

Pop quiz – doing the thing

1. What will happen when the following code snippet gets executed:

   ```
   int[] numbers = { 1, 2, 3, 4, 5, 6, 7, 8, 9, 10, 11, 12, 13 };
   int n = numbers.Single(c => c % 2 == 0 && c % 5 == 0);
   ```

   a. It will throw an exception

   b. It will not compile

   c. It will return 10 in `n`

2. What will happen when the following code snippet gets executed:

```
int[] numbers = {3,4,5,6};
int n = numbers.Single(c => c % 2 == 0 && c>6);
```

   a. It will throw an exception
   b. It will not compile
   c. It will return 10 in `n`

SingleOrDefault()

As you can probably see, usage of `Single()` in a code can lead to an exception, if the source collection is not having exactly one element. However, to solve this problem, `SingleOrDefault()` was added to LINQ.

If no element is found in the source collection or if no element is found matching the given Lambda expression, then `SingleOrDefault()` returns the default value for the type of the source collection. For example, if the collection is of type `Strings`, then it will return `null`, if it is of `System.Int16` it will return `0`, and so on.

A few default values are listed in the following table:

Type	Default value
System.Int16	0
System.Int32	0
String	Null
DateTime	1/1/0001 12:00:00 AM
System.Double	0.0

Here is a sample usage of `SingleOrDefault()`:

Time for action – set to default if there is more than one matching elements

Follow the given steps:

1. Copy the following as a query to LINQPad:

```
int[] numbers = { 1, 2, 3, 4, 5, 6, 7, 8, 9, 10, 11};
int n = numbers.SingleOrDefault(c => c % 2 == 0 && c % 6 == 0);
n.Dump();
```

2. Run the query and you will see the following output:

Output is `6` because `numbers` has `2` and `6` and only `6` matches the predicate passed as the argument to the `SingleOrDefault()` method call.

The following diagram explains how the `SingleOrDefault()` method behaves in two different situations:

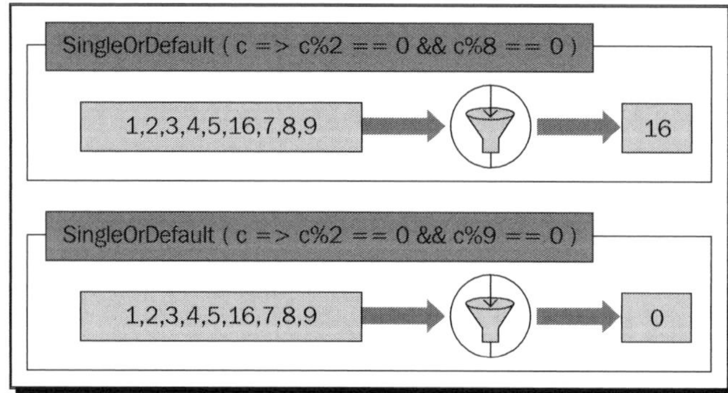

So `SingleOrDefault()` is just `Single()` with the default value attached. So, if you think usage of `Single()` can cause trouble and you wouldn't mind having the default value set to the return variable, `SingleOrDefault()` is the perfect package.

However, for obvious reasons such as you don't want to have the default value assigned to the return variable `SingleOrDefault()` can't be used to replace `Single()` calls.

Any()

This is used to find whether there are any element in the source collection. There are two overloaded versions. The first one checks whether there is any element in the source collection or not. This is more like checking whether the source collection is empty or not:

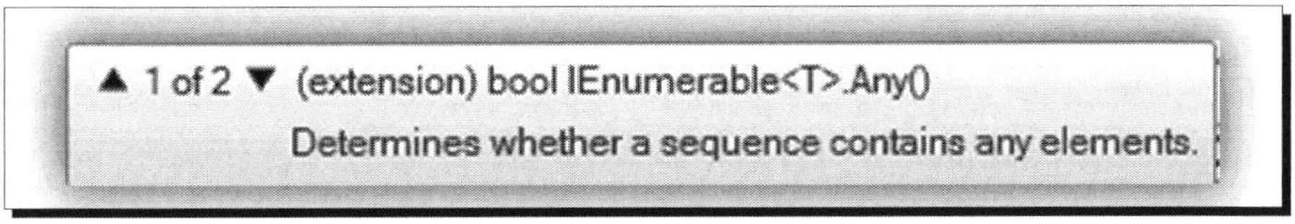

▲ 1 of 2 ▼ (extension) bool IEnumerable<T>.Any()
Determines whether a sequence contains any elements.

The other version takes a Lambda expression and returns `true` if any (can be more than one, unlike `Single()` or `SingleOrDefault()`) of the elements in the source collection satisfy the predicate described by the Lambda expression:

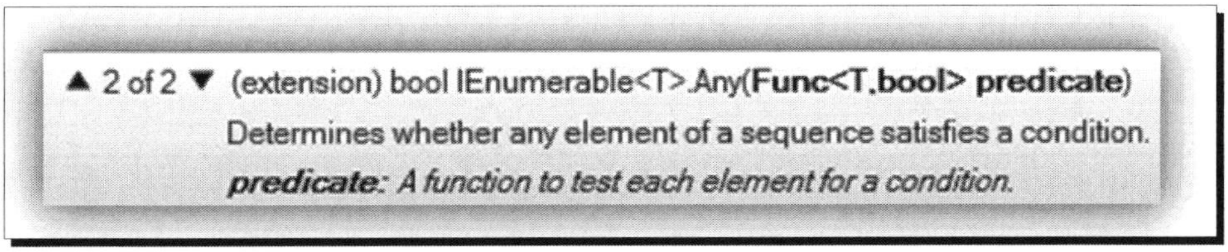

▲ 2 of 2 ▼ (extension) bool IEnumerable<T>.Any(**Func<T,bool> predicate**)
Determines whether any element of a sequence satisfies a condition.
predicate: *A function to test each element for a condition.*

Here is a snippet that describes this operator:

Time for action – checking Any()

Follow the given steps:

1. Copy the following as a query to LINQPad:

```
string[] names = {"Sam", "Danny", "Jeff", "Erik",
  "Anders","Derik"};
bool z  = names.Any();
bool x = names.Any(c => c.Length == 5);
z.Dump("There are some elements");
x.Dump("There is at least one element with length 5");
```

2. Run the query and you will get the following output:

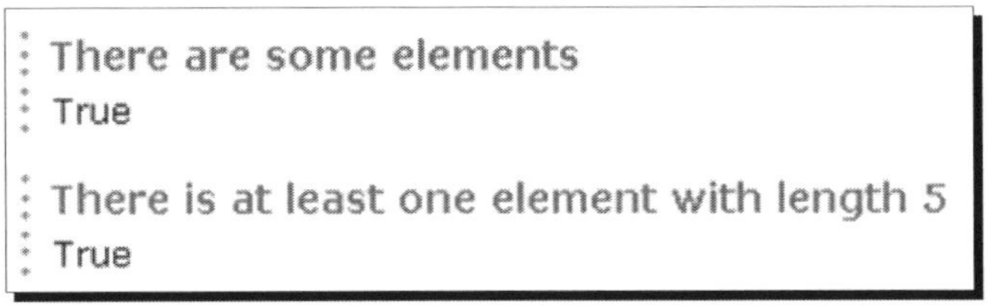

```
There are some elements
True

There is at least one element with length 5
True
```

What just happened?

Both `x` and `z` will be `true`, in this case, as the source collection (`names` in this case) has some elements and a couple of them have a length of `5`.

Unlike `Single()`, `Any()` doesn't complain if there is no element in the source collection or any that matches the Lambda expression.

All()

This operator allows us to check whether all the parameters in the source collection satisfy the given condition. This expression can be passed to the method as a Lambda expression:

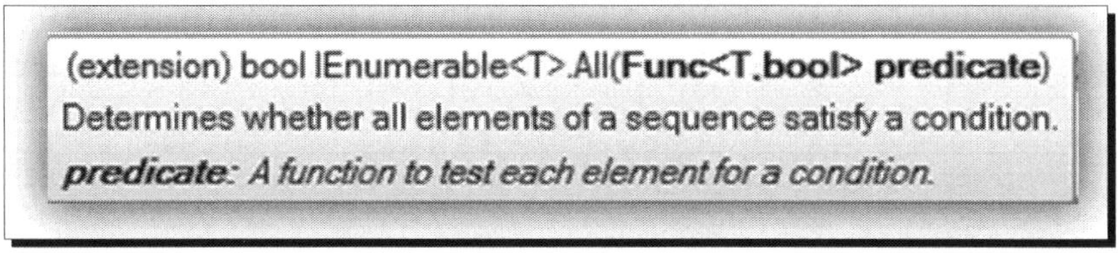

(extension) bool IEnumerable<T>.All(**Func<T,bool> predicate**)
Determines whether all elements of a sequence satisfy a condition.
predicate: *A function to test each element for a condition.*

Suppose, we have a `List` of integers and we want to check whether all of them are even or not. This is the best method to do these kinds of operations.

Time for action – how to check whether all items match a condition

Follow the given steps:

1. Copy the following as a query to LINQPad:

```
int[] numbers = { 0, 2, 34, 22, 14 };
bool allEven = numbers.All(c => c % 2 == 0);
string status = allEven? "All numbers are even":
  "All numbers are not even";
status.Dump("Status");
```

2. Run the query and you should get the following output:

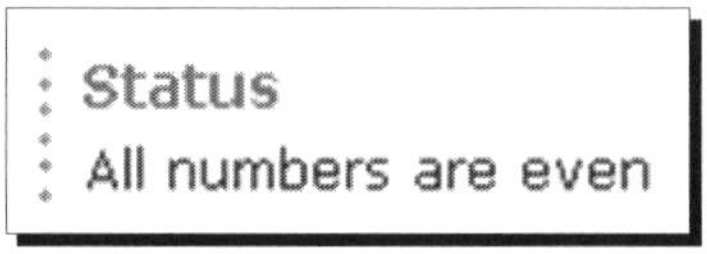

Status
All numbers are even

As all the elements in `numbers` are even, `allEven` will be set to `true`.

Merging operators

In this section, we will discuss the following Merging operators:

Zip()

This operator lets us combine the values of several collections and project them in a single collection of type `IEnumerable<T>`. This has only one version as follows:

(extension) IEnumerable<TResult> IEnumerable<T>.Zip(**IEnumerable<TSecond> second**, Func<T,TSecond,TResult> resultSelector)
Merges two sequences by using the specified predicate function.
***second**: The second sequence to merge.*

The second argument is the Lambda expression that explains how we want these projections to be made. That's why it is called `resultSelector` as it determines how the result will look. Assume this operator as a normal zipper of your bag. The following is a simple representation of how this operator works:

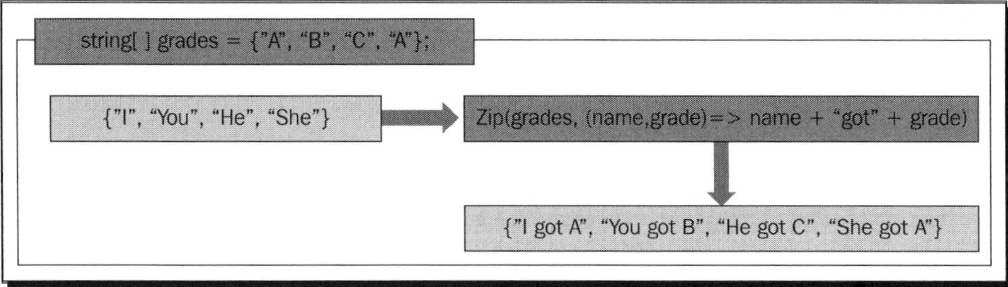

Say we have a list of first names, a last name and a set of salutations. We can zip all these together in a single `List<string>` as follows:

1. Copy the following as a query to LINQPad:

```
string[] salutations = {"Mr.", "Mrs.", "Ms", "Master"};
string[] firstNames = {"Samuel", "Jenny", "Joyace", "Sam"};
string lastName = "McEnzie";
salutations.Zip(firstNames, (sal, first) => sal + " " + first);
           .ToList();
           .ForEach(c => Console.WriteLine(c + " " + lastName));
```

2. Run the query and you should get the following output:

```
Mr. Samuel McEnzie
Mrs. Jenny McEnzie
Ms Joyace McEnzie
Master Sam McEnzie
```

What just happened?

The Lambda expression: (sal, first) => sal + " " + first does the magic of concatenating the salutation and the first name of all the "McEnzie" family members.

Now once that is done, ToList() converts the resultant IEnumerable<string> holding the concatenated salutation and first name to a List<string> such that using ForEach() last name can be concatenated to all of them in a single line of code.

That's how we get the list of names printed.

Summary

We have learned about LSQO. There is a lot of knowledge packed in to this chapter. In the later chapters, we shall use these LINQ operators to query our collection. Even in the previous chapters, I have used LINQ already whenever applicable.

5

Observable Collections

"Don't call us. We'll call you."

Changes are always happening around us. However, we don't care for all of them. But we do for some and we would like to know whether something has changed in our area of interest. The same is the case with software development. Think of the following situation:

A new entry is added/deleted to a collection or some elements are moved inside the collection. All views that are attached (also known as binded) to that collection need to be notified that something has changed, so that they can adjust.

This process of sharing news that something has happened is called **notification** *and notification can be achieved in two ways:*

1. *We keep checking for the notification every once in a while. This is called* **Polling**.
2. *The change itself knocks on your door. This is known as the* **Hollywood Principle**. *The quotation at the beginning of the chapter is known as "Hollywood Principle" in software. This means as soon as there is an event (read change), the event will notify every stakeholder. A stakeholder in software is something that has been registered for that event. There are several scenarios where notification on change of some value is vital for the proper functionality of the software system.*

The classic example is weather gadgets. Gadgets get their data from some published web service and in most instances each gadget shows their data differently from each other. So, each of these gadgets' content will need to be updated when there is a change in the data.

This can become increasingly difficult if you have more data sources to monitor, and updating the views of the collections they are bound with get modified.

.NET Generics has a set of tools packaged in the `System.Collections.ObjectModel` and `System.ComponenetModel` namespaces.

In this chapter, we will learn how to monitor for a change using the `ObservableCollection<T>` class.

Before we dig deep, let's take a second closer look at change. There is more to the dictionary definition that can be extremely relevant for software engineering. How many types of change are possible?

There are basically three types of Change:

1. **Active change/Statistical change**
2. **Passive change/Non-statistical change**
3. **Data sensitive change**

Active change/Statistical change

When some items are added or deleted from a collection, then the count of the collection changes. This is an active change that doesn't care about the existing data in the collection.

Example 1: As soon as you swipe your debit/credit card at a shopping mall, a transaction gets added to your bank account to which this debit/credit card is related.

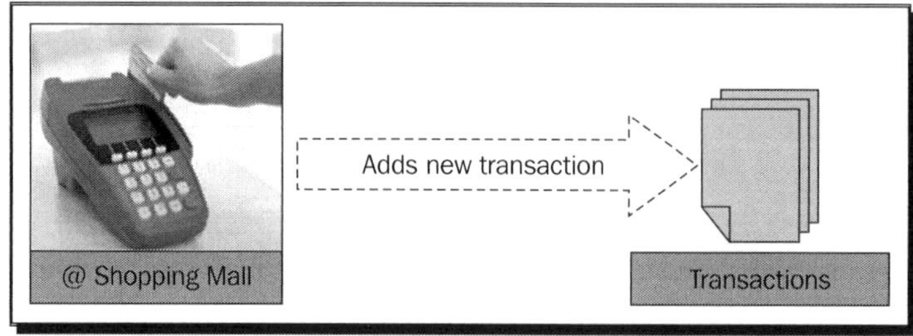

Example 2: You discovered a transaction that can't be yours. It seems fraudulent. After careful examination, your Bank Manager is convinced and she deletes the transaction that you mentioned and reverts the cash back to your account. As soon as she deletes the transaction, it gets added to a list of deleted transactions. So, in this case, an active change takes place in the deleted transaction list due to another active transaction in your bank account list.

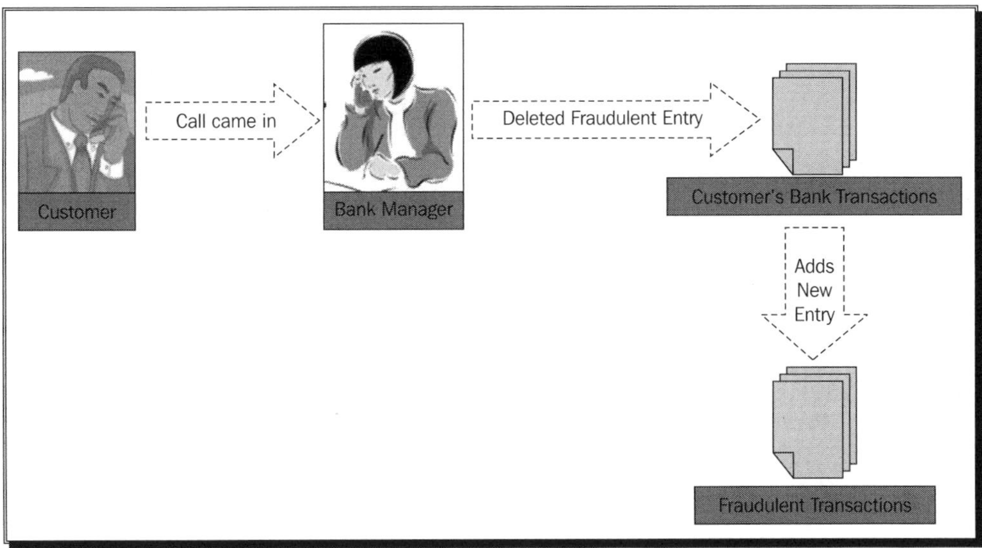

Passive change/Non-statistical change

Sometimes, the items from a collection are not deleted or added, instead they change positions or swap positions. This is a physical change in the collection; however, this doesn't change the statistics (such as length/count) of the collection.

For example, assume that you are sorting your bank account transactions according to the amount. Swapping transactions is a mandatory sub-operation, in this case, and results in a non-statistical positional change.

Data sensitive change

The preceding two changes don't care about the data already in the collection. So, if any of the elements in the collection changes, that's a data sensitive change. The physical layout of the collection doesn't change.

For example, assume that you want to monitor the weather for several locations. If any of the weather properties (such as temperature, humidity) changes in any of these locations, you want to update that detail. This is a typical scenario of a data sensitive operation.

Ok, so how do we handle these changes?

.NET 4.0 came up with an excellent way to deal with these types of changes. With .NET 4.0, a new type of generic collection, `ObservableCollection`, was introduced. This collection is a change-aware collection. So, whenever any change happens, this collection can report it.

The `ObservableCollection<T>` class implements two interfaces:

1. `INotifyCollectionChanged`
2. `INotifyPropertyChanged`

Both of these interfaces are very simple. Both of them only have one event. The `INotifyCollectionChanged` interface has an event called `CollectionChanged`, which is triggered when there is an active/statistical change. The `INotifyPropertyChanged` interface has an event, `PropertyChanged`, which can be triggered for any data sensitive change related to the Windows Presentation Foundation. I have decided to keep this interface out of discussion for this chapter. We will deal only with the `CollectionChanged` event and observable and read-only collections.

In this chapter, we will focus on the `CollectionChanged` event handler.

The `ObservableCollection<T>` class has a method called `Move()`. This method lets us swap two elements in an `ObservableCollection`.

Enough theory, now let's try our hands at this. The `ObservableCollection<T>` class can be used to monitor and help decide when to manipulate data for a source collection.

My nephew is 5 years old and he is getting used to even numbers, odd numbers, and so on. He also likes to do something on the computer. I wanted to keep him busy on the computer, so I designed a simple console that will ask him simple questions involving even and odd numbers, and will also monitor his responses. Also, I wanted to keep a track of the questions he answers, and the time he took for the response, so that I can monitor his progress.

Time for action – creating a simple math question monitor

Follow the given steps:

1. Create a Windows application and call it `NumberGame`.
2. Put a label on the form which will display the questions. Call it `lblQuestion`.
3. Put a textbox on the form where kids will type their answers. Call it `txtAnswer`.
4. Put a button to submit the answer. Call it `btnSubmit`.
5. Put a button to generate a new question. Call it `btnNewGame`.
6. Put a label to show the current time. This will be used to measure how much time the kid took to answer the question.
7. Arrange everything as shown in the following screenshot. Add a good background image. This is a screenshot of the running app. So at design time, you can use any text to initialize the labels:

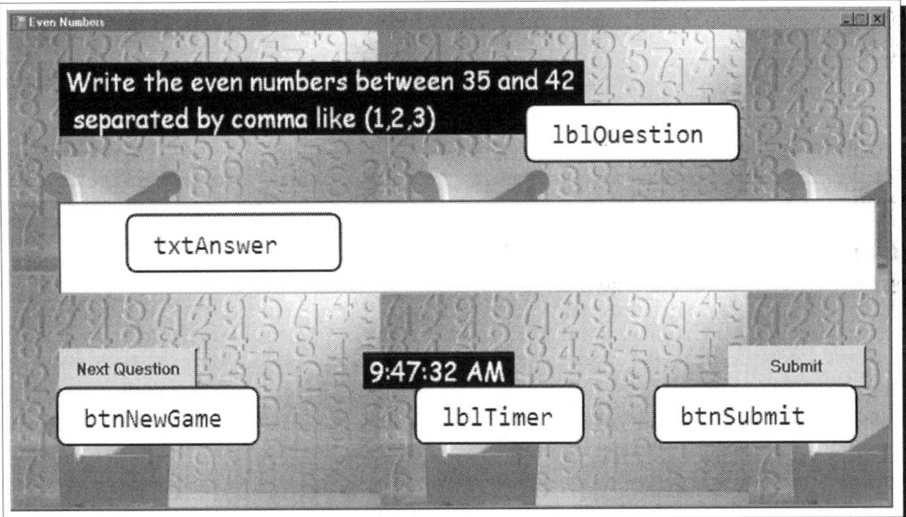

8. Put a timer control on the form. Leave the name as `Timer1`. Make sure it is enabled and the interval of the timer is set to `1000`.

What just happened?

At this point, you can run the application but nothing will happen as we are yet to glue the buttons to the code.

Time for action – creating the collections to hold questions

Now that we have the skeleton and GUI, we need collections to hold questions and answers:

1. Add the following using statement in `Form1.cs`:

   ```
   using System.Collections.ObjectModel;
   ```

   This namespace is the sweet home of our dear `ObservableCollection<T>` class.

2. Add the following code snippets to the class `Form1.cs`:

   ```
   ObservableCollection<int> numbers =
     newObservableCollection<int>();

   ObservableCollection<KeyValuePair<string, TimeSpan>>questions =
     newObservableCollection<KeyValuePair<string, TimeSpan>>();

   List<int> evenNumbersInRange;
   DateTime startingTime;
   DateTime endingTime;

   int start;
   int end;

   bool isAllRight = true;
   ```

What just happened?

The program is not yet ready to run the way we want it to. However, let's check out the rationale behind the declaration of these variables.

We want to ask the kid questions, as shown in the previous screenshot.

The first line of the preceding code snippet, `ObservableCollection<int> numbers`, will be used to capture the response given by the kid.

The second line of the preceding code snippet, `ObservableCollection<KeyValuePair<string, TimeSpan>>questions`, which is a collection of `KeyValuePair<string, TimeSpan>`, for storing the questions asked and the response time (time taken to answer the question) of the kid to answer each question.

Following are the variables we just introduced:

- `evenNumbersInRange` will be used to store the even numbers in the range and will be used to validate the answer given by the kid.
- `startingTime` will mark the time when the question appears.
- `endingTime` will mark the time when the kid gets the question answered absolutely right.
- `start` will mark the starting number of the range. It will change with every question.
- `end` will mark the ending number of the range. It will change with every question.
- `isAllRight` will be useful to determine whether the question is fully answered or not.

Time for action – attaching the event to monitor the collections

Follow the given steps:

1. Add the following line in the `Form1_Load`:

```
numbers.CollectionChanged += new System.Collections.Specialized.
   NotifyCollectionChangedEventHandler(numbers_CollectionChanged);
```

2. Add the following line in the `Form1_Load`:

```
questions.CollectionChanged +=new System.Collections.Specialized.
NotifyCollectionChangedEventHandler(questions_CollectionChanged);
```

3. Add the following lines in the `Form1_Load`:

```
//Starting the new game
NewGame();
//Starting the timer
timer1.Start();
```

What just happened?

We just created the skeleton to be able to run the program. All the placeholders are ready and we just need to fill them. Let's see how these are connected.

We want to monitor the responses given by the kid and we also want to store the questions and response time of the kid. The `ObservableCollection<T>` class implements the `INotifyCollectionChanged` interface. This interface has only one event:

```
eventNotifyCollectionChangedEventHandlerCollectionChanged;
```

This event gets triggered whenever the collection gets changed. When a new item gets added to the collection, or an existing item gets deleted, or a couple of existing items swap their locations in the collection, this event is triggered.

We want to monitor the kid's response. The kid's response will be stored in the collection `numbers`. So, whenever that collection gets changed, we need to know. Thus, the event handler `numbers_CollectionChanged` is attached to the `CollectionChanged` event of the collection numbers by the following code listing:

```
numbers.CollectionChanged += new System.Collections.Specialized.
NotifyCollectionChangedEventHandler(numbers_CollectionChanged);
```

So, every time a new entry is added or deleted or existing items move, this event will be called.

We also want to store the questions asked to the kid and the response time taken by the kid to answer those questions. In order to do that, I have attached an event handler for the questions collection by declaring an event handler as follows:

```
questions.CollectionChanged += new System.Collections.Specialized.
NotifyCollectionChangedEventHandler(questions_CollectionChanged);
```

So, whenever a new question is added, the `questions_CollectionChanged` event handler will be called.

The method `NewGame()` loads a new question and displays it on the screen. And as soon as the new question starts, we must start the timer.

Time for action – dealing with the change as it happens

Follow the given steps:

1. Add the following code to deal with the change in the collection `numbers`:

```
void numbers_CollectionChanged(object sender,
  System.Collections.Specialized.
  NotifyCollectionChangedEventArgs e)
{
  isAllRight = true;

  if (e.Action == System.Collections.Specialized.
    NotifyCollectionChangedAction.Add)
  {
    if ((int)e.NewItems[0] % 2 != 0)
    {
      isAllRight = false;
      MessageBox.Show(String.Format("OOPS! You picked {0}
        which is not an even number",(int)e.NewItems[0]));
    }
    if ((int)e.NewItems[0] % 2 == 0 &&
      !evenNumbersInRange.Contains((int)e.NewItems[0]))
    {
      sAllRight = false;
      MessageBox.Show(String.Format(@"OOPS! You picked {0}
        which is an even number but not in the range",
        (int)e.NewItems[0]));
    }
  }
}
```

2. Add the following code to deal with the change in the questions collection:

```
void questions_CollectionChanged(object sender, System.
Collections.Specialized.NotifyCollectionChangedEventArgs e)
{
  if (e.Action ==
  System.Collections.Specialized.
  NotifyCollectionChangedAction.Add)
  {
    KeyValuePair<string,TimeSpan> record =
      (KeyValuePair<string,TimeSpan>)
    e.NewItems[0];
```

```
            StreamWriter questionWriter =
              new StreamWriter("C:\\questions.txt", true);
            questionWriter.WriteLine(record.Key + " Time Taken " +
              record.Value);
            questionWriter.Close();
          }
        }
```

What just happened?

The `System.Collections.Specialized.NotifyCollectionChangedEventArgs` namespace has an enum called `Action` and it's of type `NotifyCollectionChangedAction`, which has the values as shown in the following screenshot:

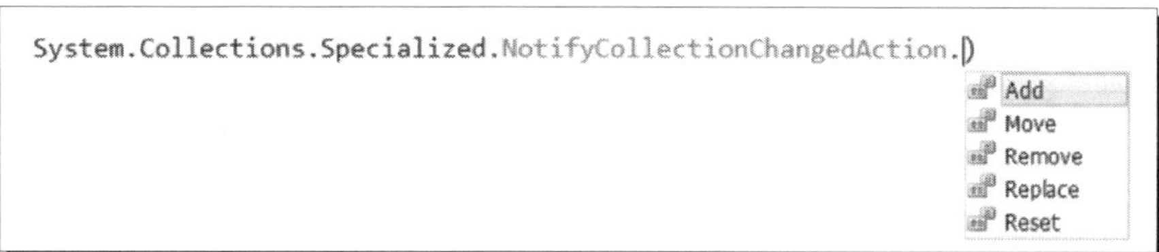

When a new item is added to the collection, the `Action` is internally set to `Add`. When an item is removed from the collection, the `Action` is set to `Remove`. When two existing items in the collection swap their location, `Action` is set to `Move`. When an existing item is replaced with another element, `Replace` is set as the `Action`. If all the elements in the collection are deleted, then `Action` is set to `Reset`.

When new items are added to the collection, these items are stored in the collection called `NewItems`, which is of type `IList`.

The first event handler, that is:

```
e.Action == System.Collections.
  Specialized.NotifyCollectionChangedAction.Add
```

will be `true` whenever a new element is being added to the `numbers` collection.

The `(int)e.NewItems[0]()` method returns the last integer added, as the `NewItems` collection returns `IList<object>` typecasting it to `int` is necessary.

If the last element added to this collection—which is actually entered by the kid—is not an even number, then it gets reported. If, however, the kid selects a number that is even, but not in the given range, then that is also a wrong answer and the application must be able to catch that. That's what happens in these two if-blocks in the preceding event handler.

When the kid finally answers the question correctly, we want to log the question asked and the response time taken by the kid to answer the question. That's what happens in the second event handler.

Note that the `ObservableCollection<T>` class is similar to any another collection, as it inherits from the `Collection<T>` class, so we can monitor any collection of any type.

Actually, there are two overloaded constructors to create an *observable* copy of an existing collection as follows:

```
List<int>firstHundredNaturalNumbers = Enumerable.Range(1,
  100).ToList();
ObservableCollection<int>observableFirstHundredNaturalNumbers =
  new ObservableCollection<int>(firstHundredNaturalNumbers);
```

In this case, `observableFirstHundredNaturalNumbers` is an *observable* copy of the `firstHundredNaturalNumbers` collection. So if you make changes to the `firstHundredNaturalNumbers` collection, it will not be monitored unless you have specific home-grown event handlers dedicated for that job. However, `firstHundredNaturalNumbers` is `ObservableCollection` and so you can use the `CollectionChanged` event to monitor any change that happens to this copy.

There is another overloaded version to create an *observable* copy from an `IEnumerable<T>` interface. This helps to form a bridge between the non-generic collection and generic collection as `IEnumerable<T>` implements `IEnumerable`.

So, using this overloaded constructor, we can create an *observable* copy of a non-generic collection, such as `Array` or `ArrayList`.

Time for action – dealing with the change as it happens

Follow the given step:

1. Add these methods to `Form1.cs`:

```
privatevoidNewGame()
{
  start = newRandom().Next(100);
  end = start + newRandom().Next(20);
  lblQuestion.Text = "Write the even numbers between " +
    start.ToString() + " and " + end.ToString()
    + "\n separated by comma like (1,2,3)";

  evenNumbersInRange = Enumerable.Range(start, end - start +
    1).Where(c => c % 2 == 0).ToList();
```

```
    startingTime = DateTime.Now;
  }

  private voidbtnNewGame_Click(object sender, EventArgs e)
  {
    txtAnswer.Clear();
    NewGame();
    txtAnswer.Focus();
    timer1.Start();
  }
```

What just happened?

We need some code to start a new game by loading a new question with a new range. Every time we need to do the same thing. So, putting that logic inside a method makes a lot of sense. The method `NewGame()` does just that.

When the **Next Question** button is clicked, the answer field must be cleared out so that the kid can enter a new answer there. Also, the timer has to be restarted so that we can capture the new response time.

Time for action – putting it all together

Follow the given step:

1. Add the following event handler to deal with the submission of the answer:

```
private void btnSubmit_Click(object sender, EventArgs e)
{
  numbers.Clear();
  string[] toks = txtAnswer.Text.Split(new char[] { ',' },
    StringSplitOptions.RemoveEmptyEntries);

  foreach (string t in toks)
  numbers.Add(Convert.ToInt16(t));

  if (isAllRight && numbers.Count == evenNumbersInRange.Count)
  {
    MessageBox.Show("Congratulations! You got it all right");
    timer1.Stop();
    endingTime = DateTime.Now;
    questions.Add(new KeyValuePair<string,
      TimeSpan>(lblQuestion.Text,
```

```
            endingTime.Subtract(startingTime)));
        }
        if (isAllRight && numbers.Count != evenNumbersInRange.Count)
        {
            MessageBox.Show("You are partially right. There are
              one or more even numbers left in the range.");
        }
    }
```

What just happened?

When the kid clicks on the **Submit** button, the program evaluates the answer. Only if it is absolutely correctly answered, the timer is stopped. At this point, the question gets added to the log along with the time taken to answer the question.

The call:

```
questions.Add(newKeyValuePair<string, TimeSpan>(lblQuestion.Text,
              endingTime.Subtract(startingTime)));
```

will in turn call the `question_CollectionChanged` event handler, where the question and the time the kid took to answer the question correctly is logged in a text file.

Later, teachers/parents can review this log to see how the kid is progressing. A large response time for an easy question will be a bad indication.

The following screenshot shows a few entries that are logged in the questions log file:

```
Write the even numbers between 96 and 115 separated by comma like (1,2,3) Time Taken 00:00:20.9218750
Write the even numbers between 2 and 2 separated by comma like (1,2,3) Time Taken 00:00:05.8125000
Write the even numbers between 18 and 21 separated by comma like (1,2,3) Time Taken 00:00:06.8906250
Write the even numbers between 0 and 0 separated by comma like (1,2,3) Time Taken 00:00:06.0625000
```

Time for action – creating a Twitter browser

Twitter is a remarkable application. It is great at getting real-time data from several people in different parts of the world. Most of us follow a lot of folks on Twitter. So, whenever they add a new tweet, we get notified.

However, people figured out long ago that seeing all the tweets from the people they follow in a single space is probably more helpful than visiting each one's page. Some applications exist to cater to this special need. I find that most of them are full of features that I don't use.

Moreover, I wanted to create a very easy application that even my granny can use. All we have to do is to put together a list of Twitter user IDs that we want to follow, and the application will get their latest tweets. If we don't want to follow a certain person for now, we can just remove her/his Twitter user ID from our list.

I guess you've understood the problem. Let's get down to business.

Time for action – creating the interface

Follow the given steps:

1. Create a new Windows application and call it `MyTweetDeck`.
2. Add a tab control to the `Form1.cs`.
3. Add two tab pages in the tab control.
4. Change the `Text` property of the tab pages to `Names` and `Tweet View`, as shown in the next screenshot.
5. Add a textbox to the first tab called `Names`. Change the `Dock` property of the textbox to `Fill` so that it fills the entire tab page. Leave its name as `textBox1`:

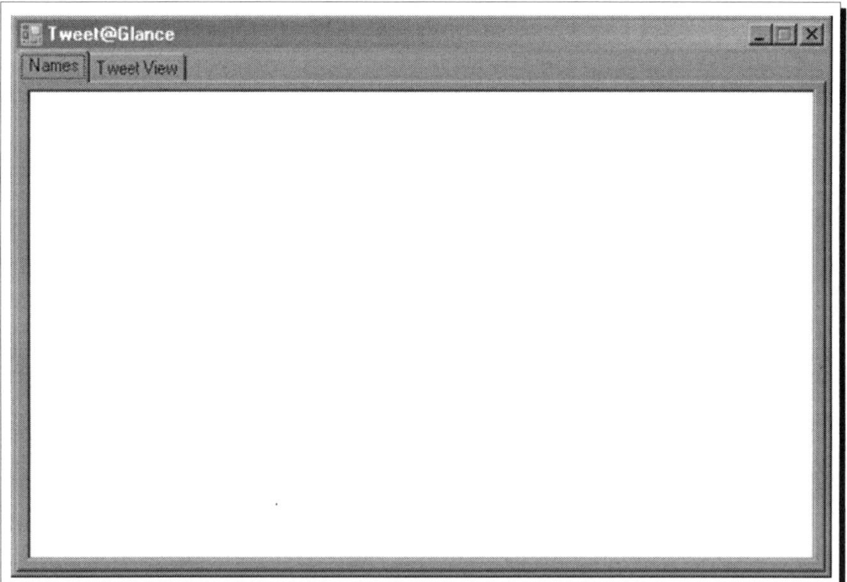

We are done with designing the basic UI. Oh! Change the `Text` of the `Form1.cs` to `Tweet@Glance`. How's that name? Well, I leave it up to you to decide.

Time for action – creating the TweetViewer user control design

We want to show the tweet on a control where the user's profile photo will be visible. The username will be just below the profile photo and the latest tweet will appear to the right. Here is a sample of what I mean. You can take a look at the control in action at `http://sudipta.posterous.com/twitview-control-for-net`.

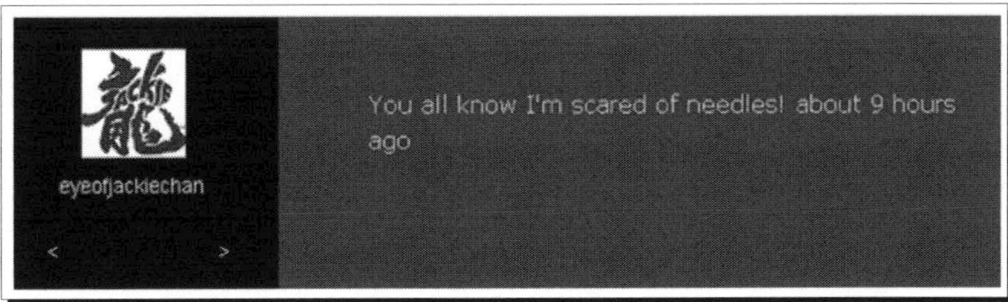

This tweet is from *Jackie Chan*. Who knew he was scared of needles! Twitter is amazing!

In this section, we are going to create a control that will help us lay out the information as shown in the preceding screenshot:

1. Create a new project of Windows control library type and call it `TwitterControl`.
2. Change the name of the `UserControl1.cs` to `TweetViewer.cs`. The control will be named as `TweetViewer`.
3. Add the following controls to the Designer. Arrange them as shown in the following image. Separate the real estates of the Designer into two segments using a splitter control. Call it `splitter1`.

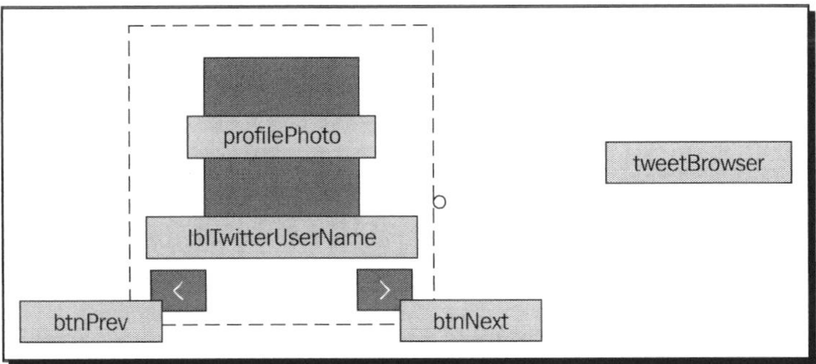

As shown in the preceding screenshot, the left part has four controls: a PictureBox called `profilePhoto`, a label called `lblTwitterUserName`, and a couple of buttons `btnPrev` and `btnNext` to move to the next and the previous tweet. The right part has a web browser. Make sure that the web browser is docked to fill the entire right part of the splitter. You can download the entire project from the website for this book. Add a context menu to this control as follows:

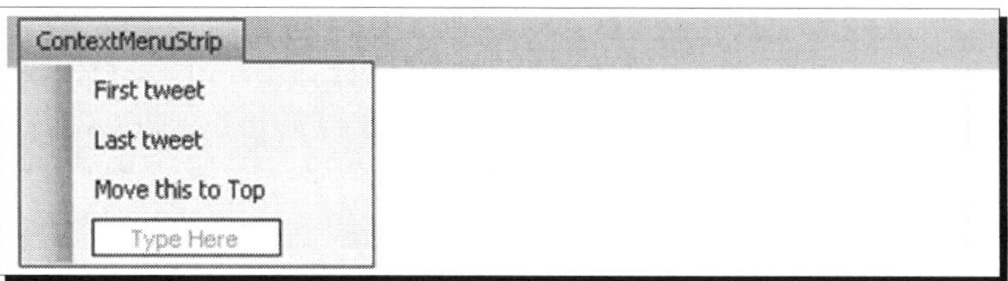

Also, attach it to the splitter control, as shown in the following screenshot:

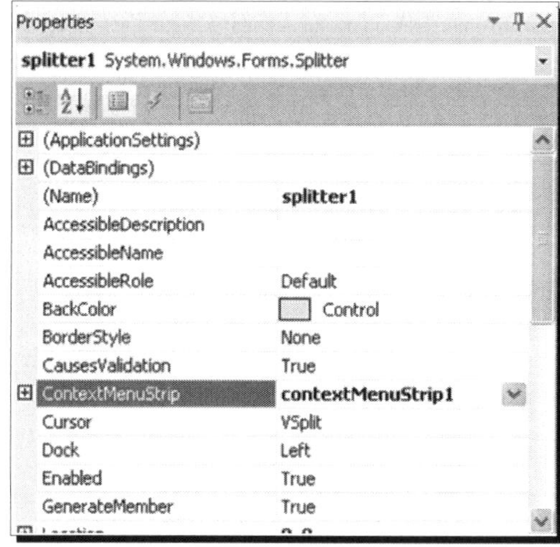

So, whenever users right-click on the left side, they will see this context menu to move a particular tweet to the top, or directly navigate to the first or last tweet. Take a look at this feature in action at `http://sudipta.posterous.com/contextmenu-on-twitview-to-move-to-the-first`.

Time for action – gluing the TweetViewer control

Now that we have all the controls in place, let's write some code to expose a few properties so that this control can be filled with Twitter data:

1. Add the following code in the `TweetViewer.cs` file:

```
public partial class TweetViewer : UserControl
{
  private int newTweetCount;
  private bool newTweetAvailable;

  public int NewTweetCount
  {
    get { return newTweetCount;}
    set { newTweetCount = value;}
  }

  private Label _tweeterUserName;
  public Label TweeterUserName
  {
    get { return this.lblTwitterUserName; }
    set { this.lblTwitterUserName = value; }
  }

  private Image _tweeterProfilePic;

  public Image TweeterProfilePic
  {
    get { return profilePhoto.Image;}
    set { profilePhoto.Image = value;}
  }
  private string _latestTweet;

  public string LatestTweet
  {
    get {return this.tweetBrowser.DocumentText;}
    set {this.tweetBrowser.DocumentText = value;}
  }

  private ObservableCollection<string> tweets;

  public ObservableCollection<string> Tweets
  {
```

```
    get { return tweets;}
    set { tweets = value;}
  }

  private Color _tweeterPicBackColor;

  public Color TweeterPicBackColor
  {
    get { return splitter1.BackColor;}
    set { splitter1.BackColor = value;}
  }

  private int currentTweetIndex;

  public int CurrentTweetIndex
  {
    get { return currentTweetIndex;}
    set { currentTweetIndex = value;}
  }

  private List<string> movedTweets;
  public TweetViewer()
  {
    movedTweets = new List<string>();
    Tweets = new ObservableCollection<string>();
    InitializeComponent();
  }
  private string Quote(string x)
  {
    return "\"" + x + "\"";
  }
  private void SetTweet(int currentTweetIndex)
  {
    tweetBrowser.DocumentText = @"<HTML> <HEAD>" + "<meta
                     http-equiv=\"Page-Enter\"
                     content=\"RevealTrans(Duration=0.5,
                     Transition=23)\" /> "
                     + "<LINK href="
                     + Quote("http://dbaron.org/style/forest")
                     + "rel="
                     + Quote("stylesheet")
                     + "type="
                     + Quote("text/css")
                     + "></HEAD>"
```

```
                        + @"<body>"
                        + Tweets[currentTweetIndex];
}
private void btnNext_Click(object sender, EventArgs e)
{
  if (this.NewTweetCount > 0 && currentTweetIndex >=
    this.NewTweetCount)
  {
    TweeterPicBackColor = Color.Black;
  }
  if (currentTweetIndex < Tweets.Count - 1)
  currentTweetIndex++;
  else
  currentTweetIndex = 0;
  SetTweet(currentTweetIndex);
}
private void btnPrev_Click(object sender, EventArgs e)
{
  if (currentTweetIndex >0)
  currentTweetIndex--;
  else
  currentTweetIndex = Tweets.Count - 1;
  SetTweet(currentTweetIndex);
}

private void firstTweetToolStripMenuItem_Click(object
  sender, EventArgs e)
{
  SetTweet(0);
}

private void lastTweetToolStripMenuItem_Click(object
  sender, EventArgs e)
{
  SetTweet(Tweets.Count - 1);
}

private void moveThisToTopToolStripMenuItem_Click(object
  sender, EventArgs e)
{
  Tweets.CollectionChanged += new
               System.Collections.Specialized
               .NotifyCollectionChangedEventHandler
               (Tweets_CollectionChanged);
  this.Tweets.Move(currentTweetIndex, 0);
```

```
        for (int k = 0; k < movedTweets.Count; k++)
        this.Tweets.RemoveAt(k);

        movedTweets.ForEach(movedTweet => this.Tweets.Insert
          (0, movedTweet));
      }
      void Tweets_CollectionChanged(object sender,
        System.Collections.Specialized
        .NotifyCollectionChangedEventArgs e)
      {
        if (e.Action ==
        System.Collections.Specialized
        .NotifyCollectionChangedAction.Move)
        {
          if(!movedTweets.Contains("[MOVED] " +
            Tweets[e.NewStartingIndex]))
          movedTweets.Add("[MOVED] " +
            Tweets[e.NewStartingIndex]);
        }
      }
    }
```

We will use NTwitter for getting the tweets of the users. You can get NTwitter at `http://ntwitter.codeplex.com/`.

Time for action – putting everything together

Now that we have every piece of code, let's put these things together:

1. Add the following variables in the `Form1.cs`:

```
TableLayoutPanel tableLayoutPanel1;
intCurrentRow = 0;
ObservableCollection<string>tweeterUserNames =
  newObservableCollection<string>();
List<string> names = newList<string>();
List<BackgroundWorker> twitterDemons = newList<BackgroundWorker>();
List<TweetViewer>twitViews = newList<TweetViewer>();
```

What just happened?

The variables mentioned in the previous code are going to be used for the following purposes:

- `tableLayoutPanel1` will be used to lay out the `TweetViewer` controls on the form.
- `CurrentRow` will be used to keep track of the row we are at, for the `tableLayoutPanel1`.
- `tweeterUserNames` will be used to store Twitter user IDs of the people who we want to follow.
- `names` will be used to store the names. This will be used closely with the `tweeterUserNames` collection in order to achieve the functionality.
- `twitterDemons` is a list of `BackgroundWorker` that will help us get the latest Twitter details.
- `twitViews` is a list of `TweetView` controls. This will be populated with the controls.

Time for action – dealing with the change in the list of names in the first tab

Follow the given step:

1. Add the following event handler in `Form1.cs`:

```
private void textBox1_Leave(object sender, EventArgs e)
{
  string[] toks = textBox1.Text.Split(new char[]{ '\r', '\n' },
  StringSplitOptions.RemoveEmptyEntries);
  foreach (string tok in toks)
  if(!tweeterUserNames.Contains(tok))
  tweeterUserNames.Add(tok);
  List<string> copyNames = tweeterUserNames.ToList();
  foreach (string tok in copyNames)
  {
    if (!toks.Contains(tok))//The name is deleted
    {
      tweeterUserNames.Remove(tok);
    }
  }
}
```

What just happened?

We want to monitor the changes being made in the list of Twitter user IDs in the first tab. So, whenever the control leaves this textbox, we want to see whether there is any change.

The first loop in the preceding code snippet checks whether any of the names are new in the current list. If yes, then it will try to add that name to the `tweeterUserNames` collection. The call to the `Add()` method of the collection by the statement `tweeterUserNames.Add(tok)` will raise the `CollectionChanged` event handler and the action is of type add.

However, we are also interested to know whether some names have been deleted from the list. In order to do that, we maintain a copy of the `tweeterUserNames` collection. This copy is needed because we can't modify a collection while iterating over it. So, if a name is found that exists in the `tweeterUserNames` collection but is not present in the current list in the first tab, then we know for sure that the user doesn't want to follow this name any further and that gets deleted from the `tweeterUserNames` collection as well.

Time for action – a few things to beware of at the form load

Follow the given step:

1. Add the following event handler in `Form1.cs`:

```
privatevoid Form1_Load(object sender, EventArgs e)
{
  tweeterUserNames.CollectionChanged +=
                    newSystem.Collections.Specialized
                    .NotifyCollectionChangedEventHandler
                    (tweeterUserNames_CollectionChanged);
}
```

What just happened?

The first time the form loads, we want to make sure that the `CollectionChanged` event handler is properly attached. So, whenever a name gets added to the collection `tweeterUserNames` or gets deleted from it, we can monitor it.

Time for action – things to do when names get added or deleted

Follow the given step:

1. Add the following event handler in `Form1.cs`:

```
void tweeterUserNames_CollectionChanged(object sender,
                       System.Collections.Specialized
                       .NotifyCollectionChangedEventArgs e)
{
  if (e.Action == System.Collections.Specialized
    .NotifyCollectionChangedAction.Add)
  {
    for (int i = e.NewStartingIndex; i <
    tweeterUserNames.Count; i++)
    {
      names.Add(tweeterUserNames[i]);
      TweetViewer twitView = new TweetViewer();
      twitView.TweeterUserName.Text = tweeterUserNames[i];
      twitView.Font = new Font("Arial", 10);
      if (tableLayoutPanel1 == null)
      {
        tableLayoutPanel1 = new TableLayoutPanel();
        tableLayoutPanel1.Dock = DockStyle.Fill;
        tableLayoutPanel1.AutoScroll = true;
        this.tabPage2.Controls.Add(tableLayoutPanel1);
        this.tableLayoutPanel1.Controls.Add(twitView, 0,
          CurrentRow);
        CurrentRow++;
        twitViews.Add(twitView);
      }
      else
      {
        this.tableLayoutPanel1.Controls.Add
          (twitView, 0, CurrentRow);
        CurrentRow++;
        twitViews.Add(twitView);
      }
      BackgroundWorker twitterDemon = new BackgroundWorker();
      twitterDemon.WorkerSupportsCancellation = true;
      twitterDemon.WorkerReportsProgress = true;
      twitterDemon.DoWork +=
        new DoWorkEventHandler(twitterDemon_DoWork);
```

```
            twitterDemon.RunWorkerCompleted += new
              RunWorkerCompletedEventHandler
              (twitterDemon_RunWorkerCompleted);
            twitterDemons.Add(twitterDemon);
          }

          for (int i = twitterDemons.Count - 1; i < names.Count; i++)
          {
            twitterDemons[i].RunWorkerAsync(i.ToString() +
              "-"+ names[i]);
          }
        }

        if (e.Action ==
          System.Collections.Specialized
          .NotifyCollectionChangedAction.Remove)
        {
          int deletedIndex = e.OldStartingIndex;
          tableLayoutPanel1.Controls.RemoveAt(deletedIndex);
        }
      }
```

What just happened?

When a name gets added to the list of Twitter user IDs that we want to follow, the `tweeterUserNames_CollectionsChanged()` method gets called and `e.Action` will be of type `Add`.

`e.NewStartingIndex` returns the index of the newly added item in the list. If the `tableLayoutPanel1` doesn't already exist, we will have to create that and add a newly created `TweetViewer` control in that. However, if it already exists, then we just have to add the newly created `TweetViewer` control and increase the current row count of the table layout panel by unity.

Once this `TweetViewer` control is added, a new `BackgroundWorker` object has to be created to get the details for this particular Twitter user ID that just got added to the list.

After that we have to run the newly created `BackgroundWorker` with the argument. Every time a new name gets added, it increases the count of names by unity. Thus, this last loop in the first if block in the preceding code, will run only once, every time.

When an existing username gets deleted from the list of names in the first tab, this event will be raised and `e.Action` will be of type `Remove`. `e.OldStartingIndex` returns the index of the item that gets deleted. So, once we know which one to delete by `e.OldStartingIndex`, the code just deletes that particular row of the `tableLayoutPanel1`.

Time for action – sharing the load and creating a task for each BackgroundWorker

Follow the given step:

1. Add the following event handler in `Form1.cs`:

```
void twitterDemon_DoWork(object sender, DoWorkEventArgs e)
{
  string[] tokens = e.Argument.ToString().Split('-');
  int index = Convert.ToInt16(tokens[0]);
  string name = tokens[1];
  twitViews[index].TweeterPicBackColor =
    System.Drawing.Color.Black;
  twitViews[index].TweeterUserName.BackColor = Color.Black;
  twitViews[index].TweeterUserName.ForeColor = Color.White;

  Stream webStream = new
    WebClient().OpenRead(GetProfilePicImage(name));
  twitViews[index].TweeterProfilePic =
    Image.FromStream(webStream);

  if (twitViews[index].Tweets.Count == 0 ||
    twitViews[index].Tweets.Count == 50)
  {
    twitViews[index].Tweets = new
                     ObservableCollection<string>(new
                     Twitter().GetUserTimeline(name).Select
                     (status => status.Text));
  }
  else
  {
    IEnumerable<string> tweetsSofar =
      twitViews[index].Tweets;
    IEnumerable<string> newTweets = new
      Twitter().GetUserTimeline(name).Select
      (status => status.Text);

    twitViews[index].NewTweetCount =
    newTweets.ToList().IndexOf(tweetsSofar.ElementAt(0));
```

```
            for (int l = 0; l < twitViews[index].NewTweetCount; l++)
            {
              twitViews[index].Tweets.Insert(l, newTweets.ElementAt(l));
            }

          }
          if (twitViews[index].NewTweetCount > 0)
          {
            twitViews[index].TweeterPicBackColor = Color.DarkSlateBlue;
          }
          twitViews[index].CurrentTweetIndex = 0;
          twitViews[index].LatestTweet
                          = @"<HTML> <HEAD><LINK href="
                          + "\"http://dbaron.org/style/forest\""
                          + "rel="
                          + "\"stylesheet\""
                          + "type="
                          + "\"text/css\""
                          + "></HEAD>"
                          + @"<body>"
                          + twitViews[index].Tweets
                            [twitViews[index].CurrentTweetIndex];
        }
```

The code for the `GetProfilePicImage()` method is omitted. You can get it from the book website.

What just happened?

If you want to get the details for all the Twitter user IDs sequentially, then it's going to take forever and the operation might leave the app screen frozen. To avoid this situation, we must share the workload evenly among many threads. `BackgroundWorker` classes are very handy in these type of situations.

The `GetUserTimeline()` method of the NTwitter API fetches the last 19 tweets, by default, of the user whose screen name is passed as an argument.

We don't want to stare at this `twitView` list all the time to check whether some of the users whom we are monitoring have tweeted recently or not. So, the `Tweets` property of the `TwitView` control is an `ObservableCollection`. So, whenever some new tweets come in, we want to be able to identify the person who tweeted recently.

That's why the `NewTweetCount` property has been introduced. The following code initializes the `NewTweetCount` property to the number of new tweets the person at *index* has created in the last monitoring frequency (which I have set to 20 minutes):

```
twitViews[index].NewTweetCount =
                newTweets.ToList().IndexOf(tweetsSofar.ElementAt(0));
```

`tweetsSofar` is the list of tweets acquired since the last time. And `newTweets` is the list of new tweets that we gathered just now.

If there is a new tweet available, we want to make sure that we identify the person who tweeted. So, we are changing the back color to some other color as follows:

```
if (twitViews[index].NewTweetCount > 0)
{
    twitViews[index].TweeterPicBackColor = Color.DarkSlateBlue;
}
```

So that we can easily identify the person who has tweeted recently, if we click on the next or previous button, we can go to the next or the previous tweet. As long as there is a new tweet available apart from those we have already seen in the past scan, the color will stay as `DarkSlateBlue`, as shown in the previous screenshot.

You can take a look at this behavior at `http://sudipta.posterous.com/twitview-control-for-net-changing-backcolor-w`.

Now that we have everything in place, let's query every now and then to check whether anything has changed. To do that, we need to add one timer to `Form1` and add the following event handler:

```
private void timer1_Tick(object sender, EventArgs e)
{
  try
  {
    for (int i = twitterDemons.Count - 1; i >= 0; i--)
    {
      if (!twitterDemons[i].IsBusy)
```

```
            {
              twitterDemons[i].RunWorkerAsync(i.ToString() + "-" +
                names[i]);
            }
          }
        }
        catch
        {
          return;
        }
      }
```

Time for action – a sample run of the application

Follow the given steps:

1. Add the following Twitter user IDs in the first tab of the application:

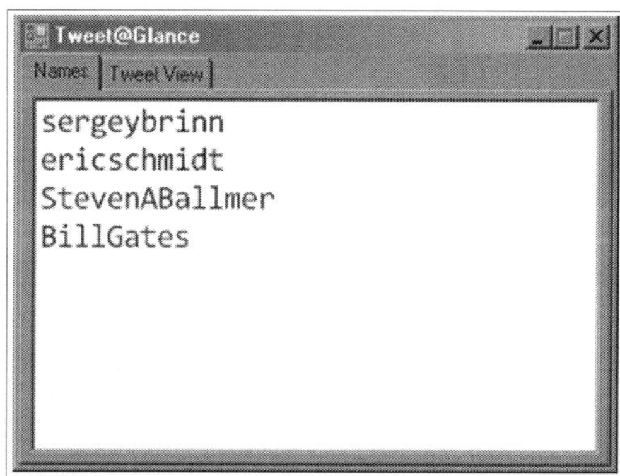

2. Click on the **Tweet View** tab. Within a few seconds, you will see something similar to the following:

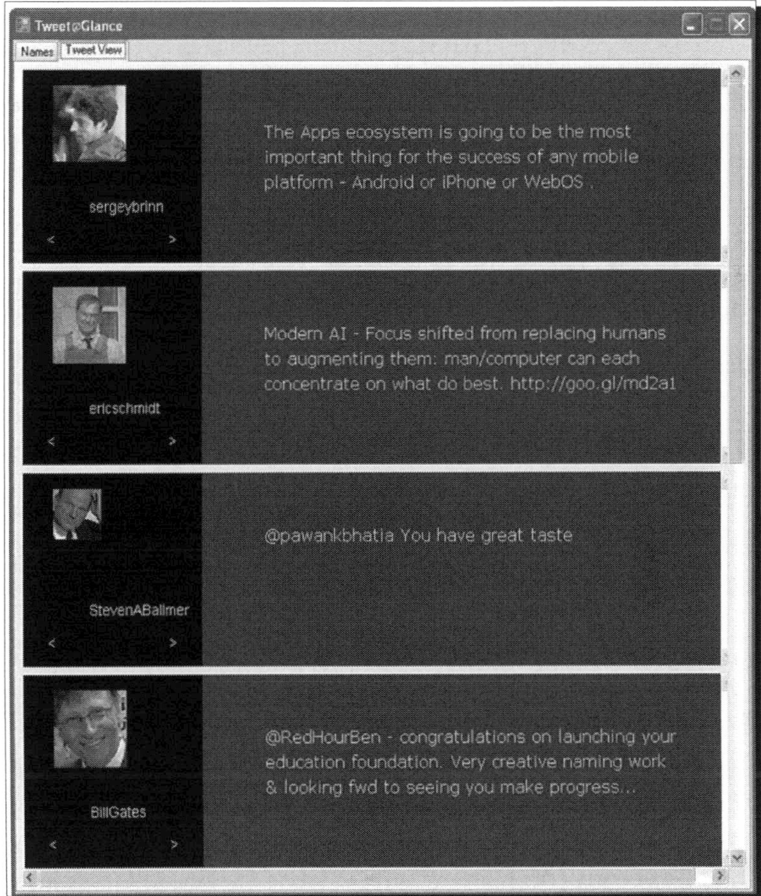

You can take a look at this application in action at `http://sudipta.posterous.com/twitglance-demo-using-a-list-of-twitview-cont`.

Have a go hero – archive tweets

The application offers a functionality to move a particular tweet of any person to the top. This way we will ensure that a tweet stays in our visibility for a long time because the last tweet gets deleted when new ones show up.

Remember that we added a context menu strip to directly go to the first and last tweet and to mark a tweet as "Moved" so that it can stay there for a longer period. The application stores only the last 19 tweets of the individual. After downloading the app from the website, try checking this functionality.

Can you explain how it works? Moreover, can you tweak it to monitor tweets from different people containing any of the keywords from a given list of keywords. Think of it as an exercise to monitor some Twitter trend.

Have a go hero – monitoring weather/stock

Using a similar structure, can you write a program to monitor weather at different locations? You can create a similar control to show a picture of the weather. You can download the startup code from the website for this book—search for **WeatherDeck** in the chapter's source.

You can use the Anima Online Weather API. It provides a nice wrapper against the Google weather API. You can download the API from `http://awapi.codeplex.com/`.

I have created a control similar to `TweetViewer` for weather monitoring called `WeatherBlock`. You can get it from the website for this book. With this control and the previously mentioned API, you can get and set weather conditions for any location as follows:

```
private void Form1_Load(object sender, EventArgs e)
{
  WeatherBlock wblock = new WeatherBlock();
  string place = "NYC";
  GoogleWeatherData nycWeather =
    GoogleWeatherAPI.GetWeather
    (Animaonline.Globals.LanguageCode.en_US,
    place);
  WebClient client = new WebClient();
  client.DownloadFile("http://www.google.com/" +
    nycWeather.CurrentConditions.Icon,
    "Temp.png");
  wblock.Location = place;
  wblock.ConditionTempCel =
    nycWeather.CurrentConditions.Temperature.Celsius.ToString()
    + "C";
  wblock.ConditionTempFer =
    nycWeather.CurrentConditions.Temperature.Fahrenheit.ToString()
    + "F";
  wblock.WeatherImage = Image.FromFile("Temp.png");
  wblock.WeatherText.Text = nycWeather.CurrentConditions.Condition;
  wblock.WeatherHumidity = nycWeather.CurrentConditions.Humidity;
  wblock.WeatherWind = nycWeather.CurrentConditions.WindCondition;
  wblock.BackColor = Color.Black;
  this.Controls.Add(wblock);
}
```

It generated the following output. It shows the weather conditions in NYC (New York City, U.S.):

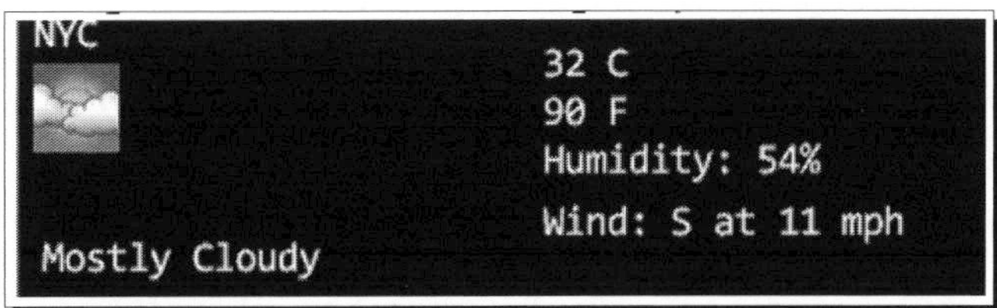

Summary

In this chapter, we have learned how to deal with some physical changes of elements being added in Generic collections. In the next chapter, we will learn about several concurrent collections to see how to deal with concurrency at the data structure level.

6
Concurrent Collections

Me! Me! Me!

Thread safety has been a major concern for API (Application Programming Interface) or framework developers for many years. Achieving thread safety had been inherently hard. These developers have always dreamt of collections that are primitively thread-safe, not requiring any locking mechanism when consumed in a multi-threaded environment.

Moreover, applications that can do more than one thing (also known as multi-threaded applications) are almost taken for granted these days. If an application fails to live up to this expectation, then it has little chance of surviving.

Thanks to **Concurrent Collections** *from Microsoft! These collections make writing thread-safe code a breeze. They encapsulate all locking mechanisms inside the generic data structures, so that the developers don't have to worry about it.*

In this chapter, we shall learn how concurrent collections are making writing synchronized code easy. To learn about this power, in this chapter we shall create applications to:

- Create bank queue simulation
- Develop a survey engine simulation system
- Devise a new generic data structure to find the most in-demand item at a store

Creating and running asynchronous tasks

This chapter deals with concurrency. We have to simulate that too. We will use the **Task Parallelization Library** (also known as **TPL**) to simulate several concurrent tasks that will deal with concurrent collections. TPL is available in .NET 4.0 for creating and running asynchronous tasks. Following are few of the patterns we'll use in this chapter. Task is a specialized class and it abstracts the creation of primitive threads.

With this API, writing asynchronous routines becomes more conceptual.

Pattern 1: Creating and starting a new asynchronous task

```
Task.Factory.StartNew(() => AddNewFruitNames());
```

Pattern 2: Creating a task and starting it off a little later

```
Task keepAdding = new Task(() => AddNewFruitNames());
//Some other code that has to be done before this task gets started.
keepAdding.Start();
```

Pattern 3: Waiting for all running tasks to complete

```
Task.WaitAll(task1, task2, task3, task4, task5, task6, task7, task8);
```

Pattern 4: Waiting for any particular task

```
Task.WaitAny(someTask);
```

Pattern 5: Starting a task with an initial parameter

```
Task voting1 = new Task((obj) => VoteThisOne(obj), "initial value");
```

Warning! This is by no means a chapter on TPL. These are just the patterns we will use in this chapter.

Simulating a survey (which is, of course, simultaneous by nature)

Surveys could be very concurrent in nature. Assume that someone from every part of the world is taking part in a survey and their responses to a single survey question could come in at the same time.

In this example, we shall simulate such a situation using concurrent collection and TPL. Following are the assumptions about the simulation:

- People can add more options at runtime for a given survey question
- Many people can take the survey at the same time, which means it will be concurrent in nature

Time for action – creating the blocks

Follow the given steps:

1. Create a console application. Call it `SurveyDonkeyTest`.
2. Make sure you add the following directives:

```
using System.Collections.Concurrent;
using System.IO;
using System.Threading.Tasks;//Needed for TPL
```

3. Add the following variables to the file `Program.cs`:

```
static ConcurrentDictionary<string, int> votes = new
  ConcurrentDictionary<string, int>();

static ConcurrentBag<string> options = new
  ConcurrentBag<string>();

static List<string> fruits = new List<string>();
```

4. Add the following code to read all fruit names:

```
//You can create your own version of Fruits.txt to store names of
//few fruits
//or you can download it from the book website
StreamReader optionReader = new StreamReader("Fruits.txt");

fruits.AddRange(optionReader.ReadToEnd().Split(new char[] { '\r',
  '\n' }, StringSplitOptions.RemoveEmptyEntries));

optionReader.Close();
```

5. Add a few initial options in `Main()`:

```
//Initial options
options.Add("Apple");
options.Add("Banana");
options.Add("Orange");

//Adding initial options to vote for
votes.TryAdd("Apple", 0);
votes.TryAdd("Banana", 0);
votes.TryAdd("Orange", 0);
//Start adding random fruits from the fruits.txt file as we
//vote. This is similar to the situation where people started
//buying and suddenly more options become available for them
//to choose from.
keepAdding.Start();
```

6. Add the following tasks, start them and wait on them:

```
Task showResult = new Task(() => ShowVotingResult());
Task keepAdding = new Task(() => AddNewFruitNames());
//Creating tasks that will act as voters
List<Task> voters = new List<Task>();

for (int i = 0; i < 100; i++)
{
  //Creating a new task with a randomly chosen object from the
  //options pool
  Task voter = new Task((obj) => VoteThisOne(obj),
              options.ElementAt((new
              Random()).Next(options.Count)));
  //Wait for some time, otherwise we might get the same random
  //element.
  //This is done to make sure we get an evenly distributed voting
  //:) Might not
```

```
    //happen in real world though. You can delete this line to see
    //what happens.
    System.Threading.Thread.Sleep(5);
    //Adding this voter to the list of voters
    voters.Add(voter);
  }
  //Let's start the voting process
  voters.ForEach(voter => voter.Start());

  //Wait till the voting is completed
  Task.WaitAll(voters.ToArray());

  //Show the result
  showResult.Start();

  //Wait for the results to be shown properly
  Task.WaitAny(showResult);
```

7. Add the following method to add new options at runtime:

```
///<summary>
///Make 10 tries to add new fruit options to the voting.
///It is like having new nominations during the voting process :)
///</summary>
private static void AddNewFruitNames()
{
  for(int i=0 ;i<10; i++)
  {
    string newFruit = fruits[(new
      Random()).Next(fruits.Count)];
    if (!options.Contains(newFruit))
    {
      options.Add(newFruit);
      votes.TryAdd(newFruit, 0);
    }
  }
}
```

8. Add the following method to vote for an option:

```
///<summary>
///Voting process by individual voters.
///</summary>
///<param name="obj"> The option for which this voter is voting.
///</param>
private static void VoteThisOne(object obj)
```

```
{
  string option = (string)obj;
  votes[option]++;
}
```

9. Add the following method to show voting results:

```
private static void ShowVotingResult()
{
  Console.WriteLine("Voting Result");
  Console.WriteLine("-------------");
  foreach (string fruitName in votes.Keys)
  {
    int thisManyPeople = 0;
    votes.TryGetValue(fruitName,out  thisManyPeople );
    Console.WriteLine(thisManyPeople.ToString() + "people
    like " + key);
  }
}
```

10. Add the following line at the beginning of the `Main()` method:

```
Console.WriteLine("Voting is in progress...");
```

We are now ready to execute our test. As you run the program, you will get the following output:

```
Voting is in progress...
Voting Result
-------------
150 people like Orange
153 people like Plum
143 people like Banana
150 people like Apple
```

What just happened?

At the heart of any survey is a table, and essentially a dictionary, which tracks the number of votes each option has got. In the previous code, we have created 100 voting tasks that vote random options.

In the previous example, two concurrent collections are used. A `ConcurrentBag` collection is used to update the available voting options at runtime. `ConcurrentBag` is optimized for addition and deletion from the same thread. `votes` is a `ConcurrentDictionary` that holds the response of individual voter tasks. The `TryAdd()` method is used to add initial options to the dictionary. This method is the implementation of the `IProducerConsumerCollection()` interface method.

`Try`, in the beginning of this method, means that it might fail in a multi-threaded environment if primitive `Add` is used. Imagine a situation where you are trying to add a few values against a dictionary key, while it was deleted by some other thread.

`ConcurrentDictionary`, similar to the thread-unsafe dictionary, still provides support for key indexers. So, `votes[option]++;` will increase the voting count for the options mentioned.

`ConcurrentBag` is a collection that implements an `IEnumerable<T>` interface; so, it supports all the LINQ Standard Query Operators.

As `votes` is a concurrent collection, and it is being accessed by several threads at runtime, it might so happen that it runs out of elements when we want to get the associated value for a given key.

The `votes.TryGetValue(fruitName, out thisManyPeople)` method returns the value for the key `fruitName` in `votes` and stores it in the variable `thisManyPeople`, or in other words, it stores the number of votes that the fruit with the name `fruitName` has received from voting.

Devising a data structure for finding the most in-demand item

In this section, we will develop a generic concurrent, move-to-front list with the following functionalities:

- It will allow the addition of new elements.
- It will show the top element and how many times that element has been accessed.
- It will let users take the top *n* elements sorted by demand. So, the item that is sought most should be available as the first item on the list.

Time for action – creating the concurrent move-to-front list

Follow the given steps:

1. Create a new class library project. Call it `TSList`.
2. Change the name of the class from `Class1.cs` to `ConcurrentMTFList.cs`.
3. Change the class header as follows:

```
public class ConcurrentMTFList<T> where T:IComparable
```

4. Add the following variable and the constructor:

```
ConcurrentDictionary<T,int> _innerDS;
///<summary>
///Initializes the internal data structure.
///</summary>
public ConcurrentMTFList()
{
  _innerDS = new ConcurrentDictionary<T, int>();
}
```

5. Add the following method to add new items to the list:

```
///<summary>
///Adds an item to the concurrent list.
///</summary>
///<param name="item">item to be added.</param>
public void Add(T item)
{
  _innerDS.AddOrUpdate(item, 0, (i, c) => _innerDS[i]=1);
}
```

6. Add the following method to check whether an item is present in the list or not:

```
///<summary>
///Checks whether an element is present in the collection.
///</summary>
///<param name="item">item to be sought</param>
///<returns>return true, </returns>
public bool Contains(T item)
{
  return _innerDS.ContainsKey(item);
}
```

7. Add the following method to perform the **active search** on the list:

```
///<summary>
///Active search of the collection.
///If the item found, it moves it to the top of the collection.
///</summary>
///<param name="item"> Item to search in the collection. </param>
///<returns> True if the search is found else returns False
///</returns>
public bool Search(T item)
{
  if (Contains(item))
  {
    _innerDS[item]++;
    return true;
  }
  else
  {
    _innerDS.GetOrAdd(item, 0);
    return false;
  }
}
```

8. Add the following property to find the top-most sought-after element in the list:

```
///<summary>
///Find the most sought after item.
///</summary>
public T Top
{
  get
  {
    try
    {
      return _innerDS.Where(c => c.Value ==
        _innerDS.Values.Max()).Select(c => c.Key).ElementAt(0);
    }
    catch
    {
      return default(T);
    }
  }
}
```

9. Add the following property to find out those elements that were sought after, but not found in the list:

```
///<summary>
///Returns a collection of items that are sought after.
///however not found in the list.
///</summary>
public ConcurrentBag<T> ItemsInDemandButNotFound
{
  get
  {
    return new ConcurrentBag<T>(_innerDS.Where(c =>
      GetFrequency(c.Key) == 0).Select(c=>c.Key));
  }
}
```

10. Add the following method to find out how many times an item is sought:

```
///<summary>
///Number of times an item is being sought.
///</summary>
///<param name="item">The item</param>
///<returns>How many times <code>item</code> is sought.</returns>
public int GetFrequency(T item)
{
  return _innerDS.GetOrAdd(item, 0);
}
```

11. Add the following public property to return a list of all items sought after:

```
///<summary>
///A Concurrent Bag is returned.
///This might serve as a concurrent bridge.
///</summary>
public ConcurrentBag<T> Bag
{
  get
  {
    return new ConcurrentBag<T>(_innerDS.Select(c => c.Key));
  }
}
```

We are now ready to use this API from our application. Let's see how.

Assume that we are trying to simulate a departmental store, where many people shop in different departments.

The store management wants to install gigantic electronic boards to show which item is selling the most in each department, as they think this will increase the sales.

Our just-baked `ConcurrentMTFList<T>` class is perfect for this situation. I recommend you take a look at the video: `http://sudipta.posterous.com/move-to-front-list-most-in-demand-demo`. This shows how a *move-to-front* list works as built in *Chapter 8, C5 Collections*. In this example, we will try a multi-threaded version of the same.

12. Create a Windows application and place controls as shown in the following screenshot:

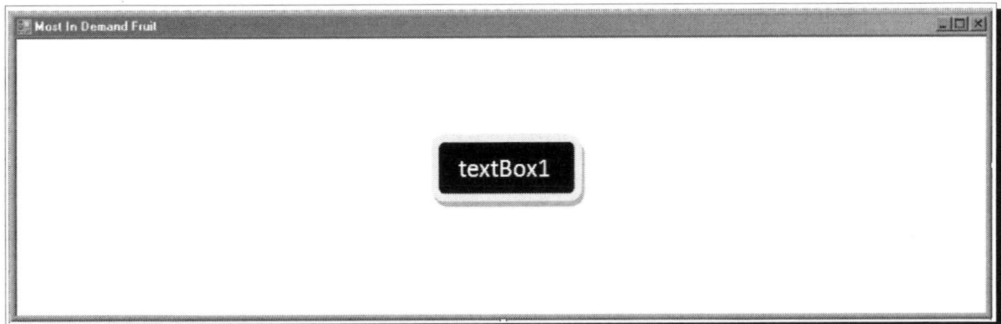

13. Attach a reference of the class library `TSList` in this project and add the `using` directives:

```
using TSList;
using System.Threading.Tasks;
using System.IO;
```

14. Add the following variables in `Form1.cs`:

```
ConcurrentMTFList<string> wantedList = new
  ConcurrentMTFList<string>();
ConcurrentBag<string> bag = new ConcurrentBag<string>();
List<Task> shoppers = new List<Task>();
```

15. Add the following private methods:

```
private void ShopFruits()
{
  wantedList.Search(bag.ElementAt((new
    Random()).Next(bag.Count)));
  System.Threading.Thread.Sleep(5000);
}

private void MakeFruitsAvailable()
```

```
{
  StreamReader fruitListReader = new
    StreamReader("fruits.txt");
  fruitListReader.ReadToEnd().Split(new char[] { '\r', '\n' },
  StringSplitOptions.RemoveEmptyEntries)
  .ToList()
  .ForEach(c => wantedList.Add(c));
  fruitListReader.Close();
}
```

16. Add the following code in the `Form_Load` event:

```
private void Form1_Load(object sender, EventArgs e)
{
  //one task for adding
  //multiple tasks for searching
  wantedList = new ConcurrentMTFList<string>();
  Task.Factory.StartNew(() => MakeFruitsAvailable()).Wait();
  Task.Factory.StartNew(() => wantedList.Bag.ToList()
    .ForEach(c => bag.Add(c))).Wait();
  //Create some virtual shoppers
  for (int i = 0; i < 100; i++)
  {
    Task shopper = new Task(() => ShopFruits());
    shoppers.Add(shopper);
  }
  //Let these shoppers start shopping
  shoppers.ForEach(shopper => shopper.Start());
}
```

17. Add a timer in the form and enable it with an interval value of `2000`.

18. Add the following code in the `timer_Tick` event:

```
private void timer1_Tick(object sender, EventArgs e)
{
  textBox1.Text = wantedList.Top + @"is the most in demand fruit
                  now."
                  + Environment.NewLine
                  +  "It is bought "
                  + wantedList.GetFrequency(wantedList.Top) +
                  "times.";
}
```

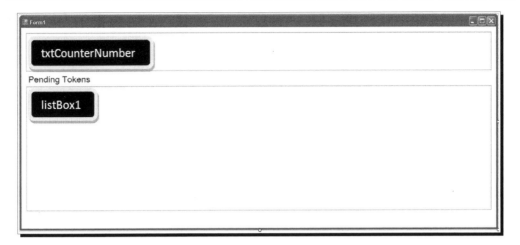

Also, add the following reference to your project and add them at the start of `Form1.cs`:

```
using System.Collections.Concurrent;
using System.Threading;
using System.Threading.Tasks;
```

2. Add the following variables and delegate in `Form1.cs`:

```
ConcurrentQueue<string> tickets = new ConcurrentQueue<string>();
bool stillAddingTickets = false;
private delegate void ChangeCurrentToken(string oldItem, string
  newItem);
```

3. Add the following methods in `Form1.cs` to generate random token numbers:

```
public string GetTokenNumber()
{
  List<string> words = new List<string>()
  { "alpha", "beta", "gamma", "kappa", "delta", "zeta" };
  //A large range, so probability of generating same number gets
  //reduced.
  List<int> ints = Enumerable.Range(1, 5000).ToList();
  Thread.Sleep(1000);
  return words[new Random().Next(0, words.Count - 1)] + ints[new
    Random().Next(0, ints.Count - 1)].ToString();
}
```

4. Add the following method to simulate servicing a request by a teller:

```
private void ServiceToken(object obj)
{
  do
  {
    string counter = (string)obj;
    string deq = string.Empty;

    tickets.TryDequeue(out deq);
    if (deq != null)
    {
      AddNewToken(txtCounterNumber.Text, deq + " At " + counter);
      System.Threading.Thread.Sleep(2000);
    }
    Thread.Sleep(10000);
  }
  while (stillAddingTickets || tickets.Count > 0);
}
```

5. Add the following methods to add a generated random token to the concurrent queue:

```
private void AddToken()
{
  string deq = string.Empty;
  for (int i = 0; i < 100; i++)
  {
    stillAddingTickets = true;
    string token = GetTokenNumber();
    tickets.Enqueue(token);
  }
  stillAddingTickets = false;
}
```

6. Note the delegate implementation to change the current displayed token and counter number in the textbox. As there will be multiple threads operating, the task to update the content of the textbox has to be delegated to the UI thread, otherwise it will throw a cross-thread exception:

```
private void AddNewToken(string oldItem, string newItem)
{
  if (this.txtCounterNumber.InvokeRequired)
  {
    //This is a worker thread so delegate the task.
```

```
        this.txtCounterNumber.Invoke(new
          ChangeCurrentToken(this.AddNewToken), oldItem, newItem);
      }
      else
      {
        // This is the UI thread so perform the task.
        try
        {
          txtCounterNumber.Text = newItem;
        }
        catch
        {
          return;
        }
      }
    }
```

7. Finally, put all of them to work, create a few tellers and a token generator:

```
private void Form1_Load(object sender, EventArgs e)
{
  Task tokenGenerator = new Task(() => AddToken());
  Task teller1 = new Task((obj) => ServiceToken(obj),
    "Counter #1");
  Task teller2 = new Task((obj) => ServiceToken(obj),
    "Counter #2");
  Task teller3 = new Task((obj) => ServiceToken(obj),
    "Counter #3");

  tokenGenerator.Start();//Staring the generator
  teller1.Start();//Starting teller #1
  teller2.Start();//Starting teller #2
  teller3.Start();//Starting teller #3
}
```

8. Add two timers to the project named `timer1` and `timer3`.

9. Add the following event handlers for the two timers:

```
private void timer1_Tick(object sender, EventArgs e)
{
  listBox1.Items.Clear();
  if (tickets.Count > 0)
  {
    foreach (string pendingToken in tickets)
```

```
            {
              listBox1.Items.Add(pendingToken);
            }
          }
        }

        private void timer3_Tick(object sender, EventArgs e)
        {
          if (!tickets.IsEmpty)
          {
            lblCount.Text = "There are " + tickets.Count.ToString() +
              " people in the queue";
          }
          else
          {
            lblCount.Text = "Queue is empty!";
            txtCounterNumber.Text = string.Empty;
          }
        }
```

We are now ready to run this app. As you run this app, for a moment you will get an output similar to the following screenshot:

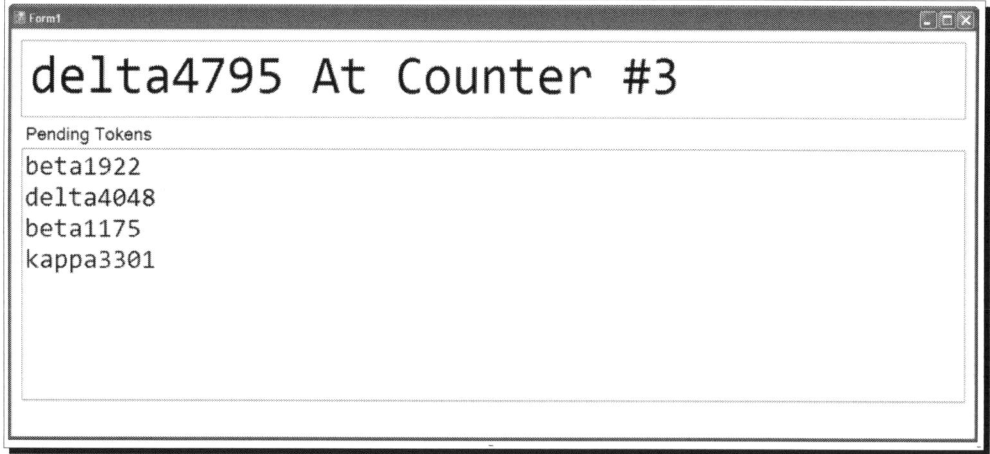

I recommend you check out the video that shows this application in action at `http://sudipta.posterous.com/queue-simulation-bank-demo`.

What just happened?

`ConcurrentQueue` is a thread-safe version of the plain old queue. As you can imagine, adding elements to a queue in a multi-threaded environment is fine as it does not lead to any exceptional error situation. However, we have to be wary while taking an element out from the collection, because by the time we reach out to get the element, the queue might be empty already.

`ConcurrentQueue` offers functionalities to do this very easily. The `Enqueue()` method works as with a normal thread-unsafe generic queue collection. However, the method `TryDequeue()` returns a `null` value if the queue is empty, otherwise it returns the first item in the queue.

The queue simulation we built is rudimentary. There is a lot of scope for improvement. One such improvement could be to run another parallel task that will monitor the queue all the time and it would return the *next three tokens to be serviced* as we have only simulated three tellers. On the other hand, the tellers would like to know *how many people are waiting*. Moreover, it will be nice if it displayed the *expected time* before they are attended to by a teller. All these tasks are easily achievable using concurrent collections.

Let's see how we can make the changes.

Time for action – making our bank queue simulator more useful

Follow the given steps:

1. Add the following two controls in the form, as shown in the following screenshot:

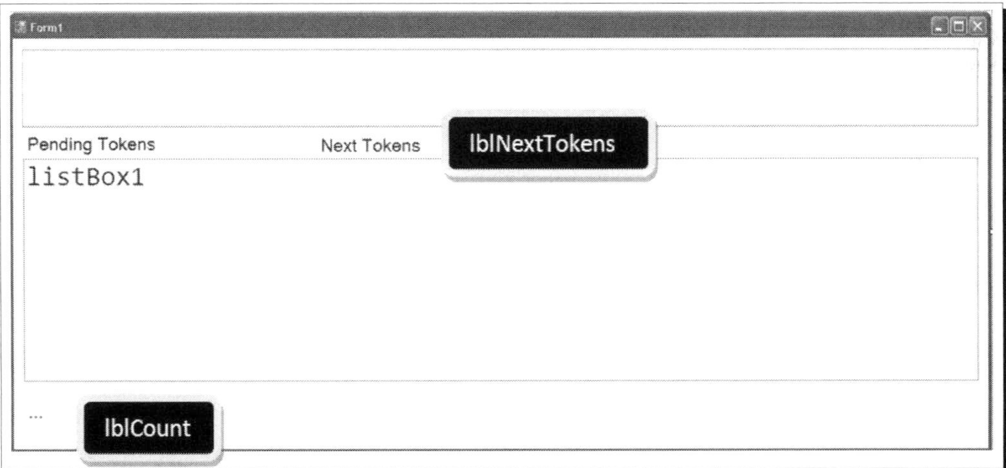

2. Change the code in `timer1_Tick` as shown:

   Replace `listBox1.Items.Add(pendingToken);` with

```
float expectedDelay = tickets.ToList().IndexOf(pendingToken) * 10;
listBox1.Items.Add(pendingToken +  " Approximate Waiting time " +
  expectedDelay  + " seconds");
```

3. Add the following variable in the `Form1` class:

```
string pendingStatusTemplate = "Next three tokens are [Queue]";
```

4. Add a timer. Name it `timer_2` and add the following code to it. Activate the timer and set the time interval for `2` seconds:

```
private void timer2_Tick(object sender, EventArgs e)
{
  lblNextTokens.Text = pendingStatusTemplate.Replace("[Queue]",
    NextTokens(tickets));
}
```

5. Add the following method:

```
private string NextTokens(IProducerConsumerCollection<string>
  queue)
{
  StringBuilder nexttokensBuilder = new StringBuilder();
  tickets.Take(3)
         .ToList()
         .ForEach(token => nexttokensBuilder.Append (token + " "));
  return nexttokensBuilder.ToString();
}
```

Now if you run the app, you will see an output similar to the following screenshot at any given point in time:

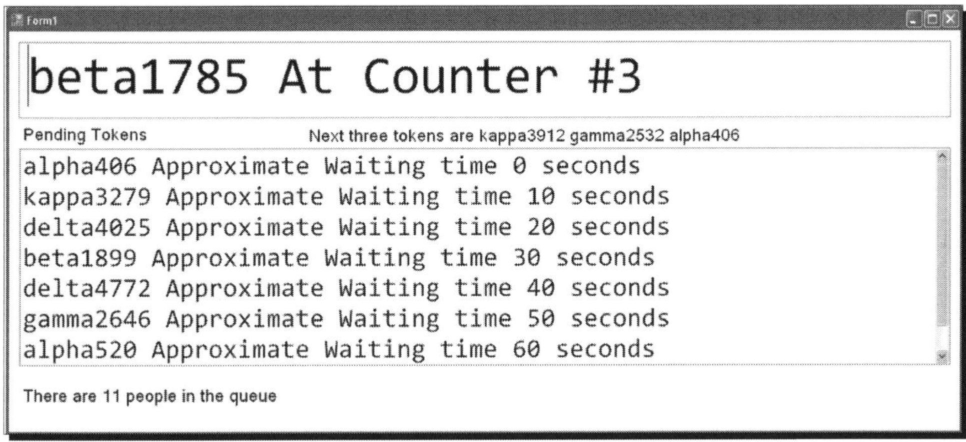

I recommend you check out the video at http://sudipta.posterous.com/private/nhnAmivcCv to see how the program works.

What just happened?

These concurrent collections support LINQ, because they implement the IEnumerable<T> interface. As we have created three tellers, so simultaneously only three people can get their request addressed at three teller locations. However, a little delay is introduced to make sure that the people waiting to get their request serviced don't miss their token number shown on the screen. In the meantime, people find it easier to be told a little in advance that their turn is coming. So, the first three tokens are shown alongside the entire list of pending tokens. This is achieved by using the Take() LINQ operator. Note that the timer runs on a different thread. Even then, the program always returns correct values.

Be a smart consumer, don't wait till you have it all

You have a situation where you want to ensure thread safety for your collection, but you don't care for the order of insertion, or in other words, you don't care whether it is a FIFO or a LIFO list. The elements in the collection can be in any order. In this situation, you need a vanilla implementation of the IProducerConsumerCollection<T> interface and that is BlockingCollection<T>, the wrapper collection of IProducerConsumerCollection<T>. All others except ConcurrentDictionary also implement IProducerConsumerCollection<T>.

There is another situation where `BlockingCollection<T>` can prove to be extremely handy. While waiting on some producer tasks to generate results and then iterate over them, this might be a bad experience for the user as they have to wait till the producer queues have finished. If we want to perform some other jobs on the results as they start appearing, we can use the `GetConsumableEnumerable()` method of `BlockingCollection<T>`.

`BlockingCollection<T>` also offers some methods to deal with many concurrent collections. We will learn them as a reference in the later chapters.

Exploring data structure mapping

Before we wrap this chapter, let's see what we have learned about thread-safe and thread-unsafe data structure mapping:

Thread-unsafe Generics	**Thread-safe Generics**
`Stack<T>`	`ConcurrentStack<T>`
`Queue<T>`	`ConcurrentQueue<T>`
`Dictionary<TKey,TValue>`	`ConcurrentDictionary<TKey,TValue>`
`List<T>`	`ConcurrentBag<T>`
`LinkedList<T>`	`ConcurrentBag<T>`
`SortedList<TKey,TValue>`	`ConcurrentDictionary<TKey,TValue>` There is no direct mapping in the thread-safe collection world that offers `SortedList` functionalities in a thread-safe way. You can use the LINQ operator `OrderBy()` lazily, as you need sorting capabilities and use this concurrent dictionary as the basic data structure.

Some of the thread-unsafe generic collections are not present as is; however, with a little bit of thought they can be mapped using the concurrent primitives.

`IList<KeyValuePair<TKey,TValue>>` can be represented as `ConcurrentDictionary<TKey, ConcurrentBag<TValue>>`.

`SortedDictionary<TKey,TValue>` can be represented as `ConcurrentDictionary<T, int>(EqualityComparer<T>.Default)`, where `T` is the data type.

For example:

```
ConcurrentDictionary<string, int> conSorted = new
  ConcurrentDictionary<string, int>(EqualityComparer<string>.Default);
```

However, this will store the keys in descending order. You can always use the `OrderBy()` LINQ operator to sort the keys in such a concurrent dictionary in ascending order.

`SortedSet<T>` doesn't have a direct mapping. However, using the `Distinct()` and `OrderByDescending()` operator and `ConcurrentBag`, we can get a sorted set flavor, as follows:

```
ConcurrentBag<string> randomWithDuplicates = new
                      ConcurrentBag<string>();
randomWithDuplicates.Add("A");
randomWithDuplicates.Add("A");
randomWithDuplicates.Add("B");
randomWithDuplicates.Add("D");
randomWithDuplicates.Add("C");
randomWithDuplicates.Add("E");

ConcurrentBag<string> set = new ConcurrentBag<string>
(
  randomWithDuplicates

  .Distinct()
  .OrderByDescending(c => c)
);
```

Summary

We learned about new concurrent collections and how they can be used with the Task Parallelization Library. The things that are not discussed in this chapter include advanced partitioning logic offered by the framework.

In the next chapter, we will learn about power algorithms from Wintellect's Power Collections API. Though with the new .NET Framework most of the generic data structures available there are not relevant any more. However the API is a great place for good algorithms to complement .NET data structures.

7
Power Collections

Plug-n-Play

Power Collections came into existence during 2005, followed by the introduction of the .NET Framework 2.0. Wintellect is the company that created Power Collections. At the time of writing, with the introduction of LINQ and some data structures in .NET 4.0, Power Collections look dated. However, there are some data structures, such as `OrderedBag` *and* `Deque`*, and some great algorithms in Power Collections that become all the more easy to use with LINQ. To this day, this collection is being used.*

In this chapter, we will discuss some of the algorithms available in this API that are difficult to reproduce with standard LINQ operators. In the latter half of this chapter, we will see how some of the algorithms that we had skipped can be reproduced through LINQ operators. It does make a lot of sense to make these algorithms as LINQ Standard Query Operators (LSQO) so that they can be used on all IEnumerable<T> implementations. *Wintellect* has shared the code as an open source project on `http://powercollections.codeplex.com/`.

Setting up the environment

First we need to get the binary files for the API. Go to `http://powercollections.codeplex.com/` and download the API ZIP file. The DLL will be available under the `PowerCollections\Binaries` folder after you unzip the file.

Now that we have the API, let's put it with LINQPad 4 (that we had used in *Chapter 5, Observable Collections*).

1. Open LINQPad 4.
2. Press *F4*. You will see the following screen:

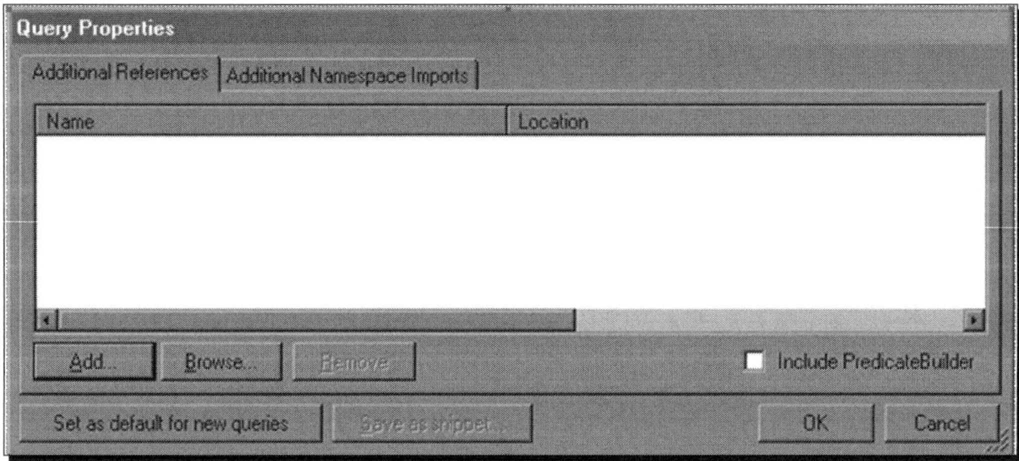

3. Click on **Browse** to locate the following binary file:

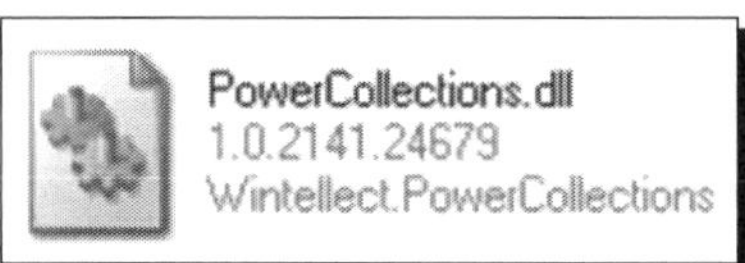

4. Once you add the file, it will be displayed in the list of **Additional References**, as follows:

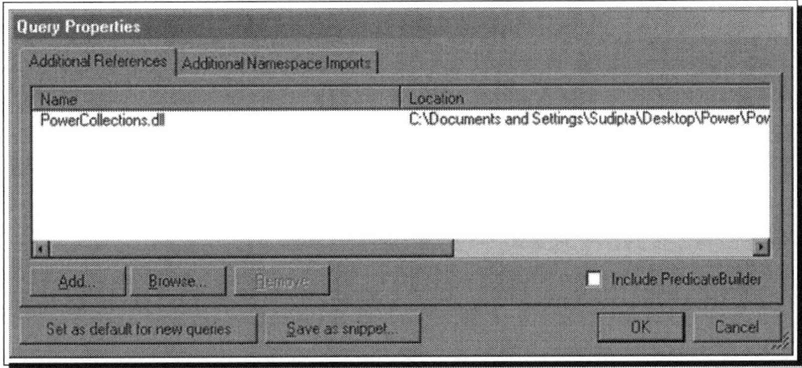

Click on **OK** to complete this process.

5. Click on the next tab, **Additional Namespace Imports,** and write `Wintellect.PowerCollections` in the textbox:

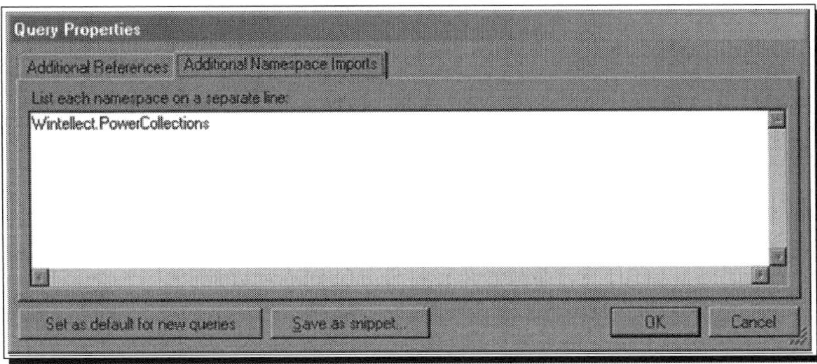

Every time you open LINQPad, you have to repeat step 4 and step 5 explained earlier. So, I recommend not to close your LINQPad instance when you are practicing.

Just change the **Language** drop-down value to `C# Statement` in the LINQPad editor header. We are now ready to play with all the power algorithms (if you will) in LINQPad.

Let's start exploring algorithms that I think are interesting and which Power Collections has to offer.

BinarySearch()

This query operator allows the user to search for an item from an `IList<T>` instance using the binary search algorithm. As you know, a prerequisite for a binary search is that the array must be sorted. The `BinarySearch()` method takes care of the sorting internally, so you don't have to actually sort the list.

There are three overloads of this generic method:

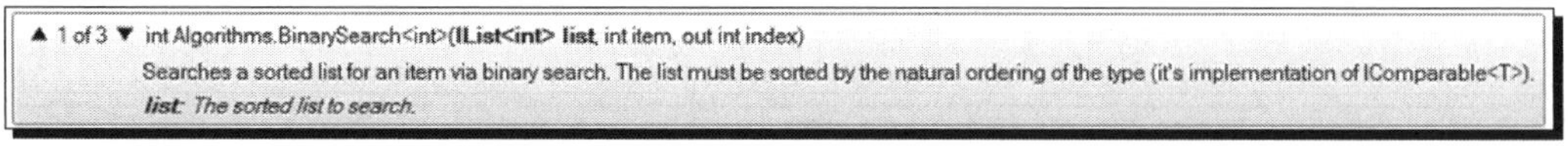

▲ 1 of 3 ▼ int Algorithms.BinarySearch<int>(**IList<int> list**, int item, out int index)
Searches a sorted list for an item via binary search. The list must be sorted by the natural ordering of the type (it's implementation of IComparable<T>).
***list**: The sorted list to search.*

This overload takes a type of list and item to search for, and an index where the index of the sought item will be stored.

Time for action – finding a name from a list of names

Problem 1: Say we have a list of names and we want to find the index of a given name:

1. Copy the following code in LINQPad:

```
int index;
string[] names = {"Sam", "Pamela", "Dave", "Pascal", "Erik"};

Algorithms.BinarySearch(names, "Dave", out index);
index.Dump("\"Dave\" is found at");

Algorithms.BinarySearch(names, "Sam", out index);
index.Dump("\"Sam\" is found at");
```

2. Run the code snippet. Make sure `C# Statements` is selected in the **Language** drop-down, otherwise it will not work. Once successfully run, you should expect the following output:

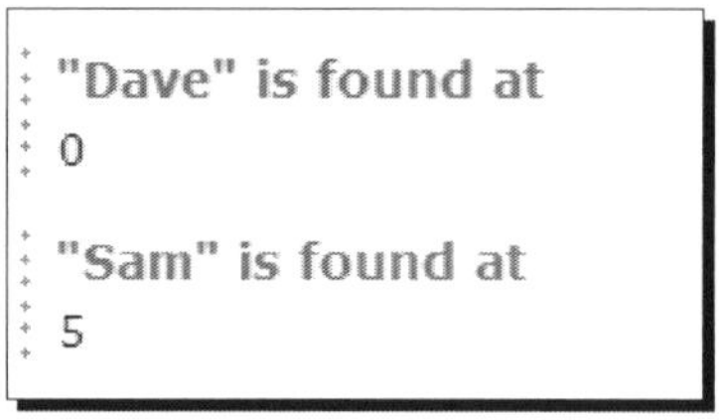

```
"Dave" is found at
0

"Sam" is found at
5
```

What just happened?

The `BinarySearch()` method first sorts the provided list of elements. In this case, it sorts the string array in alphabetical order. So after sorting, the list would be as follows:

```
"Dave", "Erik", "Pamela", "Pascal", "Sam"
```

Now, a binary search algorithm is applied on this string array to find the index of a given element from the array. So, you see the index returned by the binary search is the index of the sought element in the sorted collection. Thus, when we searched for `Dave`, the index returned was `0` and when we searched for `Sam`, the index returned was `5`, which should ideally be `4`. So, when you use `BinarySearch()` to find the index, always check whether the index is within bounds before dereferencing the index.

CartesianProduct()

This generic method generates the Cartesian product of two given lists. The lists can have a different number of items in them. Let's see how this method can help in a real-life situation.

Time for action – generating names of all the 52 playing cards

Follow the given steps:

1. Copy the following code snippet as a query in LINQPad:

```
List<Pair<string, string>> deck =

Algorithms.CartesianProduct
(
  new List<string>() {"Ace", "2", "3", "4", "5", "6", "7", "8",
    "9", "10", "Jack", "Queen", "King"},

  new List<string>() { "Spade", "Heart", "Diamond", "Club" }
)

.ToList();

List<string> cardNames = deck
  .Select(c => c.First + " of " + c.Second)
  .ToList ();

cardNames.Dump("Names of all the Playing Cards");
```

2. Run the query. You will get the list of all the 52 cards. A few of them are listed in the following screenshot:

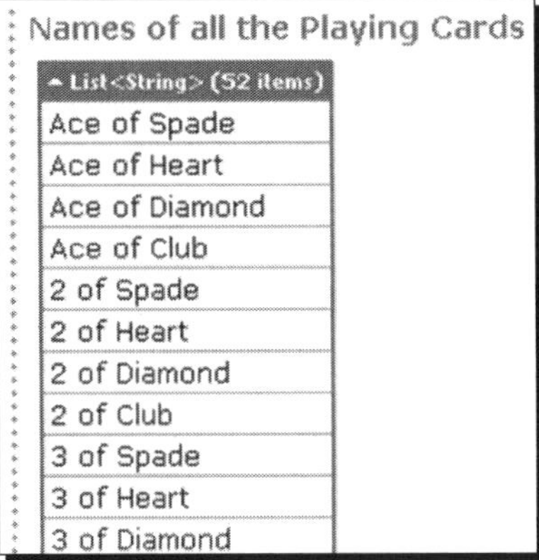

What just happened?

The `CartesianProduct()` method returns a list of `Pair<string, string>`. In this case, `c.First` refers to the first element of the pair and `c.Second` refers to the second element of the pair. Thus, the part of the code, `c.First + " of " + c.Second`, generates the output **Ace of Heart**. Using the `Select()` LINQ operator, we are converting each `Pair<string, string>` object in the final result.

RandomShuffle()

Now that we have created a deck of cards, it would be great to shuffle them. The `RandomShuffle()` method does that and returns a randomly shuffled list. The in-place version, `RandomShuffleInPlace()`, modifies the original list and stores the shuffled list.

Time for action – randomly shuffling the deck

Follow the given steps:

1. Copy the following code snippet as a query in LINQPad:

```
//Using the deck of cards we created earlier.
List<string> cardNames = deck.Select(c => c.First + " of " +
c.Second)
  .ToList ();

cardNames.Take(13).Dump("Before Shuffling first 13 cards");
List<string> shuffledDeck =
```

```
            Algorithms.RandomShuffle(cardNames).ToList();

shuffledDeck.Take(13).Dump("After Shuffling first 13 cards");
```

2. Run the query. You will get the following output. The actual names of the card that appear may differ:

What just happened?

The `RandomShuffle()` method randomly shuffles the collections passed as an argument. This method internally uses a random number generator. However, there is another overloaded version of this method where you can specify a random number generator. However, it is not recommended to use any hardcoded random number generator as it will always produce the same result.

For example, the following code snippet:

```
Algorithms.RandomShuffle(cardNames, new Random(1)).ToList();
```

will always return the same list. However, you can pass `new Random()`, which is essentially the same as omitting it as an argument to the algorithm.

NCopiesOf()

Sometimes we want to create multiple copies of the same object or value. Suppose you have a class, creating an object of which is computationally very expensive.

The `NCopiesOf()` generic method comes in very handy when creating such a list.

Time for action – creating random numbers of any given length

Follow the given steps:

1. Copy the following code snippet as a query in LINQPad:

```
StringBuilder bigRandomNumber = new StringBuilder();
List<string> allRandomNumbers = new List<string>();

for (int i = 0; i < 5; i++)
{
  bigRandomNumber = new StringBuilder();
  Algorithms.NCopiesOf(10, new Random())
            .Select(c => c.Next(100).ToString("000"))
            .ToList()
            .ForEach
  (
    c => bigRandomNumber.Append(c.ToString())
  );

  allRandomNumbers.Add(bigRandomNumber.ToString());
  System.Threading.Thread.Sleep(20);
}

allRandomNumbers.Dump("5 Random Numbers");
```

2. Run the query. You will get an output similar to the following screenshot:

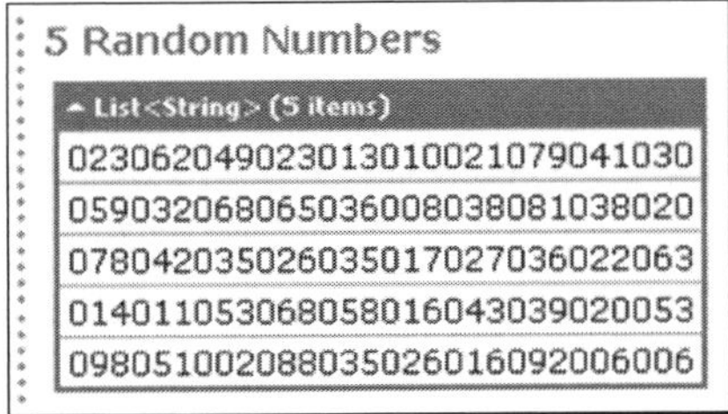

What just happened?

If you notice carefully, you will see that all of these numbers are of 30 digits. That's because they are a concatenation of 10 three digit random numbers generated from 10 copies of the `Random` class.

The following code:

```
Algorithms.NCopiesOf(10, new Random())
```

creates 10 `Random` objects. LINQ Standard Query Operator, `Select()`, is then used to format the numbers as three digit numbers. So, if the random number generated is `14`, the `Select()` method will make it `014`, because of the `ToString("000")` method call. So at this point, we have 10 random numbers of three digits each. Now, we have to stitch them together to create a 30 digit number. So, we convert this into a list of strings so that we can use the `ForEach` operator on list to concatenate the results on the `StringBuilder` object.

Once done, the number is added to the list of random numbers called `allRandomNumbers`.

Random number generators work with the system clock. A `Thread.Sleep` call is made to make sure that we don't get the same random numbers again.

Time for action – creating a custom random number generator

Now, let's take a step ahead and create a custom random number generator that can generate random numbers of any digit. As many people could use this, I thought it would be a nice idea to make this a web app. In this section, I will take you through the Windows clone:

1. Create a Windows app and place the controls as shown in the following screenshot:

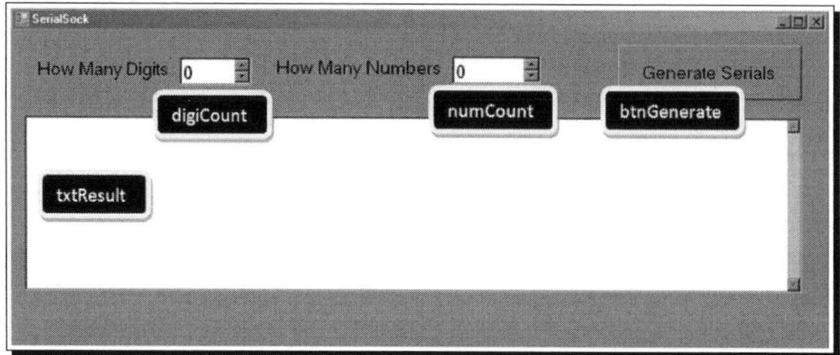

2. Add the following code in the click event of the **Generate Serials** button:

```
private void btnGenerate_Click(object sender, EventArgs e)
{
  txtResult.Clear();
  int howManyDigit = Convert.ToInt16(digitCount.Value);
  int howManyNumbers = Convert.ToInt16(numCount.Value);
  int basicDigitCount = 3;
  int numberOfRandomInstances = howManyDigit / basicDigitCount;
  StringBuilder bigRandomNumber = new StringBuilder();
  List<string> allRandomNumbers = new List<string>();
  for (int i = 0; i < howManyNumbers;)
  {
    bigRandomNumber = new StringBuilder();
    Algorithms.ForEach(Algorithms.NCopiesOf
                        (numberOfRandomInstances, new
                         Random()).ToList().Select(c =>
                         c.Next(100).ToString("100")), c =>
                         bigRandomNumber.Append(c.ToString()));
    if(bigRandomNumber.ToString().Length < howManyDigit)
    {
      for (int k = 0; k <= howManyDigit -
      bigRandomNumber.ToString().Length; k++)
      bigRandomNumber.Append("0");
    }
    if(bigRandomNumber.ToString().Length > howManyDigit)
    {
      for (int k = bigRandomNumber.ToString().Length; k <=
      bigRandomNumber.ToString().Length - howManyDigit; k++)
      bigRandomNumber.Remove(k, 1);
    }
```

```
        if(!allRandomNumbers.Contains(bigRandomNumber.ToString()))
        {
          allRandomNumbers.Add(bigRandomNumber.ToString());
          i++;
        }
        System.Threading.Thread.Sleep(20);
      }
      int duplicates = allRandomNumbers.Count -
        allRandomNumbers.Distinct().Count();
      Algorithms.ForEach(allRandomNumbers, c => txtResult.Text =
        txtResult.Text + c + Environment.NewLine);
    }
```

3. Following is the output of the program:

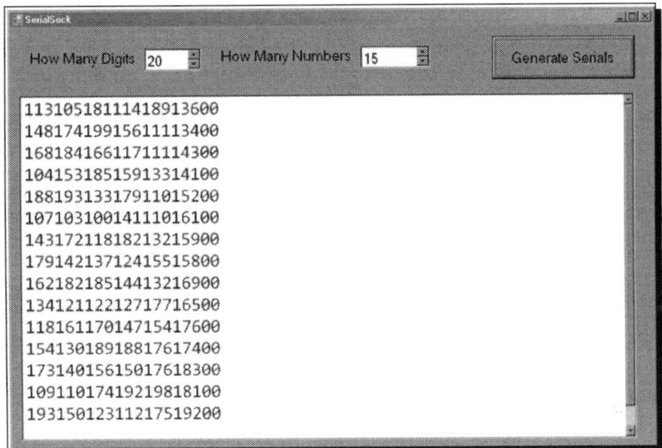

What just happened?

The program relies on the following code to generate random numbers:

```
Algorithms.ForEach
(
  Algorithms.NCopiesOf
  (
    numberOfRandomInstances
    ,new Random()
  )
  .ToList()
  .Select(c => c.Next(100).ToString("100"))
  ,c => bigRandomNumber.Append(c.ToString())
);
```

Calls to the method, `Algorithms.NCopiesOf()`, generates random numbers (with the maximum value `100`). However, if there is a number less than 100, then it will prepend `1` before that number due to the method call: `ToString("100")`. For example, if the random number generated is `4` then it will become `104`—this is because otherwise the numbers won't be of the same digit count.

`ForEach()` puts all these numbers together to the `StringBuilder` object. However, if there is a mismatch in the number of digits, zeros are either appended at the end of the number or some numbers are trimmed from the right end. These numbers are then put in a collection and added to the textbox.

You can find the web-based version at `www.consulttoday.com/SerialSock`.

ForEach()

In the previous example, we had to convert the result to a list so that we can use the `ForEach()` method of the `List` class to concatenate the numbers together. However, by using the `ForEach()` method, we can do that without converting the result to a list. Let's see how.

Time for action – creating a few random numbers of given any length

Follow the given steps:

1. Copy the following code snippet as a query in LINQPad:

```
StringBuilder bigRandomNumber = new StringBuilder();
List<string> allRandomNumbers = new List<string>();
for (int i = 0; i < 5; i++)
{
  bigRandomNumber = new StringBuilder();
  Algorithms.ForEach
  (
    Algorithms.NCopiesOf(10, new Random())
    .Select(c => c.Next(100).ToString("000")),
    c => bigRandomNumber.Append(c.ToString())
  );
  allRandomNumbers.Add(bigRandomNumber.ToString());
  System.Threading.Thread.Sleep(20);
}
```

2. Run the query. You will get an output similar to the following screenshot:

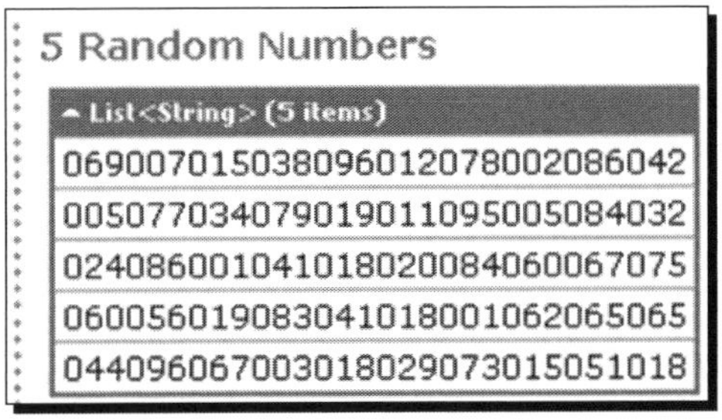

5 Random Numbers

List<String> (5 items)
069007015038096012078002086042
005077034079019011095005084032
024086001041018020084060067075
060056019083041018001062065065
044096067003018029073015051018

What just happened?

The `ForEach()` generic method takes two arguments. The first one is the collection through which to iterate and the second one is an **Action** delegate that is to be applied on each of the items in the collection:

void Algorithms.ForEach<string>(**IEnumerable<string> collection**, Action<string> action)
Performs the specified action on each item in a collection.
collection: *The collection to process.*

The **Action** delegate can be replaced with a Func or a Lambda Expression at runtime. So, we replaced that with the following delegate:

```
c => bigRandomNumber.Append(c.ToString())
```

Rotate() and RotateInPlace()

`Rotate()` and `RotateInPlace()` algorithms can rotate a represented sequence, which implements `IList<T>` interface, to a given amount. This doesn't change the original sequence. However, the in-place cousin does so.

The second argument determines the amount of rotation. If `4` is given as the rotation amount then the fifth element in the current list becomes the first element in the rotated list; because what we are passing as a rotation amount is an index to rotate. On the other hand, if `-4` is given as the rotation amount then the fourth element from the end of the collection becomes the first element in the rotated collection.

Time for action – rotating a word

Follow the given steps:

1. Copy the following code snippet as a query in LINQPad:

```
StringBuilder builder = new StringBuilder();
string word = "Generics";
word.Dump("Original Word");

List<char> wr = Algorithms.Rotate(word.ToList(), 4).ToList();

wr.ForEach(c => builder.Append(c.ToString()));
builder.ToString().Dump("After rotation is called with
  amountToRotate = 4");
builder = new StringBuilder();

List<char> wrr = Algorithms.Rotate(wr.ToList(), -4).ToList();
wrr.ForEach(c => builder.Append(c.ToString()));
builder.ToString().Dump("Going back to original one");
```

2. Run the query. You will get the following output:

```
Original Word
Generics

After rotation is called with amountToRotate = 4
ricsGene

Going back to original one
Generics
```

What just happened?

In the first `Rotate()` method call, the word becomes **ricsGene** and the second `Rotate()` method call made it turn back to the original one **Generics**. As the fourth letter from the end of **ricsGene** is *G*, the second call returned **Generics**.

Time for action – creating a word guessing game

Using `Rotate()` and `RandomShufflle()` algorithms, I created a small game that asks the users to guess a randomly shuffled or rotated word. On successful guess, it loads a different word. The game has two options namely: **Let Me Win** and **Bring It On**.

1. Create a user interface and place the controls as follows:

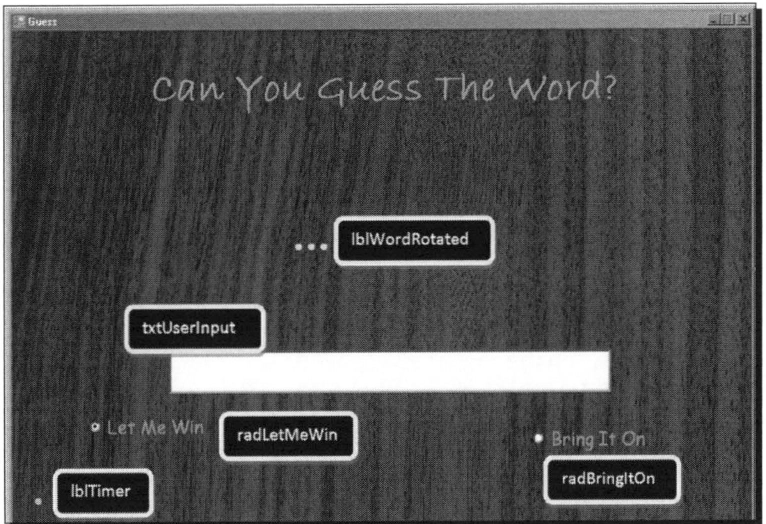

2. Add the following variables in `Form1.cs`:

```
List<string> allWords = new List<string>();
int seconds = 0;
int rotated = 0;
string word;
```

3. Add a timer to the project. Leave its name as `Timer1` and enable it. Change its `Interval` value to `1000` so that it ticks every second.

4. Add the following code in the `Form_Load` event:

```
StreamReader sr = new StreamReader("C:\\T9.txt");
allWords.AddRange(sr.ReadToEnd().Split(new char[]{
  '','\r','\n'},StringSplitOptions.RemoveEmptyEntries));
sr.Close();
LoadNextWord();
```

5. Add the following method to load the next word:

```
private void LoadNextWord()
{
  lblWordRotated.Text = "";
  rotated = (new Random()).Next(100);
  word = allWords[(new Random()).Next(0, allWords.Count - 1)];
  if (radLetMeWin.Checked)
  {
```

```
      Algorithms.ForEach
      (
        Algorithms.Rotate(word.ToList(), rotated).ToList(),
        c => lblWordRotated.Text =
        lblWordRotated.Text + c.ToString()
      );
      if (lblWordRotated.Text.Equals(word))
      LoadNextWord();
    }
    else
    {
      Algorithms.ForEach
      (
        Algorithms.RandomShuffle(word.ToList()).ToList(),
          c => lblWordRotated.Text =
          lblWordRotated.Text +
          c.ToString()
      );
      if (lblWordRotated.Text.Equals(word))
      LoadNextWord();

    }
    timer1.Start();
  }
```

6. Deal with the change as users attempt to guess the rotated or shuffled word:

```
private void txtUserInput_TextChanged(object sender, EventArgs e)
{
  if (txtUserInput.Text == word)
  {
    System.Media.SoundPlayer player = new
      System.Media.SoundPlayer(@"tada.wav");
    player.Play();
    lblTimer.Text = "";
    txtUserInput.Clear();
    LoadNextWord();
  }
}
```

7. Let's give the users an emotional stress. Let's show them a progress bar:

```
private void timer1_Tick(object sender, EventArgs e)
{
  lblTimer.Text = lblTimer.Text + " .";
  seconds++;
```

```
      if (seconds == 24)
      {
        lblTimer.Text = "";
        seconds = 0;
      }
    }
```

8. Once you run the program, you will be presented with a screen similar to the following screenshot:

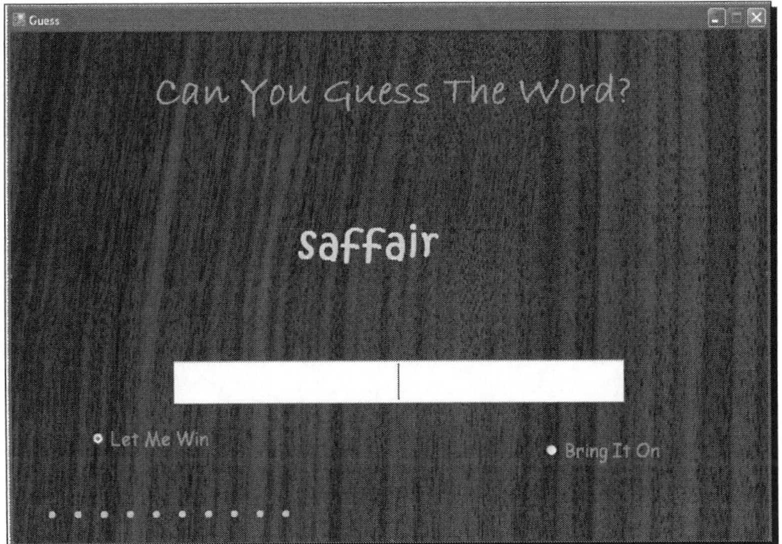

What just happened?

Can you guess the word in the preceding screenshot? It's *affairs*. The **Let Me Win** radio button uses the `Rotate()` method to generate a rotated version of the word, which is kind of easy to figure out. However, the **Bring It On** radio button uses the `RandomShuffle()` method to generate a more difficult version of the word.

The `Algorithms.Rotate(word.ToList(), rotated)` method returns an instance of `IEnumerable<T>` interface. Using the `ToList()` method, the instance is converted to a list so that the `ForEach()` method can iterate through the collection.

The following Lambda expression:

```
c => lblWordRotated.Text = lblWordRotated.Text + c.ToString()
```

appends each character generated from the rotation of the character list and puts them at the end of `lblWordRotated`.

Have a go hero

However, there could be a possible buggy situation for **Bring It On** when there are anagrams in the dictionary. For example, the words "DEAR" and "READ" both could become "AERD" when randomly shuffled. However, if the program picked "DEAR" and the user enters "READ" then the program will not be able to identify that as a correct response.

Can you provide a fix for this? **Hint**: You can use `MultiDictionary` described in *Chapter 3, Dictionaries*.

RandomSubset()

`RandomSubset()` is the method to sample a collection. If you want to randomly select a subset of a given set, this is the method for you. Let's see how it works.

Time for action – picking a set of random elements

Follow the given steps:

1. Copy the following code in LINQPad:

```
string[] names = { "Sam", "Pamela", "Dave", "Pascal", "Erik" };
string[] sub = Algorithms.RandomSubset(names, 3);
sub.Dump("A Random Sample of 3 names");
```

2. Run the query. You should get the following output:

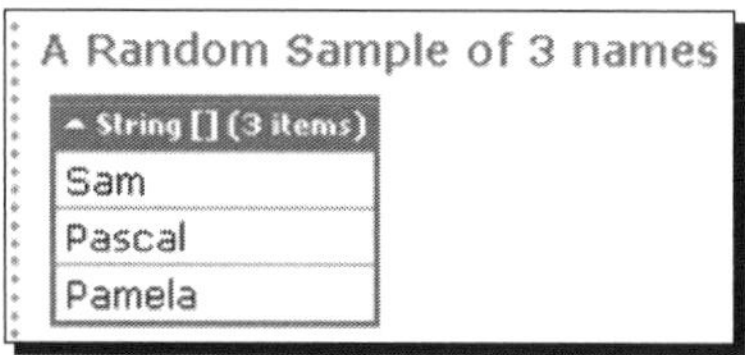

What just happened?

The `RandomSubset()` method takes two arguments. The first one is the collection on which the method has to operate and the second one is the number of elements to be selected in the subset.

This method will come particularly handy in designing systems where the computer has to pick a handful from a haystack of elements.

Reverse()

This method is capable of reversing a collection of any type. Let's see how it works.

Time for action – reversing any collection

Follow the given steps:

1. Copy the following code in LINQPad:

```
string[] names = { "Sam", "Pamela", "Dave", "Pascal", "Erik" };
names.Dump("People joined the party in this order");
string[] sub  = Algorithms.Reverse(names).ToArray();
sub.Dump("The reverse order is");
```

2. Run the query. It will generate the following output:

What just happened?

The `Reverse()` method returns a reversed collection which is just the opposite of the input sequence. Check the input. **Sam** appeared at the first index. In the output **Sam** appeared at the end. This is same as the Reverse operator in LINQ Operators.

EqualCollections()

The `EqualCollections()` method helps compare two collections. If two collections have exactly the same number of elements, then this method returns `true`. For the primitive type, it knows how to do the comparison of elements. However, for the user-defined type, it needs a comparer object or a binary predicate to do the comparison. The order in which elements appear in the collection is important. If the order is not the same and still both collections hold the same elements, even then they are not considered as *equal collections*.

Time for action – revisiting the palindrome problem

With the two methods, `Reverse()` and `EqualCollections()`, finding whether a sequence is palindromic or not becomes a single line of code. Let's see how:

1. Copy the following code in LINQPad:

```
string word = "rotor";
bool isPalindrome =
Algorithms.EqualCollections(word.ToCharArray(),
  Algorithms.Reverse(word.ToCharArray()));
string status = word + " is ";
if (isPalindrome)
    status += "Palindromic";
else
    status += "Not Palindromic";
status.Dump();
```

2. Run the query. It will generate the following output:

```
rotor is Palindromic
```

This method can work with any type of collection.

What just happened?

The `Reverse()` method is used to reverse the character array representation of the word `"rotor"`. The following line:

```
Algorithms.EqualCollections(word.ToCharArray()
                            ,Algorithms.Reverse(word.ToCharArray()));
```

checks whether two collections, the character array representation of the word and its reverse, are equal or not. Two collections are said to be equal only if they contain the same elements in the same order. As `"rotor"` and its reversed version are the same, `EqualCollections()` returns `true` in this case.

DisjointSets()

Sometimes we need to check whether two collections contain the same element or not. However, that's a quadratic time operation at the least and .NET doesn't have any method to check that directly. Although you can convert any collection to a .NET set implementation and then do such a check. But that would be computationally expensive.

However, the `DisjointSets()` method does that. It considers each collection as a set and returns `false` if they have the same elements in any order; and `true` otherwise. Think of this method as the complementary method to the `EqualCollections()` method.

Time for action – checking for common stuff

Follow the given steps:

1. Copy the following code in LINQPad:

```
string[] cities = { "Boston", "Berlin", "Chicago" };
string[] otherCities = { "Berlin", "Chicago", "Boston" };

bool isDisjoint = Algorithms.DisjointSets(cities, otherCities);
isDisjoint.Dump();
```

2. Run the query. It will generate the following output:

```
False
```

What just happened?

Because both the collections (arrays in this case) `cities` and `otherCities` have the same elements, though in different order, they turn out to be equal sets so they are not disjoint to each other. Thus, the method returns `false`. Unlike `EqualCollections()`, order in the sequence of elements in the collections is not important.

Time for action – finding anagrams the easiest way

As they say, *if all you have is a hammer, every problem would seem like a nail*. Finding an anagram is similar to finding whether two sorted character sets exactly match with each other or not. `OrderedBag<T>` collection from Power Collections is *perfect* for this job. I can't emphasize this more. Let's see how we can do it:

1. Create a Console Application project and call it `AnaCheck`.
2. Add `PowerCollections.dll` reference to the project.
3. Now add the following lines of code in the `Main()` method:

```
static void Main(string[] args)
{
  OrderedBag<char> first = new OrderedBag<char>("dad");
  OrderedBag<char> second = new OrderedBag<char>("add");
  bool isAna = Algorithms.EqualCollections(first, second);
  if(isAna)
  Console.Write("\"dad\" and \"add\" are anagrams");
}
```

4. Now, we are ready to run the application. When you run the application, you will see the following output:

```
"dad" and "add" are anagrams
```

What just happened?

"dad" and "add" are anagrams as both of them have the same character set with the same frequency of occurrence of each character. If the characters are sorted, both words "add" and "dad" become "add". That's exactly what `OrderedBag<char>` does for us. It sorts the elements and doesn't care whether you pass duplicates, as I did in this case.

So internally, first and second, both the `OrderedBag<char>` instances hold "a", "d", and "d" as the characters are in that order. Thus, when we check whether the collections are the same or not, we get the answer as true. If you are familiar with C++, you would find the `OrderedBag<T>` class similar to the `MultiMap<T, V>` class.

Have a go hero

Create a generic anagramic sequence checker using the `OrderedBag<T>` class.

Creating an efficient arbitrary floating point representation

Scientists in number theory sometimes need to represent a floating point to some reasonably big decimal places, say to the 20,000th digit after the decimal. However, the largest available data type in .NET (decimal) supports only to the 28th digit after the decimal.

Following is what scientists want and what we can assume:

- To be able to store as many digits after the decimal as possible.
- To be able to know what the digit is after the decimal at any given index at constant time. This means, no matter which value they want to get at whichever index after the decimal, be it at index 0 or at index 100; it should take the same constant time. Users can't wait long.
- To know which digit occurred most in the decimal places. Again they can't wait. So, the faster the better.
- The floating point number will always be represented in the p/q format where p and q are integers within the `System.Int32` range.

Let's see how we can help them.

Time for action – creating a huge number API

Follow the given steps:

1. Create a Class Library project and call it `Huge`.
2. Add `PowerCollections.dll` in the reference for this project.
3. Add the following class, `HugeInteger`, in this Class Library project:

```
public class HugeInteger
{
  /// <summary>
  /// Internal representation of the huge integer
  /// </summary>
  private Dictionary<int, BigList<decimal>> _huge;
  /// <summary>
  /// Creating such an empty huge integer
```

```
/// </summary>
public HugeInteger()
{
  _huge = new Dictionary<int, BigList<decimal>>();
  Enumerable.Range(0, 10).ToList()
  .ForEach(i => _huge.Add(i, new BigList<decimal>()));
}
/// <summary>
/// Length of the huge integer
/// </summary>
public decimal Length
{
  get
  {
    //As it deals with zero based indexing
    //so the actual length would be one more.
    Dictionary<int, BigList<decimal>> temp = new
      Dictionary<int, BigList<decimal>>();
    Enumerable.Range(0, 10).ToList()
    .ForEach(i => temp.Add(i, new BigList<decimal>()));
    foreach (int k in _huge.Keys)
    temp[k] = _huge[k];
    return
    Algorithms.Maximum(new
                   decimal[]{temp[0].LastOrDefault(),
                   temp[1].LastOrDefault(),
                   temp[2].LastOrDefault(),
                   temp[3].LastOrDefault(),
                   temp[4].LastOrDefault(),
                   temp[5].LastOrDefault(),
                   temp[6].LastOrDefault(),
                   temp[7].LastOrDefault(),
                   temp[8].LastOrDefault(),
                   temp[9].LastOrDefault()}) + 1;
  }
}
/// <summary>
/// Represents the huge integer as a string format
/// </summary>
public override string ToString()
{
  StringBuilder builder = new StringBuilder();
  for (int i = 0; i < this.Length; i++)
  {
```

```
      builder.Append(this.huge.First(indices =>
      indices.Value.Contains(i)).Key.ToString());
    }
    return builder.ToString();
  }
  /// <summary>
  /// Adds a digit to the huge integer
  /// </summary>
  /// <param name="digit">The digit</param>
  /// <param name="index">Where should we add it</param>
  public void AddDigit(int digit, decimal index)
  {
    _huge[digit].Add(index);
  }
}
```

4. Add the following class, `HugeFloatingPoint`, in the Class Library project:

```
/// <summary>
/// Class to represent floating point numbers
/// </summary>
public class HugeFloatingPoint
{
  int IntegralPart;
  HugeInteger decimalPart;
  decimal digitsAfterDecimal;
  public HugeFloatingPoint(string floatingPoint)
  {
    IntegralPart =
    Convert.ToInt32(floatingPoint.Split('.')[0].Trim());
    decimalPart = new
      HugeInteger(floatingPoint.Split('.')[1].Trim());
    digitsAfterDecimal = decimalPart.Length;
  }
  /// <summary>
  /// Create an Irrational number with arbitrary
  /// number of digits after decimal.
  /// </summary>
  /// <param name="numerator">The numerator or the p or p/q
  /// format</param>
  /// <param name="denominator">The denominator or the q or p/q
  /// format</param>
  /// <param name="digits">Requested number of digits after
  /// decimal</param>
  public HugeFloatingPoint(int numerator, int denominator,
```

```
        decimal digits)
    {
        IntegralPart = numerator / denominator;
        digitsAfterDecimal = digits;
        decimalPart = new HugeInteger();
        decimal count = 0;
        do
        {
            int digit = numerator / denominator;
            int div = numerator % denominator;
            if (div < denominator)
            numerator = div * 10;
            if (digit > 9 || digit == IntegralPart)
            continue;
            decimalPart.AddDigit(digit, count);
            count++;
        }
        while (count != digitsAfterDecimal);
    }
    /// <summary>
    /// Overridden ToString() to represent a the floating
    /// point number as a string.
    /// </summary>
    /// <returns></returns>
    public override string ToString()
    {
        return IntegralPart.ToString() + "." +
        decimalPart.ToString().Substring(1);
    }
}
```

5. Now we are ready to consume these classes and create an irrational number with an arbitrary number of digits after the decimal. Create a Console Application project in the same solution and call it `HugeTest`.

6. Stay in the `HugeTest` project. Set it as the **StartUp Project** by right-clicking on it. Add the following code in the `Main()` method:

```
static void Main(string[] args)
{
    //Square root of 3.
    //approximated as 97/56 as per Wikipedia
    //(http://en.wikipedia.org/wiki/Square_root_of_3)
    HugeFloatingPoint fp = new HugeFloatingPoint(97, 56, 60);
    string sqRoot3 = fp.ToString();
    Console.WriteLine(@"Square root of 3 approximated to 60 digits
        after decimal is");
```

```
        Console.WriteLine(sqRoot3);
        Console.ReadKey();
    }
```

7. Ok! Now we are ready to run the application. As you run the application, you will get the following output:

```
Squre root of 3 approximated to 60 digits after decimal is
1.7321428571428571428571428571428571428571428571428571428571 4
```

What just happened?

The arbitrary floating point is represented as a dictionary of integers and the indices where the integers occur in the given number. For example, the number 1230913233 will be stored, as shown in the following screenshot:

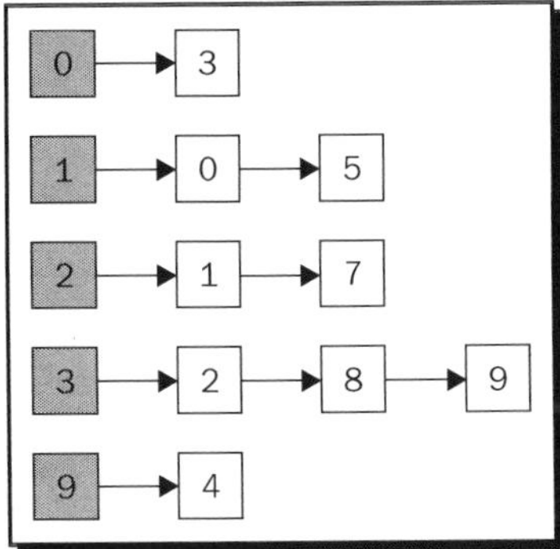

The keys of this dictionary would be `0` to `9` and where they occur in the number will be stored in the associated values, which is a `BigList<T>` instance.

To determine the length of the digit, it will be sufficient to find the maximum of the values stored as follows:

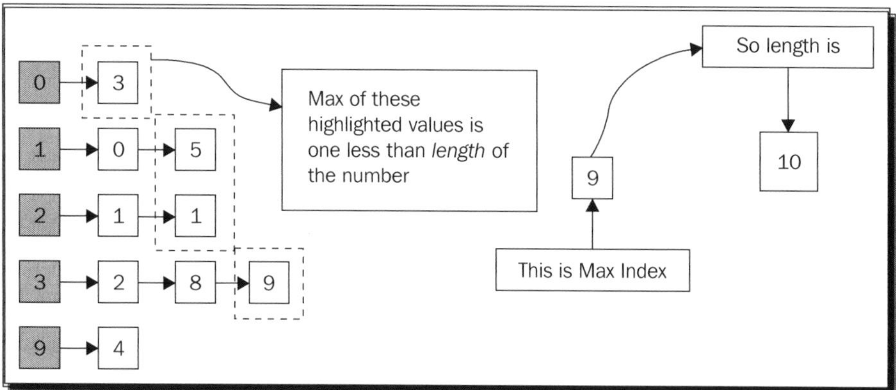

The preceding screenshot explains the logic of the `Length` property of the `HugeInteger` class. A `HugeFloatingPoint` class is just a combination of the following two parts:

1. An integral number.
2. A decimal part after decimal, which is also a `HugeInteger` class.

That's why in the constructor of the `HugeFloatingPoint` class, digits are being added to the huge number list through the `AddDigit()` method. Following is a screenshot showing how the internal dictionary, `_huge`, looks for the square root of 3, as previously approximated:

_huge	Count = 10
[0]	{[0, {}]}
[1]	{[1, {}]}
[2]	{[2, {2,4,9,14,19,24,29,34,39,44,49,54,59}]}
[3]	{[3, {1}]}
[4]	{[4, {3,8,13,18,23,28,33,38,43,48,53,58}]}
[5]	{[5, {6,11,16,21,26,31,36,41,46,51,56}]}
[6]	{[6, {}]}
[7]	{[7, {0,7,12,17,22,27,32,37,42,47,52,57}]}
[8]	{[8, {5,10,15,20,25,30,35,40,45,50,55}]}
[9]	{[9, {}]}
Raw View	

With .NET 4.0, a `BigInteger` class implementation is available from the `System.Numerics` namespace. However, that doesn't quite help to create a big floating point representation as we did in this section.

Have a go hero

I didn't add code to find the digit that occurs the maximum number of times after the decimal and the digit at any given index after the decimal. Both of these tasks are quite simple. Add these methods in the `HugeFloatingPoint` class.

Creating an API for customizable default values

LINQ Standard Query Operators: `FirstOrDefault()`, `LastOrDefault()`, or any operator that ends with "Default" in its name throws a useless `null`, as the default value, for user-defined objects.

Now, if you have several situations where you have to deal with such values, you would prefer to be able to set a default value of your choice to these collections.

Power Collections offer an algorithm called `Fill` and a range version called `FillRange`, which offer functionality to fill a collection or an array with a given default value.

I thought it would be really useful if we can use these two algorithms to brew some default value initialization framework using the LINQ extension method style. Suppose we have a `List<string>` with 10 entries and we want to set the first four to `#` and that's needed for our application. In such situations, we can use the framework that we are about to build.

Time for action – creating a default value API

Follow the given steps:

1. Create a Class Library project and call it `DefaultValues`.
2. Change the default name `Class1` and rename it to `DefaultValueMap`.
3. Add the following code in the class:

```
public static  class DefaultValueMap
{
  public static Dictionary<string, object> DefaultValueMapping =
    null;
  /// <summary>
  /// Allows to add new default value at runtime.
  /// </summary>
  /// <param name="fullTypeName">Fully Qualified name of the
    object for which the default value is being set</param>
  /// <param name="value">The default value</param>
  public static void AddDefaultValue(string fullTypeName, object
    value)
```

```
{
  if(!DefaultValueMapping.ContainsKey(fullTypeName))
  DefaultValueMapping.Add(fullTypeName, value);
}
/// <summary>
/// Initializes the default values for the type we care about
/// Only once
private static void InitDefaultValues()
{
  //this check is to make sure that initialization happens
  //only once.
  if (DefaultValueMapping == null)
  {
    DefaultValueMapping = new Dictionary<string, object>();
    DefaultValueMapping.Add("System.String", "*");
    DefaultValueMapping.Add("System.Int32", 10);
    DefaultValueMapping.Add("DefaultValues.Student", new
      Student(name: "new student", age: 10));
  }
  /// <summary>
  /// Sets a range of values in a collection by the pre-
  ///defined default value
  /// </summary>
  /// <typeparam name="T">Type of the collection</typeparam>
  /// <param name="list">The collection for which default
  ///values have to be set</param>
  /// <param name="start">The starting index of the
  ///range</param>
  /// <param name="count">Element count in the range</param>
  /// <returns></returns>
  public static IEnumerable<T> SetDefault<T>(this IEnumerable<T>
    list, int start, int count)
  {
    InitDefaultValues();
    T[] internalArray = list.ToArray();
    Algorithms.FillRange(internalArray, start, count,
      (T)DefaultValueMapping[list.ElementAt(0).
      GetType().FullName]);
    return internalArray.AsEnumerable();
  }

  /// <summary>
  /// Sets the first few values to default value for the type
  /// </summary>
  /// <typeparam name="T">The type of the
```

```
    ///collection</typeparam>
    /// <param name="list">The collection for which the values
    ///have to be set to default</param>
    /// <param name="tillThis">Till this item all the values
    ///must be set to default</param>
    /// <returns></returns>
    public static IEnumerable<T> SetDefault<T>(this IEnumerable<T>
      list, int tillThis)
    {
      InitDefaultValues();
      IEnumerable<T> temp;
      try
      {
        temp = list.Take(tillThis);
      }
      catch
      {
        throw new ArgumentOutOfRangeException("There is not
          enough element to set to default");
      }
      T[] internalArray = temp.ToArray();
      Algorithms.Fill(internalArray,
        (T)DefaultValueMapping
        [list.ElementAt(0).GetType().FullName]);
      return internalArray.Concat(list.Skip(tillThis));
    }
  }
}
```

4. Create a new Console Application project to test this API and call it `DefaultValuesTest`.

5. Add the following code in the `Main()` method:

```
static void Main(string[] args)
{
  List<string> codes = new
  List<string>(5){"a", "b", "c", "d", "e"};
  List<string> codes1 = codes.SetDefault(3).ToList();
  List<string> codes2 =  codes.SetDefault(1).ToList();
  List<string> codes3 = codes
    .SetDefault(codes.Count-2, 2).ToList();

  Console.WriteLine("Original List is ");
  codes.ForEach(Console.WriteLine);
  Console.WriteLine("First 3 values set to default as *");
  codes1.ForEach(Console.WriteLine);
```

```
        Console.WriteLine("First value set to default as *");
        codes2.ForEach(Console.WriteLine);
        Console.WriteLine("Last 2 value set to default as *");
        codes3.ForEach(Console.WriteLine);
        Console.ReadKey();
    }
```

6. Now we are ready to run the application. As you run the application, you will get the following output:

```
Original List is
a b c d e
First 3 values set to default as *
* * * d e
First value set to default as *
* b c d e
Last 2 value set to default as *
a b c * *
```

What just happened?

This is a clever use of the `Fill()` and the `FillRange()` methods available in Power Collections. Both these methods operate on either `IList<T>` or `T[]` inputs. However, I wanted to make sure that the `SetDefault<T>()` method works on `IEnumerable<T>`, similar to all the **LINQ Standard Query Operators**.

The following line of code converts the input to an array by the projection LSQO `ToArray()`:

```
T[] internalArray = temp.ToArray();
```

In the following line:

```
Algorithms.Fill(internalArray,
    (T)DefaultValueMapping[list.ElementAt(0).GetType().FullName]);
```

`internalArray` is being filled with the default value assigned for the type.

As the dictionary, `DefaultValueMapping`, stores the default value as an object, we must cast it to type `T` before we can use it in the `Fill()` or `FillRange()` algorithm, as they expect a strongly typed value of type `T` to be used as the default value.

The `list.ElementAt(0).GetType()` method returns the type of the collection and `FullName` property returns the fully qualified name of the type. For example, a collection `List<string>` returns `System.String` and a collection `List<int>` returns `System.Int32`.

In the end, LSQO Concat is used to concatenate the part filled with default values to the rest and then this combined collection is returned by the method SetDefault<T>().

Mapping data structure

Before we wrap this chapter, it would be great to know what Power Collections data structures brought to the table and how they can now be replaced with System.Collections.Generics collection classes:

Power Collections class	.NET Generics class	Comments
Pair<TKey, TValue>	KeyValuePair<TKey, TValue>	
Set<T>	HashSet<T>	
MultiDictionary<TKey, TValue>	Not available	You can use the MultiDictionary that we have created in *Chapter 3, Dictionaries.*
OrderedSet<T>	SortedSet<T>	
Bag<T>	List<T>	
OrderedBag<T>	Not available	This is basically a sorted list that allows duplication.
Deque<T>	LinkedList<T>	You can add/remove elements from both ends of a LinkedList<T>.
Triple<T1, T2, T3>	Tuple<T1, T2, T3>	This is a special case of Tuple.
BigList<T>	List<T>	

Algorithm conversion strategy

As you might have noticed, we haven't covered all the algorithms that Power Collections has to offer. The reason is that the skipped set of algorithms can be easily constructed using several LSQOs.

For example, let's consider the following line of code:

```
public static ICollection<T> RemoveWhere<T> (ICollection<T>
  collection, Predicate<T> predicate);
```

First, we can use the `Where()` operator to filter the values and then call the `Remove()` method to delete them.

Algorithms in Power Collections use `Predicate<T>` and `BinaryPredicate<T>`. This is because Power Collections was written before Func came into existence. You can replace `Predicate<T>` with `Func<T, bool>` and `BinaryPredicate<T>` with `Func<T, T, bool>`.

In order to convert the input to these algorithms to be compatible with LSQOs, use the following projection operators `ToArray()`, `ToList()`, and `AsEnumerable()`.

Summary

We have studied various algorithms and the `OrderedBag` and BigList data structures that Power Collections has to offer. Although most of the functionalities offered by these algorithms and data structures can be achieved otherwise, it still makes sense to know about them because these are still being used for the sheer simplicity it brings to the table.

If you are craving for more data structures and algorithms, hold on. In the next chapter, we will study another well-known and reputed generic collection API called C5, which is home to different great algorithms and data structures.

8
C5 Collections

From Denmark with love

Generic Collections from .NET and Power Collections offer great abstraction over very low-level implementations. You can use a dictionary to represent an indexed, associative list; however, you will have no idea what the internal data structure under the hood is, and if you don't like the internal implementation of dictionary, you don't have any other option than to come up with your own Generic Collection, which is a lot of work. Seriously!

The fine folks at IT University of Copenhagen thought about it a lot and have come up with a brilliant Generic Collection API known as C5. C5 is not an acronym to be exact. However, the creators of the API termed this and it could possibly be **Copenhagen Comprehensive Collection Classes for C#**. *However, this API can also be used from VB.NET. This comes as a loaded third-party API in Mono project, which is a .NET port for Linux systems.*

The most basic goal of this API is to allow users to choose different concrete classes for the same type of abstraction depending on the need. For example, there are dictionary abstractions where the interface is almost similar to `System.Collections.Generic.Dictionary<TKey, TValue>`; however, these dictionaries in C5 have two variants; namely **hash based** and **tree based**, giving us more control over the selection of the data structure. Again, the point is, most of these can be conceptually duplicated using Generic Collections available from the `System.Collections.Generic` namespace; but these let the user decide whether they want a hash-based, tree-based, array-based, and/or LinkedList-based container.

In this chapter, we will deal with some real-world problems using C5, Power Collection, and LINQ. Along the way, we will learn about some of the following collection classes and how to use them wisely. Collections that conceptually belong to the same family, such as HashBag and TreeBag, LinkedList and ArrayList can be used interchangeably with some modifications.

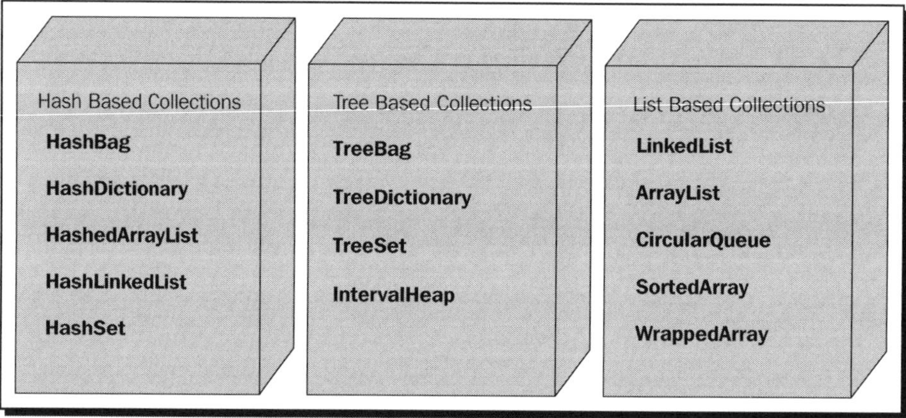

The goal is to learn how they fit into our real-world problem-solving strategy. These collections offer some really cool methods that will otherwise be quite some work on the client code developer's part. So, the stress will be more towards exploring these.

Hash-based collections use a hashing method to store the elements. So, checking whether an item is available in such a collection is a constant time operation `O(1)`. However, the order of insertions is not preserved in these collections. So, you can't expect to get the elements in the same location as you added them. Apart from `HashSet`, other hash-based collections allow duplicate items.

Tree-based collections use Red Black Tree, which is a variation of the balanced binary search tree to store the elements. So, for primitive data types, items always get added in a sorted fashion. Accessing elements is also fast, `O(logn)`, but not as fast as in hash-based collections. `IntervalHeap` is a heap-based implementation of Priority Queue.

In *Chapter 9, Patterns, Practices, and Performance* we shall see how these containers perform against containers in the `System.Collections.Generic` namespace

Setting up the environment

Get the C5 binaries from `http://www.itu.dk/research/c5/Release1.1/C5.bin.zip`.

You need to attach `C5.dll` to the project's reference.

Time for action – cloning Gender Genie!

Gender Genie (`http://bookblog.net/gender/genie.php`) is an online web application that tries to guess the gender of the author from a digital content. I always wanted to use this offline. Few methods and collection classes of C5 make it really simple.

1. Create a Windows application and attach `C5.dll` and `PowerCollections.dll` to the project's reference (instructions on *How to get Power Collections* can be found in *Chapter 7, Power Collections*).

2. Add the following `using` directives to the project:

```
using C5;
using Wintellect.PowerCollections;
```

3. Add the following variables:

```
C5.ArrayList<string> femaleWords = new ArrayList<string>()
{"with", "if", "not", "where", "be", "when", "your", "her", "we",
"should", "she", "and", "me", "myself", "hers", "was"};

C5.ArrayList<int> femaleWordPoints = new ArrayList<int>()
{52, 47, 27, 18, 17, 17, 17, 9, 8, 7, 6, 4, 4, 4, 3, 1};

C5.ArrayList<string> maleWords = new ArrayList<string>()
{"around", "what", "more", "are", "as", "who", "below", "is",
"these", "the", "a", "at", "it", "many", "said", "above", "to"};

C5.ArrayList<int> maleWordPoints = new ArrayList<int>()
{42, 35, 34, 28, 23, 19, 8, 8, 8, 7, 6, 6, 6, 6, 5, 4, 2};
```

4. Add the following controls on the form, as shown in the following screenshot:

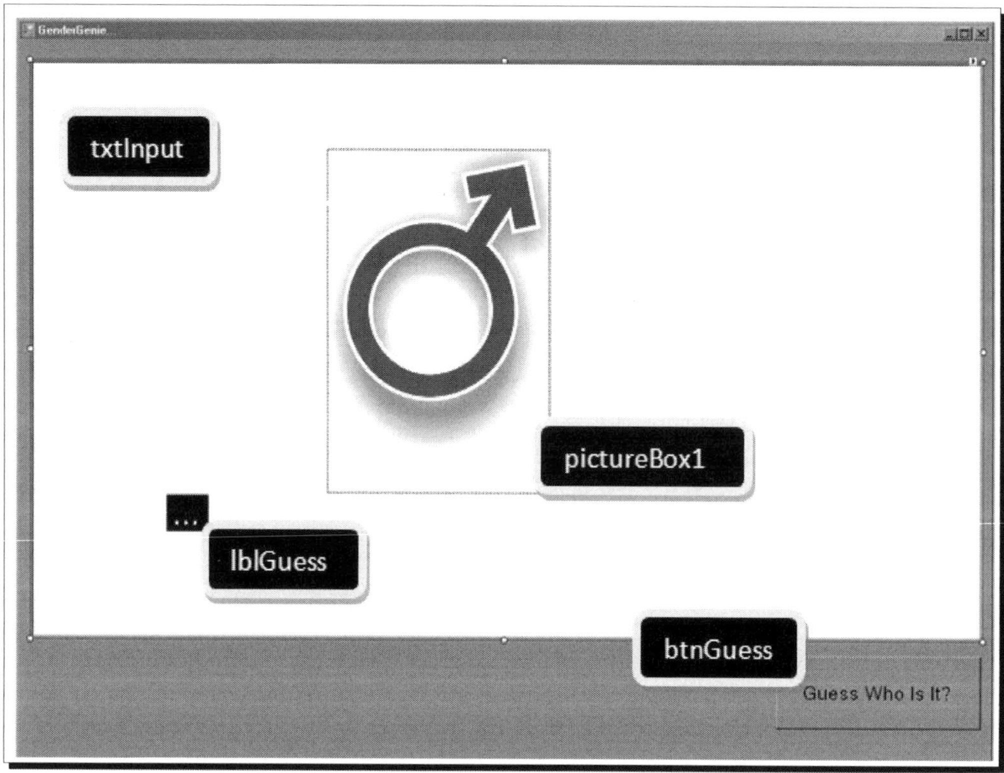

5. Add the following code to the click event of `btnGuess`:

```
private void btnGuess_Click(object sender, EventArgs e)
{
  int maleScore = 0;
  int femaleScore = 0;
  C5.ArrayList<string> words = new ArrayList<string>();
  words.AddAll(txtInput.Text.ToLower().Split(new
    char[]{'\r','\n',' ','.','?','!',';',',','\''},
    StringSplitOptions.RemoveEmptyEntries));
  //Generating word histogram that stores words and their
  //frequency.
  var histogram = words.ItemMultiplicities();

  //Copying only those words that are mostly used by women
  var femaleDic = histogram.Filter(c =>
    femaleWords.Contains(c.Key.ToLower()));
  //Copying only those words that are mostly used by men
```

```
var maleDic = histogram.Filter(c =>
  maleWords.Contains(c.Key.ToLower()));

//Calculating female score. This measure is an indication that
//the document is written by a lady
Algorithms.ForEach
(
  femaleDic,
  c => femaleScore +=
  femaleWordPoints[femaleWords.IndexOf(c.Key.ToLower())] *
  c.Value
);
//Calculating male score. This measure is an indication that
//the document is written by a gentleman
Algorithms.ForEach
(
  maleDic,
  c => maleScore +=
  maleWordPoints[maleWords.IndexOf(c.Key.ToLower())] *
  c.Value
);

//Show the response
if (maleScore > femaleScore)
{
  pictureBox1.ImageLocation = Application.StartupPath +
    "\\male.bmp";
  lblGuess.Text = "The Author of this document is probably a
    gentleman";
}
else
{
  pictureBox1.ImageLocation = Application.StartupPath +
    "\\female.bmp";
  lblGuess.Text = "The Author of this document is probably a
    lady";
}
lblGuess.Visible = true;
pictureBox1.Visible = true;
}
```

6. To hide the response, add the following code to the click event of `pictureBox1`:

```
private void pictureBox1_Click(object sender, EventArgs e)
{
  pictureBox1.Visible = false;
  lblGuess.Visible = false;
}
```

7. Run the app, and paste some text copied from anywhere. It will try to predict whether the author of the document is a man or a woman, as shown in the following screenshot:

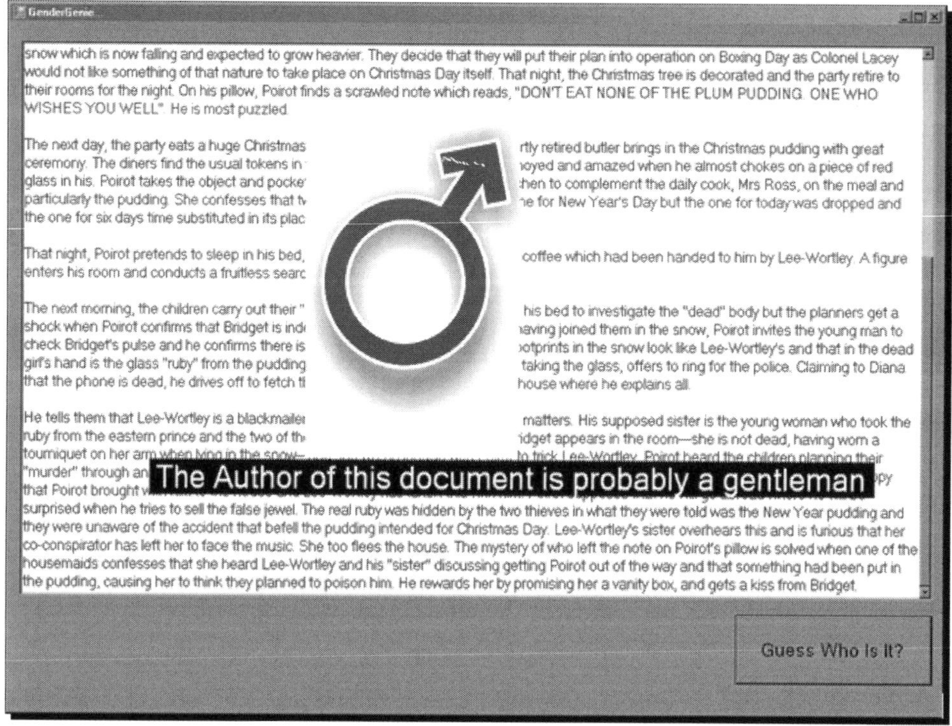

You can see this application in action at `http://sudipta.posterous.com/gender-genie-clone`.

What just happened?

The following line:

```
var histogram = words.ItemMultiplicities();
```

generates a histogram for words. `ItemMultiplicities()` is a method of the C5. `ArrayList` class that returns the elements in the array list along with their frequency. The return type of this method is `ICollectionValue<C5.KeyValuePair<string,int>>` for this case because words is a collection of the string type.

To understand how the values are stored in a histogram conceptually, I applied the `ToList()` LINQ operator and the result looked similar to the following screenshot:

Watch 1

Name	Value
histogram.ToList()	Count = 238
[0]	{(will, 3)}
[1]	{(4th, 4)}
[2]	{(considerate, 1)}
[3]	{(furthest, 1)}
[4]	{(b, 1)}
[5]	{(4, 3)}
[6]	{(status, 1)}
[7]	{(in, 7)}
[8]	{(but, 2)}
[9]	{(other, 1)}
[10]	{(off, 1)}

This means the word "in" occurred seven times. If you dig one level deep, you can see a result similar to the following screenshot:

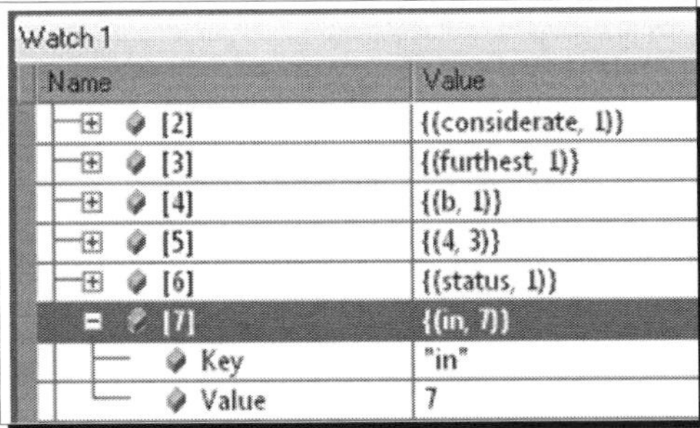

Watch 1

Name	Value
[2]	{(considerate, 1)}
[3]	{(furthest, 1)}
[4]	{(b, 1)}
[5]	{(4, 3)}
[6]	{(status, 1)}
[7]	{(in, 7)}
Key	"in"
Value	7

This means the word "in" occurred seven times in the input text.

The following line creates a dictionary instance on the fly that will have only those words that are available in both the collections `femaleWords` array and the input:

```
var femaleDic = histogram.Filter(c =>
  femaleWords.Contains(c.Key.ToLower()));
```

Note that the `Filter()` method is used as the LINQ Standard Query Operator `Where()`. C5 came into existence before LINQ. You can use `Where()` too. The `Filter()` method expects an argument of type of the function delegate so that the Lambda expressions fit nicely.

In the next line:

```
Algorithms.ForEach
(
  femaleDic,
  c => femaleScore +=
  femaleWordPoints[femaleWords.IndexOf(c.Key.ToLower())] *
  c.Value
);
```

the `ForEach()` algorithm in the Power Collection takes an action delegate to perform on each element of the passed collection; `femaleDic` in this case.

So, this statement calculates the `femaleScore`, which is a measure of the probability that the document is written by a female author. If this score is more than `maleScore`, then the document is probably authored by a woman.

The `c.Key.ToLower()` method returns the key of the current element in the `femaleDic` dictionary instance. `femaleWords.IndexOf(c.Key.ToLower())` returns the index of this word in the `femaleWords` array.

Thus, `femaleWordPoints[femaleWords.IndexOf(c.Key.ToLower())]` returns the weight of this word and `c.Value` is the frequency of occurrence of this word in the dictionary. So, by multiplying the weight and the frequency we get the score contribution of this word towards the total female score.

Time for action – revisiting the anagram problem

There is another very interesting generic method called, `UnsequencedEquals()`, which is available on the `C5.ArrayList<T>` class. Using this method, we can easily check whether two words are anagrams of each other or not. Let's see how:

1. Create a console application. Make sure you attach `C5.dll` to the reference of the project.
2. Write the following code inside `Main()`:

```
static void Main(string[] args)
{
  Console.WriteLine("Enter two phrases ");
  string first = Console.ReadLine();
  string second = Console.ReadLine();

  C5.ArrayList<char> charsFirst = new C5.ArrayList<char>();
  charsFirst.AddAll(first.ToCharArray());

  C5.ArrayList<char> charsSecond = new C5.ArrayList<char>();
  charsSecond.AddAll(second.ToCharArray());

  bool isAna = charsFirst.UnsequencedEquals(charsSecond);

  if (isAna)
  Console.WriteLine(@"The words {0} and {1} are anagrams of
    each other.", "\"" + first + "\"", "\"" + second +  "\"");
  else
  Console.WriteLine(@"The words {0} and {1} are not anagrams of
    each other.", "\"" + first + "\"", "\"" + second + "\"");

  Console.ReadKey();
}
```

Following is a sample run of the application:

```
Enter two phrases
oriental
relation
The words "oriental" and "relation" are anagrams of each other.
```

What just happened?

Finding whether two phrases are anagrams of each other or not is equivalent to finding out whether these two phrases have the same word histogram or not. A word histogram is like a dictionary where words are stored as the keys and the frequency of their occurrence is the value of the dictionary.

The method `UnsequencedEquals()` checks whether two collections have the same elements or not, disregarding the order of elements in the collections. This is exactly what we want to do to find out whether two phrases are anagrams or not. In our case, in the previous program, we wanted to check whether two words are anagrams of each other or not. So, checking the similarity of their character histogram would be sufficient.

Time for action – Google Sets idea prototype

Google Sets (`http://labs.google.com/sets`) is a nice piece of software when one wants to know what a few words mean. Given a few items, Google Sets returns similar items. In this example, we will build a small prototype that will reveal the possible data structure behind Google Sets. In the example, users will enter a few programming language keywords. The program will interpret the programming language from which these keywords are taken and then generate random small or large sets of similar keywords.

1. Create a Windows form application and place controls on it, as shown in the following screenshot:

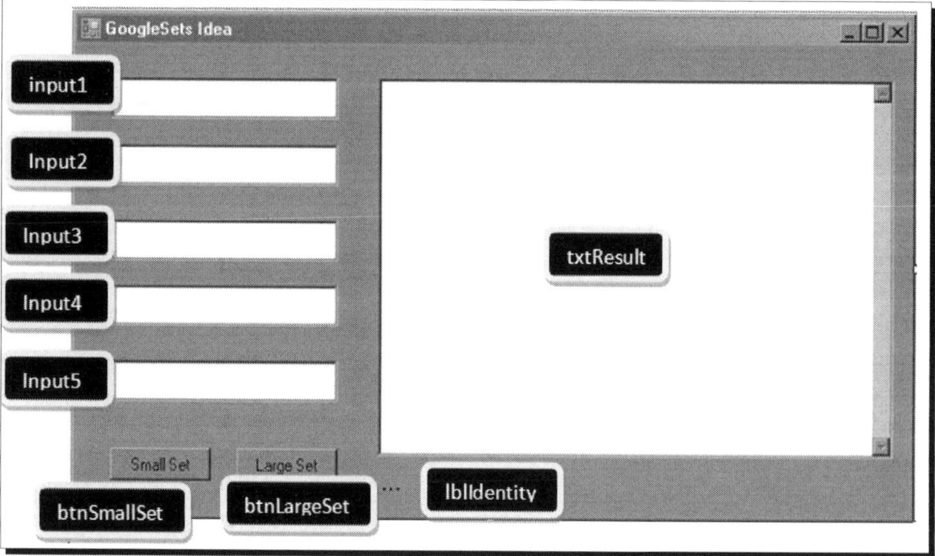

2. Add a C5 and Power Collection reference to the project:

```
using C5;
using Wintellect.PowerCollections;
```

3. Add the following variables to the `Form`:

```
enum SetType {Small, Large};
string[] smallSet;
string[] largeSet;
HashDictionary<string, HashBag<string>> languageKeywordMap = new
  HashDictionary<string, HashBag<string>>();
```

4. Add the following method to load language keywords:

```
private void LoadKeywords(string lang,string fileName)
{
  //Need to import using System.IO; to use StreamReader
  StreamReader creader = new StreamReader(fileName);
  string[] all = creader.ReadToEnd().Split(new char[]
    {' ', '\r', '\n' },
  StringSplitOptions.RemoveEmptyEntries);
  creader.Close();
  HashBag<string> allKeyWords = new HashBag<string>();
  allKeyWords.AddAll(all);
  languageKeywordMap.Add(lang, allKeyWords);
}
```

5. Call the preceding method to load several programming language keywords on `Form_Load`:

```
private void Form1_Load(object sender, EventArgs e)
{
  PopulateCKeywords();
  PopulateCPPKeywords();
  PopulatePythonKeywords();
  PopulateRubyKeywords();
  PopulateJavaKeywords();
}

private void PopulatePythonKeywords()
{
  LoadKeywords("Python","PyKeys.txt");
}
private void PopulateCPPKeywords()
{
  LoadKeywords("CPP", "CPPKeys.txt");
```

```
}
private void PopulateCKeywords()
{
  LoadKeywords("C", "CKeys.txt");
}
private void PopulateRubyKeywords()
{
  LoadKeywords("Ruby", "RubyKeys.txt");
}
private void PopulateJavaKeywords()
{
  LoadKeywords("Java", "JavaKeys.txt");
}
```

6. Add the following code to generate and show a similar small set of 15 items:

```
private void btnSmallSet_Click(object sender, EventArgs e):
{
  txtResult.Clear();
  HashSet<string> samples = new HashSet<string>();
  samples.Add(input1.Text);
  samples.Add(input2.Text);
  samples.Add(input3.Text);
  samples.Add(input4.Text);
  samples.Add(input5.Text);
  foreach (string key in languageKeywordMap.Keys)
  {
    if(Algorithms.EqualSets(languageKeywordMap[key]
      .Intersect(samples),samples))
    {
      smallSet =
      Algorithms.RandomSubset(languageKeywordMap[key], 15);
      Show(key, SetType.Small);
      break;
    }
  }
}
```

7. Add the following code to generate and show a larger set of 30 items or as many as are available (if there are less than 30):

```
private void btnLargeSet_Click(object sender, EventArgs e)
{
  //List<string> samples = new List<string>();
  txtResult.Clear();
```

```
    HashSet<string> samples = new HashSet<string>();
    samples.Add(input1.Text);
    samples.Add(input2.Text);
    samples.Add(input3.Text);
    samples.Add(input4.Text);
    samples.Add(input5.Text);

    foreach (string key in languageKeywordMap.Keys)
    {
      if(Algorithms.EqualSets(languageKeywordMap[key]
        .Intersect(samples), samples))
      {
        int bigCount = languageKeywordMap[key].Count > 30 ? 30
          : languageKeywordMap[key].Count;
        largeSet = Algorithms.RandomSubset
          (languageKeywordMap[key], bigCount);
        Show(key,SetType.Large);
        break;
      }
    }
}
```

8. Add the following method to show the results:

```
private void Show(string key,SetType whichOne)
{
  lblIdentity.Text = "These are " + key + " Keywords";
  lblIdentity.Visible = true;
  if(whichOne == SetType.Small)
  foreach (string s in smallSet)
  txtResult.Text = txtResult.Text + s +
    Environment.NewLine;
  if(whichOne == SetType.Large)
  foreach (string s in largeSet)
  txtResult.Text = txtResult.Text + s + Environment.NewLine;
}
```

9. We are all set to test this! The following is the output of a sample run:

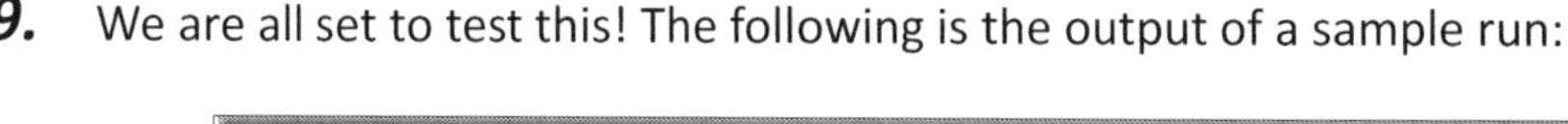

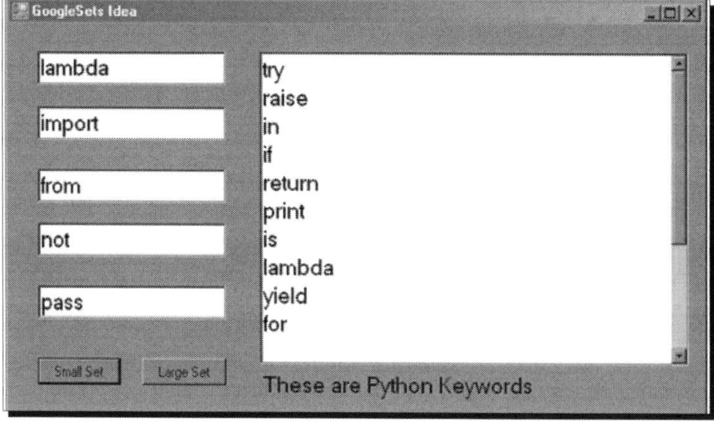

You can check out the program in action at `http://sudipta.posterous.com/google-sets-clone-mini-but-the-idea-is-correc`.

What just happened?

The following code:

```
HashDictionary<string, HashBag<string>> languageKeywordMap = new
  HashDictionary<string, HashBag<string>>();
```

creates a `HashDictionary` where keys are stored as Hash. The value for this dictionary is a `HashBag`, which is just conceptually similar to a list where all the elements are hashed for a constant time availability/membership check.

In button-click events (`btnSmallSet_Click` and `btnLargeSet_Click`), a `HashSet` is created to capture user inputs. A set is used to remove any duplicate entries. Inside the loop, within these event handlers, every entry in the dictionary is iterated using the dictionary keys.

`languageKeywordMap[key]` returns the associated `HashBag<string>` that has all the keywords associated with the language "key".

`languageKeywordMap[key].Intersect(samples)` returns the intersection set for the associated `HashBag<string>` and user input values. Now, if all entries of `samples` do exist in the intersection, this means `samples` is equal to the intersection set. `Algorithms.EqualSets` checks whether these two are equal or not. If they are, then we have hit a match.

`Algorithms.RandomSubset` returns a random subset from the given set (which is passed as the first argument).

In this example, we could have used `TreeBag`, `TreeDictionary`, and `TreeSet` also instead of the hash-based versions.

This means the following internal data structure:

```
HashDictionary<string, HashBag<string>> languageKeywordMap = new
  HashDictionary<string, HashBag<string>>();
```

could have been as follows:

```
TreeDictionary<string, TreeBag<string>> languageKeywordMap = new
  TreeDictionary<string, TreeBag<string>>();
```

or similar to the following:

```
TreeDictionary<string, TreeSet<string>> languageKeywordMap = new
  TreeDictionary<string, TreeSet<string>>();
```

Or you can choose to use a mix of these data structures. However, as the internal storage mechanisms of these data structures vary, we will have to change our calling code a little bit to make sure it still works.

For example, if you use the first alternative, then you have to change all instances of `HashBag` to `TreeBag`. However, if you use `ICollection<string>` as the value in the `languageKeywordMap` dictionary, then you can use any of these (either `TreeBag` or `HashBag` or `HashSet`) interchangeably as they are all `ICollection<T>` implementations. So, if you use `TreeBag`, you have to change the following line:

```
if(Algorithms.EqualSets(languageKeywordMap[key].Intersect(samples),
  samples))
```

to:

```
if(Algorithms.EqualSets(languageKeywordMap[key].ToArray().
  Intersect(samples), samples))
```

However, if you choose to use the second alternative, you don't have to make any changes apart from changing every instance of `HashSet<string>` to `TreeSet<string>`.

However, finding one keyword from a given list of words can be very time consuming due to the linear search in list-based collections, such as an **ArrayList**. In this situation, either a tree-based or a hash-based collection is ideal. List-based collections offer the slowest lookup speed, which is linear `O(n)`, while tree-based collections offer logarithmic time `O(n log n)` and hash-based collections offer a constant time lookup `O(1)`.

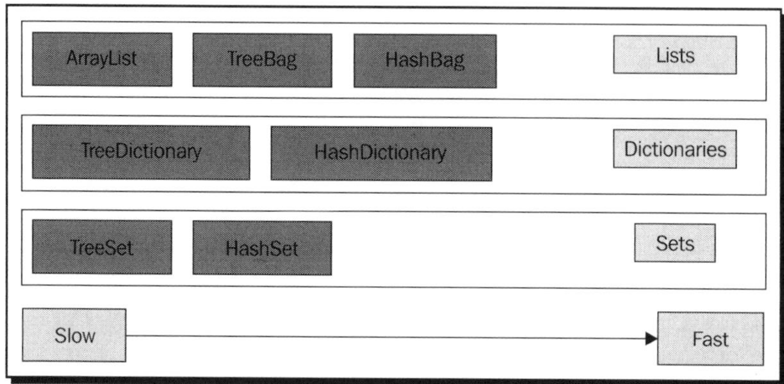

Time for action – finding the most sought-after item

The local departmental store wants to start a dynamic display system that will show high-in-demand items in each of its departments. It has a rather social impact. People shopping trust fellow shoppers more than advertisements; so, they want to know what others are buying or looking at.

In this example, we will create a generic data structure that can keep track of elements and their sale count very efficiently. At any point in time, this data structure can be queried about the top *n* (user can decide the value of *n*) items in demand. On demand, it can show how many times an item was in demand in constant time:

1. Create a class library project. Name it `MyDS` and change the name of `Class1` to `MTFList`.
2. Add `C5.dll` to the reference of the project and add the `using` directive:

   ```
   using C5;
   ```

3. Change the class header as follows:

```
public class MTFList<T>  where T:IComparable
```

4. Add the following code:

```
///<summary>
///Internal Data Structure
///</summary>
HashDictionary<T, int> _innerDS;

public MTFList()
{
  _innerDS = new HashDictionary<T, int>();
}

///<summary>
///Adds one item to the list
///</summary>
///<param name="item">item to be added</param>
public void Add(T item)
{
  _innerDS.Add(item, 1);
}

///<summary>
///Checks whether the item is in the list or not
///</summary>
///<param name="item">item for which availability has to be
///checked. </param>
///<returns>true if the item is present, false otherwise</returns>
private bool Contains(T item)
{
  return _innerDS.Contains(item);
}

///<summary>
///Searches for the item and increments its sought after count by
///unity
///</summary>
///<param name="item">item being sought</param>
///<returns>true if the item is present, false otherwise</returns>
public bool Search(T item)
{
  if (Contains(item))
```

```
    {
      _innerDS[item]++;
      return true;
    }
    return false;
  }

  ///<summary>
  ///Returns the item which is highest in demand ever.
  ///</summary>
  public T Top
  {
    get
    {
      return _innerDS.Filter(c=>c.Value ==
        _innerDS.Values.Max()).Select(c=>c.Key).ElementAt(0);
    }
  }

  ///<summary>
  ///Returns a list of top n items
  ///</summary>
  ///<param name="n">value of n</param>
  ///<returns>a list of top n items in demand</returns>
  public IEnumerable<T> TopN(int n)
  {
    if (_innerDS.Count < n)
    return new ArrayList<T>();
    else
    {
      return _innerDS.OrderByDescending(c =>
        c.Value).Select(c=>c.Key).ToList().Take(n);
    }
  }
```

At this point, we are done with the design of this structure. Time to consume it!

In the next few steps, we will see how to use this `MTFList<T>` to find the most in-demand item in a store.

5. Add the following controls to the Windows form, as shown in the following screenshot:

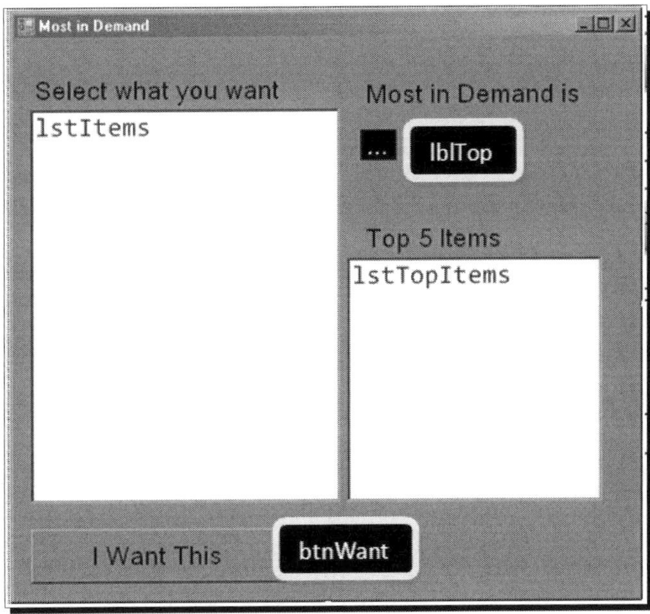

6. Add a reference of the class library in this project and make sure you add the `using` directive:

```
using MyDS;
```

7. Add the following variable to hold the most in-demand items:

```
MTFList<string> wantedGarments = new MTFList<string>();
```

8. Load this list with some values when the form loads and also add them to the list:

```
private void Form1_Load(object sender, EventArgs e)
{
  //Add using System.IO; for using StreamReader class.
  StreamReader itemReader = new StreamReader("garments.txt");
  string[] clothes = itemReader.ReadToEnd().
    Split(new char[] { ',' },
  StringSplitOptions.RemoveEmptyEntries);
  clothes.ToList().ForEach(c => lstItems.Items.Add(c.Trim()));
  clothes.ToList().ForEach(c => wantedGarments.Add(c.Trim()));
}
```

9. Deal with the button click:

```
private void btnWant_Click(object sender, EventArgs e)
{
  lstTopItems.Items.Clear();
  wantedGarments.Search(lstItems.Items[lstItems.SelectedIndex]
    .ToString());

  lblTop.Text = wantedGarments.Top;

  List<string> top5 = wantedGarments.TopN(5).ToList();

  foreach (string t in top5)
  lstTopItems.Items.Add(t);
}
```

Following is the output of a sample run of the program:

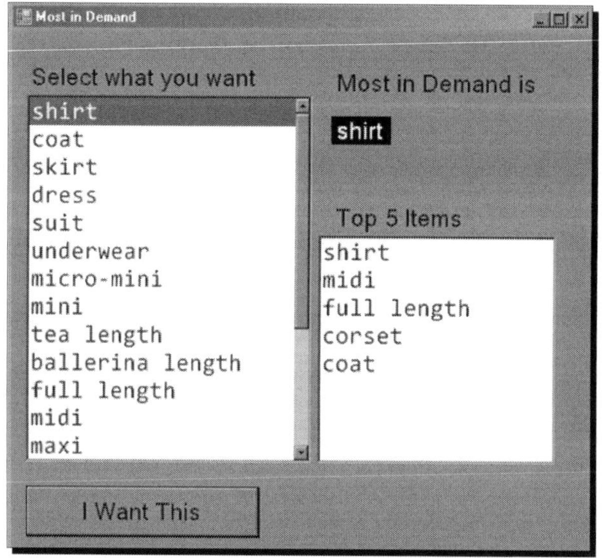

You will understand how it behaves better if you take a look at the video on my blog `http://sudipta.posterous.com/move-to-front-list-most-in-demand-demo`.

I highly recommend you see the video before you read the next section *What just happened*?

What just happened?

Unlike other search methods, the `Search()` method for this Generic Collection is active. Instead of just searching and returning `true` or `false`, it also increments the count associated with that element by unity every time that item is sought by the code line `_innerDS[item]++;`.

`HashDictionary` is used because it is the fastest of its kind—especially for strings—when localization can make actual key comparison-based structures such as `TreeDictionary` slow. `HashDictionary` offers a constant time lookup `O(1)` whereas `TreeDictionary` takes `O(log n)` for lookup where `n` is the number of elements in the dictionary.

To find the top-most item in demand, we are using the following code:

```
return _innerDS.Filter(c=>c.Value ==
        _innerDS.Values.Max()).Select(c=>c.Key).ElementAt(0);
```

The Lambda expression `c=>c.Value == _innerDS.Values.Max()` tells the `Filter()` method to find the element with the maximum value from the dictionary.

`_innerDS` is a dictionary and has keys and values. `c.Key` returns the key associated with a particular entry. As there can be many such elements, it will be sufficient to find the first one.

In the method, `TopN()`, as you can see, the dictionary is sorted by the values in descending order starting with the highest value.

Sorting algorithms

If you need some efficient sorting algorithm wrapped in a generic method, C5 has some in store for you. It has three sorting algorithms exposed as static methods of the class `Sorting`, which are as follows:

- `IntroSort`
- `HeapSort`
- `InsertionSort`

All these sorting mechanisms operate on an array of `T`, and all of these algorithms operate in-place. This means once you operate them on an array, you will be left with the sorted array and will lose the original unsorted array. We can use them to sort different collections as follows:

Pattern 1: Sorting an array of integers

`IntroSort` is an unstable version of `QuickSort` that can be used in situations where `QuickSort` fails to offer high performance, such as in the case of almost sorted collections. `HeapSort` is also as efficient as `IntroSort`. However, in practice, it is a little slower than `IntroSort`:

```
int[] a = new int[]{1, 42, 32, 22, -1, 0};
Console.WriteLine("Before Sorting");
a.ToList().ForEach(c => Console.Write(c + " "));

C5.Sorting.IntroSort(a);

Console.WriteLine("\nAfter Sorting");
a.ToList().ForEach(c=>Console.Write(c + " "));
Console.ReadLine();
```

This will generate the following output:

```
Before Sorting
1 42 32 22 -1 0
After Sorting
-1 0 1 22 32 42
```

Pattern 2: Partially sorting an array—say, sort first five numbers of a long array

Everything will remain the same. Just the call to `IntroSort` should use the overloaded version as follows:

```
C5.Sorting.IntroSort(a, 0, 5, Comparer<int>.Default);
```

This change in the preceding code snippet will generate the following output. Note that only the first five elements of the array were sorted. This is somewhat close to the `partial_sort()` method available in STL in C++:

```
Before Sorting
1 42 32 22 -1 0
After Sorting
```

```
-1 1 22 32 42 0
```

The other two sorting algorithms only offer the overload matching the second version.

Pattern 3: Sorting a list of string objects

Ideally, this is the same as *Pattern 1*; however, it shows how to use a custom comparer:

```
List<string> names = new List<string>() {"A", "C", "B", "D"};
string[] nameArray = names.ToArray();
C5.Sorting.IntroSort(nameArray, 0, nameArray.Length-1,
  Comparer<string>.Default);
```

As these methods sort in-place, an extra array is required to sort generic non-array collections.

Now, using the `MergeSorted()` method of the `PowerCollections` library, we can merge two sorted arrays as shown next:

```
int[] a = new int[] { 1, -1, 0, 4, 44, 22, 12 };
int[] b = new int[] { 2, -3, 3, 34, 14, 21, 11 };
int[] merged = Algorithms.MergeSorted(a, b).ToArray();
C5.Sorting.IntroSort(a);
C5.Sorting.IntroSort(b);
Console.WriteLine("Before sorting and merging");
Algorithms.ForEach(merged, c => Console.Write(c + " "));
Console.WriteLine("\nAfter sorting and merging");
merged = Algorithms.MergeSorted(a, b).ToArray();
Algorithms.ForEach(merged, c => Console.Write(c + " "));
```

This will generate the following output:

```
Before Sorting and Merging
1 -1 0 2 -3 3 4 34 14 21 11 44 22 12
After Sorting and Merging
-3 -1 0 1 2 3 4 11 12 14 21 22 34 44
```

These sorting methods can be applied to any type of collection as they have overloaded versions where you can pass an `IEqualityComparer<T>`. The preceding example uses integers as it is easy for most people to get the idea.

Summary

So far, we have learned all the .NET Generic classes and related algorithms. In the next and final chapter, we will discuss best practices and performance analysis; this will help you pick the correct tool (I mean correct Generic Collection and correct Generic Algorithm implementation) for efficiently solving a problem.

9

Patterns, Practices, and Performance

If all you have is a hammer, every problem would seem like a nail. Know thy tools.

We have come a long way. Starting at why Generics is important, we have learnt the basics of this API by building several applications. This chapter, however, will be different from the previous chapters. It will be a reference of best practices while dealing with Generics. The content of this chapter has been broken down into the following sections:

- Generic container patterns: There are several patterns that are used more than the others in code bases that use Generics. Here, we shall walk through some of these very popular generic structures.
- Best practices: Here we shall walk through a list of best practices with succinct causes to back them.
- Performances: Here we shall walk through a list of benchmarking including techniques and results.

Generic container patterns

There are several generic containers such as List<T>, Dictionary<Tkey,Tvalue>, and so on, which you have learnt about in the previous chapters. Now, let's take a look at some of the patterns involving these generic containers that show up more often in code.

How these are organized

Each pattern discussed in this chapter has a few sections. First is the title. This is written against the pattern sequence number. For example, the title for *Pattern 1* is *One-to-one mapping*. The *Pattern interface* section denotes the interface implementation of the pattern. So anything that conforms to that interface is a concrete implementation of that pattern. For example, Dictionary<TKey,TValue> is a concrete implementation of IDictionary<TKey,TValue>. The *Example usages* section shows some implementations where TKey and TValue are replaced with real data types such as string or int. The last section, as the name suggests, showcases some ideas where this pattern can be used.

Pattern 1: One-to-one mapping

One-to-one mapping maps one element to another.

Pattern interface

The following is an interface implementation of this pattern:

```
IDictionary<TKey,Tvalue>
```

Some concrete implementations

Some concrete implementations of this pattern are as follows:

- Dictionary<TKey,TValue>
- SortedDictionary<TKey,TValue>
- SortedList<TKey,TValue>

Example usages

The following are examples where TKey and TValue are replaced with real data types such as string or int:

- Dictionary<string,int>
- SortedDictionary<int,string>
- SortedList<string,string>
- Dictionary<string,IClass>

Some situations where this pattern can be used

One-to-one mapping can be used in the following situations:

- Mapping some class objects with a string ID
- Converting an `enum` to a string
- General conversion between types
- Find and replace algorithms where the `find` and `replace` strings become key and value pairs
- Implementing a state machine where each state has a description, which becomes the key, and the concrete implementation of the `IState` interface becomes the value of a structure such as `Dictionary<string, IState>`

Pattern 2: One-to-many unique value mapping

One-to-many unique value mapping maps one element to a set of unique values.

Pattern interface

The following is an interface implementation of this pattern:

```
IDictionary<TKey,ISet<Tvalue>>
```

Some concrete implementations

Some concrete implementations of this pattern are as follows:

- `Dictionary<TKey,HashSet<TValue>>`
- `SortedDictionary<TKey,HashSet<TValue>>`
- `SortedList<TKey,SortedSet<TValue>>`
- `Dictionary<TKey,SortedSet<TValue>>`

Example usages

The following are examples where `TKey` and `TValue` are replaced with real data types such as `string` or `int`:

- `Dictionary<int,HashSet<string>>`
- `SortedDictionary<string,HashSet<int>>`
- `Dictionary<string,SortedSet<int>>`

Some situations where this pattern can be used

One-to-many unique value mapping can be used in the following situations:

- Mapping all the anagrams of a given word
- Creating spell check where all spelling mistakes can be pre-calculated and stored as unique values

Pattern 3: One-to-many value mapping

One-to-many value mapping maps an element to a list of values. This might contain duplicates.

Pattern interface

The following are the interface implementations of this pattern:

- `IDictionary<TKey,ICollection<Tvalue>>`
- `IDictionary<TKey,Ilist<TValue>>`

Some concrete implementations

Some concrete implementations of this pattern are as follows:

- `Dictionary<TKey,List<TValue>>`
- `SortedDictionary<TKey,Queue<TValue>>`
- `SortedList<TKey,Stack<TValue>>`
- `Dictionary<TKey,LinkedList<TValue>>`

Example usages

The following are examples where `TKey` and `TValue` are replaced with real data types such as `string` or `int`:

- `Dictionary<string,List<DateTime>>`
- `SortedDictionary<string,Queue<int>>`
- `SortedList<int,Stack<float>>`
- `Dictionary<string,LinkedList<int>>`

Some situations where this pattern can be used

One-to-many value mapping can be used in the following situations:

- Mapping all the grades obtained by a student. The ID of the student can be the key and the grades obtained in each subject (which may be duplicate) can be stored as the values in a list.
- Tracking all the followers of a Twitter account. The user ID for the account will be the key and all follower IDs can be stored as values in a list.
- Scheduling all the appointments for a patient whose user ID will serve as the key.

Pattern 4: Many-to-many mapping

Many-to-many mapping maps many elements of a group to many elements in other groups. Both can have duplicate entries.

Pattern interface

The following are the interface implementations of this pattern:

- `IEnumerable<Tuple<T1,T2,..,ISet<Tresult>>`
- `IEnumerable<Tuple<T1,T2,..,ICollection<Tresult>>>`

Some concrete implementations

A concrete implementation of this pattern is as follows:

```
IList<Tuple<T1,T2,T3,HashSet<TResult>>>
```

Example usages

The following are examples where `TKey` and `TValue` are replaced with real data types such as `string` or `int`:

- `List<Tuple<string,int,int,int>>`
- `List<Tuple<string,int,int,int,HashSet<float>>`

Some situations where this pattern can be used

Many-to-many mapping can be used in the following situations:

- If many independent values can be mapped to a set of values, then these patterns should be used. `ISet<T>` implementations don't allow duplicates while `ICollection<T>` implementations, such as `IList<T>`, do.

- Imagine a company wants to give a pay hike to its employees based on certain conditions. In this situation, the parameters for conditions can be the independent variable of the Tuples, and IDs of employees eligible for the hike can be stored in an `ISet<T>` implementation.

For concurrency support, replace non-concurrent implementations with their concurrent cousins. For example, replace `Dictionary<TKey,TValue>` with `ConcurrentDictionary<TKey,TValue>`. For a complete list of mappings refer to *Appendix B, Migration Cheat Sheet*.

A special Tuple<> pattern

Since Tuple is a new inclusion in the .NET 4.0 Framework and can prove to be handy in a lot of situations, I thought it would be a great place to showcase an unusual use of this beautiful data representation technique.

Let's say we have situations involving four integers. This is generally represented using nested if-else blocks, as shown in the following code. However, we can use a Tuple to refactor this code, as we shall see in a while:

1. Create a console app and add these four variables:

```
static  int x = 11;
static  int y = 9;
static  int z = 20;
static  int w = 30;
```

2. Now, add these nested if-else blocks in the `Main()` method:

```
if (x > 9)
{
  if (y > x)
  {
    if (z > y)
    {
      if (w > 10)
      {
        Console.WriteLine(" y > x and z > y and w > 10 ");
      }
      else
      {
        Console.WriteLine(" y > x and z > y and w <= 10 ");
      }
    }
    else
```

```
        {
          if (w > 10)
          {
            Console.WriteLine(" y > x and z <= y and w > 10 ");
          }
          else
          {
            Console.WriteLine(" y > x and z <= y and w <= 10 ");
          }
        }
      }
      else
      {
        if (z > y)
        {
          if (w > 10)
          {
            Console.WriteLine(" y <= x and z > y and w > 10 ");
          }
          else
          {
            Console.WriteLine(" y <= x and z > y and w <= 10 ");
          }
        }
        else
        {
          if (w > 10)
          {
            Console.WriteLine(" y <= x and z <= y and w > 10 ");
          }
          else
          {
            Console.WriteLine(" y <= x and z <= y and w <= 10 ");
          }
        }
      }
    }
```

3. If you run this, you shall see the following output:

```
y <= x and z > y and w > 10
```

4. Although this code performs the job, it has the following problems:
    - It is very long. Most programmers will lose track of what they were reading.
    - It is impossible to re-use any part of the code that is available under a specific branching.

Time for action – refactoring deeply nested if-else blocks

Follow the given steps:

1. We must acknowledge that by using a maximum of four variables there can be 16 different branchings. Of these only eight are shown here. This type of code can be remodeled using the following structure. Now, delete everything in the `Main()` method and copy the following code:

```
//Creating rules list
List<Tuple<bool, bool, bool, bool, Func<int,int,int,int,string>>>
rules =
new List<Tuple<bool, bool, bool, bool, Func<int,int,int,int,
string>>>();

//adding rules.The benefit is that entire nested if-else is
//flatend.
rules.Add(new Tuple<bool, bool, bool, bool, Func<int, int, int,
int, string>>
(x > 9, y > x, z > y, w > 10, DoThis));
rules.Add(new Tuple<bool, bool, bool, bool, Func<int, int, int,
int, string>>
(x > 9, y > x, z > y, w <= 10, DoThis));
rules.Add(new Tuple<bool, bool, bool, bool, Func<int, int, int,
int, string>>
(x > 9, y > x, z <= y, w > 10, DoThis));
rules.Add(new Tuple<bool, bool, bool, bool, Func<int, int, int,
int, string>>
(x > 9, y > x, z <= y, w <= 10, DoThis));
rules.Add(new Tuple<bool, bool, bool, bool, Func<int, int, int,
int, string>>
(x > 9, y <= x, z > y, w > 10, DoThis));
rules.Add(new Tuple<bool, bool, bool, bool, Func<int, int, int,
int, string>>
(x > 9, y <= x, z > y, w <= 10, DoThis));
rules.Add(new Tuple<bool, bool, bool, bool, Func<int, int, int,
int, string>>
(x > 9, y <= x, z <= y, w > 10, DoThis));
```

```
rules.Add(new Tuple<bool, bool, bool, bool, Func<int, int, int,
int, string>>
(x > 9, y <= x, z <= y, w <= 10, DoThis));

Console.WriteLine ("Printing using tuple");
//Finding the first rule that matches these conditions.
Tuple<bool, bool, bool, bool, Func<int, int, int, int, string>>
matchingRule
            =  rules.First
                (
                  rule =>
                    rule.Item1 == GetExpression(x, 9)
                    //represents x > 9
                    && rule.Item2 == GetExpression(y, x)
                    //represents y > x
                    && rule.Item3 == GetExpression(z, y)
                    //represents z > y
                    && rule.Item4 == GetExpression(w, 10)
                    //represents w > 10
                );
//Find the Matching function.
Func<int, int, int, int, string> function = matchingRule.Item5;
//Invoke the function.
Console.WriteLine(function.Invoke(x,y,z,w));
```

2. This will not compile yet because the `DoThis()` and `GetExpression()` methods are not defined. So add these methods as follows:

```
private static string DoThis(int x, int y, int z, int w)
{
  string partOne = y > x ? " y > x " : " y <= x ";
  string partTwo = z > y ? " z > y " : " z <= y ";
  string partThree = w > 10 ? " w > 10 " : " w <= 10 ";
  return partOne + "and" + partTwo + "and" + partThree;
}

private static bool GetExpression(int x, int y)
{
  return x > y;
}
```

What just happened?

Now if you run the program, you shall see the same output as before:

```
y <= x and z > y and w > 10
```

So you saw how the if-else blocks were removed while the rules are still intact. Moreover, the code is more readable now.

Let's see how this worked. Notice carefully that the last parameter of the Tuples used in the rules is `Func<int,int,int,string>`. This means, we can place any function that takes four integer parameters and returns a string. The `DoThis()` method matches this requirement and so we place it in the list:

```
Tuple<bool, bool, bool, bool, Func<int, int, int, int, string>>
```

The previous list represents a relationship between four Boolean expressions and a function. These Boolean expressions are independent and the associated function is found using the following concern:

```
Func<int, int, int, int, string> function = matchingRule.Item5;
```

`Invoke()` is a method to call the function.

Best practices when using Generics

The following are the best practices to be followed while using Generics:

1. Don't use Generics when you know the situation won't always be generic.
2. Use `Stack<T>` for a Last In First Out (LIFO) list implementation.
3. Use `Queue<T>` for a First In First Out (FIFO) implementation.
4. Use `List<T>` for random access lists with zero-based indexing.
5. Use `LinkedList<T>` to implement a deque because it offers faster insertion and deletion at both ends as opposed to other collections.
6. If you have to frequently insert random locations in the list, prefer `LinkedList<T>` over `List<T>` because `LinkedList<T>` is a constant time operation to insert one item in between two elements in a linked list.
7. If the random list does not have a duplicate, use `HashSet<T>` instead. It is the fastest. Check out the performance analysis in *Appendix A, Performance Cheat Sheet*.
8. Don't use a `for` loop over a `IDictionary<TKey,TValue>` implementation. It can give incorrect results. Use a `foreach` loop over the keys collection instead.

9. Avoid using ElementAt() or, its cousin, the ElementAtOrDefault() method on generic collections that natively don't support zero-based integer indexing, (for example, Stack<T> or Dictionary<TKey,TValue>); since dictionary elements are not guaranteed to be available on an index where they were added.
10. Don't use a Tuple with more than seven parameters. Create a class with those parameters and then create a list of that class' objects. Using a Tuple with more than four parameters makes the code look messy and it's not efficient.
11. Use SortedDictionary<TKey,TValue> just to get the entries sorted. Don't use it to store simple associative "one-to-one" and "one-to-many" relationships as keeping the keys sorted isn't absolutely necessary. It is very slow compared to a normal dictionary.
12. Use HashSet<T> to create a generic set. It's the fastest set implementation available in the .NET Framework. Check out the *Performance analysis* later in the chapter.
13. Use SortedSet<T> only to create a sorted generic set. Don't use it when you don't want the set to be sorted because it is slower than HashSet<T>.
14. Don't expect indexing to work on an array or a list as it would on sets or dictionaries, because sets and dictionaries use hashing or tree-based internal data structures to place elements in the collection.
15. Use the available bare minimum implementation for your customized need or resort to creating your own custom collection class from the interfaces. This is a design guideline. Try to make sure your code is as lightweight as possible. If you want a queue, use a Queue<T> instead of a List<T>.
16. Use LinkedList<T> when you need to insert elements at arbitrary positions but you don't need to access them randomly via integer indexing.
17. Use KeyValuePair<TKey,TValue> to store a key value pair. Avoid using Tuple<T1,T2> for this purpose because KeyValuePair<TKey,TValue> is more efficient.
18. Prefer Dictionary<TKey,List<TValue>> over List<KeyValuePair<TKey,TValue>> whenever possible for representing a one-to-many relationship between two entities. Lookup speed will be much faster and client code will be less clumsy.
19. Prefer List<Tuple<..>> to represent a many-to-one relationship between two entities over Dictionary<List<TKey>,TValue> if there is a duplicate.

20. If no more entries need to be added to a collection, call `TrimExcess()` to free up the extra memory.
21. Prefer LINQ Standard Query Operator `Where()` over `Contains()`, `Exists()`, or `Find()` methods to check whether a value is present in a `List<T>` instance.
22. If you implement `IEnumerable<T>` in your custom collection, don't forget to implement IEnumerable also. This is to ensure backward compatibility and the Liskov substitution principle.
23. Use `SortedList<TKey,TValue>` if you want a concrete implementation of `IDictionary<TKey,TValue>` that supports native indexing. However, it is slower than `Dictionary<TKey,TValue>`. Avoid `SortedList<TKey,TValue>` when you don't want indexing.
24. Don't use the `ElementAt()` or the `ElementAtOrDefault()` method on `IDictionary<TKey,TValue>` implementations except `SortedList<TKey,TValue>`, because dictionary elements are not guaranteed to be in the index where they are added.
25. Avoid conversions between data structure formats (for example, array to list, or vice versa using LINQ operators) as far as possible. Use other language constructs. For example, consider using a `foreach` loop than converting an `IEnumerable<T>` instance to a list using the `ToList()` method before performing some operations on each item in the list.
26. Use the `OrderBy()` or the `OrderByDescending()` method to sort any `IEnumerable<T>`.

Selecting a generic collection

Not all generic containers are geared to do each job well, as we already know it. Here is a table that will let you pick a generic container that supports some features listed in the left-hand column.

How to pick a list?	**Stack<T>**	**Queue<T>**	**List<T>**	**LinkedList<T>**	**Hash Set<T>**	**Sorted Set<T>**
Allows duplicates	Yes	Yes	Yes	Yes	No	No
Native integer indexing	No	No	Yes	No	No	No
Keeps entries sorted	No	No	No	No	No	Yes
Native sorting capability	No	No	Yes	No	No	Yes

How to pick a dictionary?	**Dictionary <TKey,TValue>**	**SortedDictionary <TKey,TValue>**	**SortedList <TKey,TValue>**
Native sorting support	No	Yes	Yes
Zero-based indexing	No	No	Yes
Keeps entries sorted	No	Yes	Yes

You can download the **GenGuru** app from the book's website. It's a kind of wizard that will recommend the generic containers available in .NET Generics that you should use. It will ask you few questions and recommend a collection. You can see it in action at `http://sudipta.posterous.com/private/niixaeFlmk`.

Best practices when creating custom generic collections

The following are the best practices while creating custom generic collections:

1. Try to use built-in generic classes for maintaining internal data structures.
2. Try to use interfaces as return type and method arguments for publicly exposed methods for your collection. For example, consider using `IEnumerable<T>` over `List<T>`.
3. Try to keep the names aligned as much as possible towards the names available in frameworks. For example, if you are creating a concrete implementation of `IDictionary<TKey,TValue>` then try to use the suffix Dictionary in the name of the class, such as `MultiDictionary<TKey,TValue>`.
4. Try to provide overloaded constructors to offer flexibility such that the class can be created from many diverse data sources.

5. Use Generics constraints judiciously. Remember that these constraints are like boomerangs. You should know what exactly you can allow as an input parameter for a constrained generic type. Otherwise, these can backfire and hurt you and the users of your collection.
6. Make sure to always implement the `IEnumerable<T>`, `IEnumerable`, `ICollection`, `IDisposable`, and `IClonable` interfaces.
7. Make sure that your collection confirms to the Liskov substitution principle. Divide into subclasses only when it makes sense, otherwise use composition.
8. Offer a constructor overload to create a thread-safe instance of your collection.
9. Make sure it supports LINQ, which will be obvious if you implement `IEnumearble<T>` properly. LINQ is changing the way we see and solve problems. So if you miss LINQ, your collection will probably fail to impress a large section of the target audience.
10. Thrive for performance. Make sure that performance is as best as it could be. Refer to the *Performance Analysis* section later in the chapter and *Appendix A, Performance Cheat Sheet*.
11. Make sure your collection is as lightweight as possible. If a `Queue<T>` can do what you want done internally in your collection, use it. Don't consider using a more versatile list implementation such as `List<T>`.
12. Don't write raw events by yourself to monitor the collection; rather expose `ObservableCollection<T>` to offer this functionality.
13. Don't provide functionalities that can be achieved by a simple combination of exposed functions. For example, take a look at the Date Time API from the .NET Framework. There is a method called `AddDays()` that can take a positive or negative integer such that you can go to a past or a future date. However, the framework doesn't provide a method or a public property to compute `Tomorrow()` or `Yesterday()` as they can be easily calculated using the `AddDays()` method. While exposing public functions for your generic collection, remember to expose only those methods that can be used as building blocks for several reasons.
14. However, you have to strike a balance. The framework also has the `AddYears()` method because it will be cumbersome, although technically achievable, to duplicate `AddYears()` using the `AddDays()` method.

Remember these points while coming up with your own generic collection.

Performance analysis

Let's accept that we are impatient. Rather, we are becoming more and more impatient with each year. Part of this is due to the availability of processors that are a zillion times faster than the previous ones and come in pairs in almost every computer. Buying a single core machine these days is almost impossible. Computer hardware is faster than ever. Software developers have to put in extra effort to put these new powers to good use.

"*Algorithms + Data Structures = Programs*" said *Niklaus Wirth*. He was absolutely right in the title. If you add the word 'faster' to all the words in the equation mentioned earlier, it would result in "Faster Algorithms + Faster Data Structures = Faster Programs".

For a moment, forget whatever you know about data structures and think like a mathematician rather than a programmer. You should see that there are basically only a few types of data structures possible. They are Lists, Associative Containers, Sets, and sorted versions of each of these. It doesn't matter to a client code developer whether you use "Red-black tree" or "HashTable" internally to implement your dictionary as long as they both expose the same functionality. Take an ATM machine, for example. As long as the machine functions in a way people are familiar with, no one complains. But users complain if the machine requires some extra input or the interface changes.

In this chapter, we shall try to see which generic container outperforms its peers in practice even if their theoretical worst-case time complexity limit is identical. For example, `HashSet<T>` in `System.Collections.Generics` namespace and `HashSet<T>` in C5 collections, both are documented to offer constant time lookup activity. But in practice, as you will find in a little while, `HashSet<T>` in `System.Collections.Generics` is way faster than `HashSet<T>` in C5 collections.

We will investigate the following important situations for each kind of data structures:

Lists

The following are the important situations for lists:

- How much time does it take to check whether an element is present in a list-based collection?
- How much time does it take to find the index of the first occurrence of an item in a list-based collection?
- How much time does it take to find the last index of an item in a list-based collection?
- How much time does it take to insert a single element in a random location in a list-based collection?

Dictionaries/associative containers

The following are the important situations for dictionaries/associative containers:

- How fast can we look up an element in the collection?

Sets

The following are the important situations for sets:

- How quickly can we find the union of two or more sets?
- How quickly can we find the intersection of two or more sets?

  (This is a special case of union find)
- How quickly can we check whether a set is a subset of another set or not?

  This is a special case of superset find. Changing the caller and called objects in a subset find call would suffice. For example, the statements `set1.IsSubsetOf(set2)` and `set2.IsSuperSetOf(set1)` are identical.

How would we do this investigation?

We shall put all data structures under a lot of stress! We shall perform the same operations over and over again starting at 100,000 times to 2,000,000 times with a step size of 100,000 operations at a time. I have put the results in spreadsheets and have generated graphs and tables for your future reference. All source code used in these benchmarking experiements are also available for download from the book's website. Benchmarking results are recorded in tables. In this chapter, we shall use fewer rows of these tables to save some space. If you want the entire table, you can always get that from the spreadsheet.

Codes used to benchmark these data structures are given right next to the benchmarking result. Actual results (measurement figures) that you would get from running these code snippets on your system could be very different in absolute terms; however, they will surely share the same relative resemblance.

In the following tables, the figures that represent the time taken for the operation are measured in milliseconds. Create a console application and put the code and assemblies required (for example, `C5.dll` when you are using generic collections from this namespace) and the benchmarking code in the `Main()` method. You should be good to go. Further, you can download the Excel file from the book's website if you want to add some more values and see it in reference with others. Excel also enables you to add trend lines. So you can experiment with that too. The advice is don't trust documentation. Don't trust me. Do the profiling yourself. You as the developer of a program know what your requirement is better than anyone else. Use the strategies discussed in this chapter to find out the collection that works best for you. Good Luck!

Benchmarking experiment 1

How much time does it take to check whether an element is present in a list-based collection?

In order to determine whether a given item is in a collection or not, we have to call the `Contains()` method on linear containers.

The following are the steps to create the benchmarking code that I have used. You shall have to change the `Contain()` method accordingly, to alter it for the next benchmarking on another equivalent container:

1. Create a console app.
2. In the `Main()` method, add the following code:

```
static void Main(string[] args)
{
  HashSet<char> codes = new HashSet<char>();
  string alphabets = "ABCDEFGHIJKLMNOPQRSTUVWXYZ";
  foreach (char c in alphabets)
  codes.Add(c);
  Dictionary<int, double> perfMap = new Dictionary<int, double>();
  int N = 100000;

  for (; N <= 2000000; N += 100000)
  {

    DateTime start = DateTime.Now;
    for (int k = 0; k < N; k++)
    {
      codes.Contains('D');

    }
```

```
        DateTime end = DateTime.Now;
        perfMap.Add(N, end.Subtract(start).TotalMilliseconds);
    }
    foreach (int k in perfMap.Keys)
    Console.WriteLine(k + " " + perfMap[k]);
    Console.ReadLine();
}
```

3. As you run this app, you shall get a similar output. Exact figures shall vary depending on how much free memory is available on the computer you are running this code on and how busy the processors are. I recommend you close all other apps and run this. This way, the figures that you will get will convey more meaningful data about the performance of the generic container; `HashSet<T>` in this case.

```
100000 0
200000 15.625
300000 0
400000 15.625
500000 15.625
600000 0
700000 31.25
800000 15.625
900000 15.625
1000000 31.25
1100000 15.625
1200000 31.25
1300000 31.25
1400000 31.25
1500000 31.25
1600000 46.875
1700000 31.25
1800000 46.875
1900000 46.875
2000000 46.875
```

The numbers at the beginning of each line of the output denote the number of times the code snippet is executed. The second decimal number denotes total time in milliseconds taken for those many iterations of the given code execution. Looking at the figures, I can tell `HashSet<T>` is very fast. With further investigation we shall see that it is in fact the fastest of its kind in the .NET API eco-system.

What we just did, can hardly be termed as benchmarking. We have to compare the results obtained for `HashSet<T>` with other equivalent containers such as `SortedSet<T>`, `C5.HashSet<T>`, and so on. In order to do that, we have to run the previous program after changing it to use the container we want. For example, if we want to benchmark `C5.HashSet<T>` next, we'll have to perform the following steps:

1. Add a reference of C5.dll in the project.
2. Add the following using directive:

```
using C5;
```

3. As soon as you perform step 2, the compiler will return an error that HashSet<T> is ambiguous because there are two HashSet<T> now available; one from System.Collections.Generic and the other from C5. As we want to benchmark the HashSet<T> from the C5 Collection, explicitly mention that by replacing the following line of code:

```
HashSet<char> codes = new HashSet<char>();
```

   with

```
C5.HashSet<char> codes = new C5.HashSet<char>();
```

4. We are now ready to run the application again. This time the figures will represent the performance of C5.HashSet<T>.

```
100000 0
200000 15.625
300000 15.625
400000 15.625
500000 31.25
600000 31.25
700000 46.875
800000 31.25
900000 46.875
1000000 62.5
1100000 62.5
1200000 62.5
1300000 62.5
1400000 78.125
1500000 93.75
1600000 78.125
1700000 93.75
1800000 93.75
1900000 109.375
2000000 93.75
```

This is the way I got the performance figures of all linear lists such as containers by slightly changing the given benchmarking code. Once I got these numbers, I kept saving them on an Excel sheet.

Towards the end, I got something similar to the following screenshot:

Attempts	List<T>	LinkedList<T>	C5.LinkedList<T>	C5.ArrayList<T>	C5.HashedLinkedList<T>	C5.HashedArrayList<T>	C5.HashBag<T>	C5.HashSet<T>	HashSet<T>	SortedSet<T>	C5.SortedArray<T>
100000	46.875	46.875	140.625	140.625	15.625	15.625	15.625	0	0	0	15.625
200000	93.75	93.75	281.25	265.625	31.25	15.625	15.625	15.625	0	15.625	31.25
300000	140.625	140.625	421.875	390.625	46.875	31.25	31.25	15.625	0	15.625	31.25
400000	187.5	171.875	562.5	531.25	46.875	46.875	31.25	15.625	15.625	31.25	62.5
500000	250	218.75	687.5	656.25	78.125	46.875	31.25	31.25	15.625	31.25	62.5
600000	281.25	281.25	828.125	796.875	93.75	46.875	62.5	31.25	0	46.875	78.125
700000	328.125	312.5	984.375	921.875	93.75	62.5	62.5	31.25	15.625	46.875	93.75
800000	390.625	343.75	1109.375	1062.5	125	78.125	78.125	46.875	15.625	62.5	93.75
900000	437.5	406.25	1250	1187.5	140.625	78.125	78.125	46.875	31.25	62.5	125
1000000	468.75	453.125	1390.625	1312.5	156.25	93.75	93.75	46.875	15.625	62.5	125
1100000	515.625	484.375	1546.875	1453.125	156.25	109.375	109.375	62.5	31.25	78.125	140.625
1200000	578.125	531.25	1656.25	1578.125	171.875	109.375	109.375	62.5	15.625	78.125	156.25
1300000	625	578.125	1828.125	1718.75	187.5	125	125	62.5	31.25	93.75	171.875
1400000	671.875	625	1953.125	1843.75	203.125	125	125	78.125	31.25	93.75	187.5
1500000	718.75	671.875	2093.75	1984.375	234.375	156.25	140.625	62.5	31.25	109.375	187.5
1600000	765.625	718.75	2234.375	2109.375	234.375	140.625	156.25	93.75	31.25	109.375	203.125
1700000	812.5	750	2375	2234.375	250	156.25	156.25	93.75	46.875	125	218.75
1800000	859.375	812.5	2515.625	2359.375	265.625	171.875	171.875	93.75	31.25	109.375	234.375
1900000	906.25	843.75	2656.25	2500	281.25	171.875	171.875	93.75	46.875	140.625	265.625
2000000	953.125	890.625	2796.875	2640.625	296.875	187.5	187.5	93.75	31.25	140.625	250

From these data, I generated the following graph:

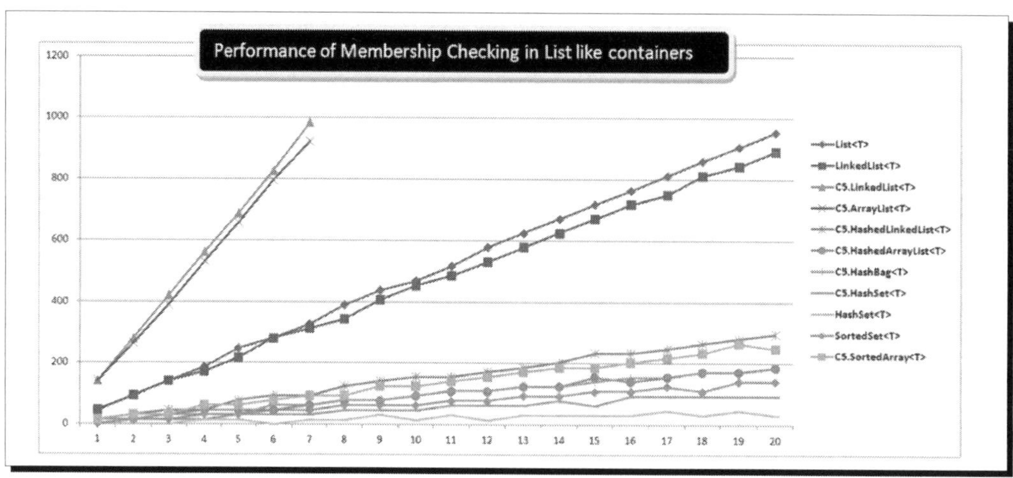

I was trying to check whether a given element is there in the list or not. This is also known as checking for membership in a given container. Thus the title of the graph is "Performance of Membership Checking".

You can download the Excel sheet with all these figures from the book's website.

It will be a great idea to create a tag cloud as a performance poster. From this data, I created the following tag cloud using Wordle (`www.wordle.net`):

I am quite happy with the end result of my benchmarking. This will stick longer in my brain than the actual figures and the graph. This means `HashSet<T>` is the fastest of all containers when it comes to membership checking. As a rule of thumb, anything that you can't read without a magnifying glass (such as **LinkedList** shown above the letter **e** in **HashSet**) should be among your last choices for this functionality.

If you are interested to know how I created this tag cloud with container names, please refer to the article at `http://sudipta.posterous.com/private/kzccCdJaDg`.

You can download benchmarking code for all these containers for membership checking from `http://sudipta.posterous.com/private/HmrocplDxg`.

I shall use the same pattern for all other benchmarking experiments in this chapter. I reckoned that it might be difficult to follow for some of you, so I created a screencast of the first experiment from start to finish. You can download this screencast (`PerformanceAnalysis_Screencast.MP4`) from the book's website.

Benchmarking experiment 2

How much time does it take to find the index of the first occurrence of an item in a list such as collection?

When dealing with a list such as containers, it is very common to face a situation where we need to know the index of a given element in the collection. Here, we shall compare the following containers to see how efficient they are in this situation:

```
List<T>
C5.LinkedList<T>
C5.ArrayList<T>
C5.HashedArrayList<T>
C5.HashedLinkedList<T>
C5.TreeSet<T>
```

The approach remains the same as the previous task. The benchmarking code is as follows:

```
using System;
using System.Collections.Generic;
using System.Linq;
using System.Text;

namespace PerformanceMap
{
  class Program
  {
    static void Main(string[] args)
    {
      List<char> codes = new List<char>();

      string alphabets = "ABCDEFGHIJKLMNOPQRSTUVWXYZ";
      foreach (char c in alphabets)
      codes.Add(c);

      Dictionary<int, double> perfMap =
      new Dictionary<int, double>();

      int N = 100000;

      int index = 0;

      for (; N <= 2000000; N += 100000)
      {
        DateTime start = DateTime.Now;
```

```
            for (int k = 0; k < N; k++)
            {
              index = codes.IndexOf('Z');
            }
            DateTime end = DateTime.Now;
            perfMap.Add(N, end.Subtract(start).TotalMilliseconds);
          }
          foreach (int k in perfMap.Keys)
          Console.WriteLine(k + " " + perfMap[k]);
          Console.ReadLine();
        }
      }
    }
```

As you run the code, you shall get an output similar to the following screenshot:

```
100000 0
200000 15.625
300000 31.25
400000 15.625
500000 31.25
600000 46.875
700000 46.875
800000 46.875
900000 62.5
1000000 78.125
1100000 62.5
1200000 93.75
1300000 78.125
1400000 93.75
1500000 109.375
1600000 93.75
1700000 125
1800000 109.375
1900000 140.625
2000000 125
```

And using the previous approach and running the program for all other containers mentioned, we get the following output in an Excel sheet:

Attempts	List<T>	C5.LinkedList<T>	C5.ArrayList<T>	C5.HashedLinkedList<T>	C5.HashedArrayList<T>
100000	15.625	109.375	125	125	0
200000	31.25	234.375	250	250	31.25
300000	31.25	328.125	406.25	390.625	15.625
400000	62.5	453.125	531.25	500	46.875
500000	62.5	562.5	656.25	640.625	46.875
600000	78.125	656.25	781.25	750	62.5
700000	109.375	781.25	921.875	875	62.5
800000	109.375	906.25	1046.875	1015.625	78.125
900000	125	1000	1187.5	1125	78.125
1000000	125	1109.375	1312.5	1265.625	93.75
1100000	156.25	1234.375	1453.125	1375	109.375
1200000	156.25	1328.125	1562.5	1515.625	109.375
1300000	187.5	1453.125	1718.75	1640.625	125
1400000	187.5	1562.5	1828.125	1765.625	140.625
1500000	203.125	1671.875	1968.75	1890.625	140.625
1600000	218.75	1781.25	2109.375	2015.625	156.25
1700000	234.375	1906.25	2234.375	2140.625	156.25
1800000	250	2015.625	2359.375	2265.625	171.875
1900000	250	2109.375	2515.625	2406.25	171.875
2000000	281.25	2234.375	2656.25	2515.625	187.5

After plotting the entire data, I got the following graph:

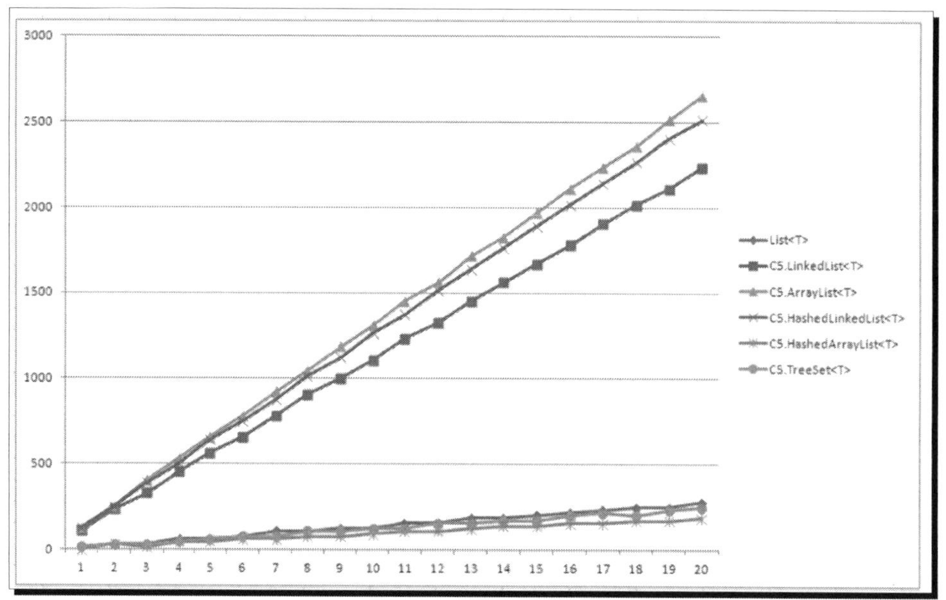

From this graph, it is evident that `C5.HashedArrayList<T>` is the fastest when it comes to finding the first index of occurrence of a given element in the container.

Following the previous approach, I got the following tag cloud:

C5.TreeSet
C5.HashedArrayList
List

Also, from the previous graph, it is evident that `C5.HashedArrayList<T>` is the fastest and `C5.HashedLinkedList<T>` is prohibitively slow. So, think twice before you call `IndexOf()` on a linked implementation.

To modify the benchmarking code for all other containers, just change the following line with the appropriate instantiation call:

```
List<char> codes = new List<char>();
```

For example, if you want to benchmark `C5.HashedArrayList<T>`, then follow the given steps:

1. Include `C5.dll` reference in the project.
2. Add the following `using` directive:

   ```
   using C5;
   ```

3. Replace the following line:

   ```
   List<char> codes = new List<char>();
   ```

   with

   ```
   C5.HashedArrayist<char> codes = new C5.HashedArrayList<char>();
   ```

Benchmarking experiment 3

How much time does it take to find the last index of an item in a list-based collection?

If you go by your intuition, it might seem obvious that the container that offers the lowest time for first index lookup of a given element will do so for the last index of occurrence too. However, soon you shall find that's not the case. Here, we shall benchmark the same containers as in the previous one.

The benchmarking code will be exactly the same. Except, instead of the `IndexOf()` method, you have to call the `LastIndexOf()` method on the containers.

The following is the result for all these containers:

Attempts	List<T>	C5.LinkedList<T>	C5.ArrayList<T>	C5.HashedLinkedList<T>	C5.HashedArrayList<T>
100000	0	0	0	125	15.625
200000	0	0	15.625	281.25	15.625
300000	15.625	15.625	0	390.625	31.25
400000	15.625	0	15.625	515.625	46.875
500000	15.625	15.625	15.625	671.875	46.875
600000	31.25	15.625	15.625	781.25	62.5
700000	15.625	15.625	15.625	906.25	62.5
800000	46.875	15.625	31.25	1046.875	93.75
900000	31.25	31.25	31.25	1187.5	78.125
1000000	31.25	31.25	31.25	1296.875	109.375
1100000	46.875	15.625	31.25	1437.5	109.375
1200000	46.875	31.25	31.25	1546.875	125
1300000	46.875	31.25	46.875	1687.5	140.625
1400000	46.875	46.875	31.25	1828.125	140.625
1500000	62.5	31.25	46.875	1953.125	156.25
1600000	62.5	46.875	46.875	2078.125	156.25
1700000	62.5	31.25	46.875	2203.125	187.5
1800000	62.5	46.875	62.5	2343.75	187.5
1900000	78.125	46.875	62.5	2453.125	187.5
2000000	78.125	62.5	46.875	2609.375	203.125

The graph depicting the relative performance of all these containers for this operation is as follows:

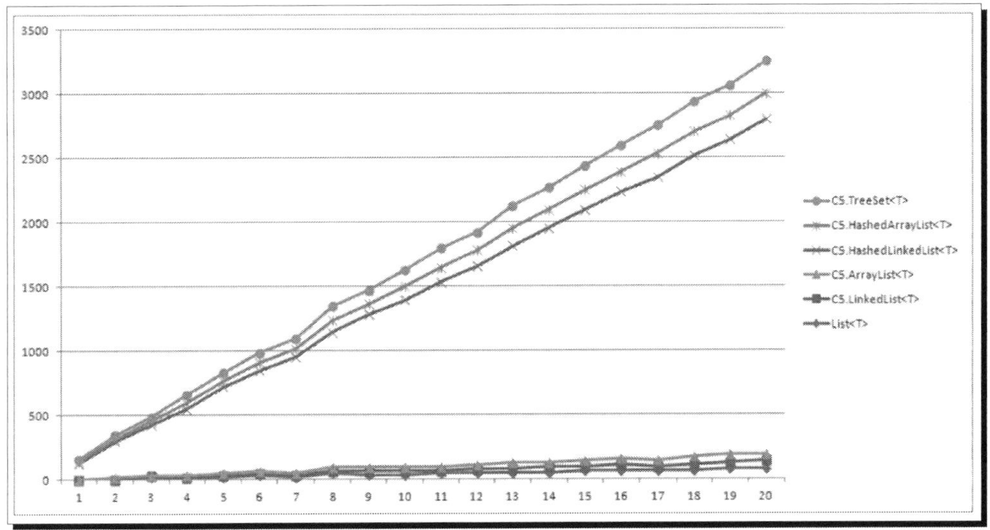

And the following is what I got putting the data to Wordle, as I did earlier:

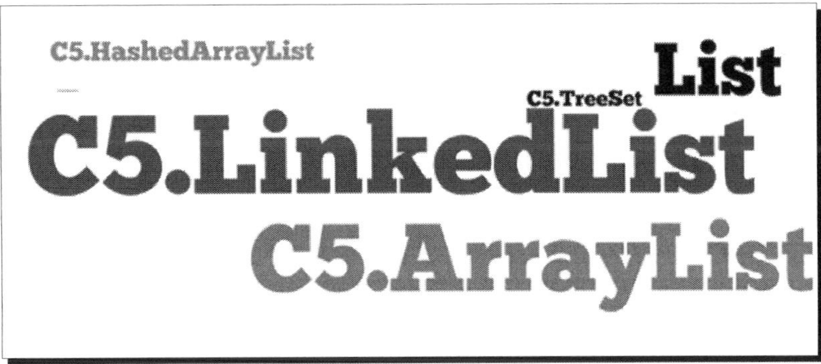

From the previous graph, it is pretty much evident that `C5.LinkedList<T>`, `C5.ArrayList<T>`, and `List<T>` offer equivalent performance. Anything beyond these collections would be an underperformer for this task.

Benchmarking experiment 4

How much time it takes to insert a single element in a random location in a list-based collection?

Sometimes we need to insert an element at a random location. Think about sorting, for example. Not all collections are geared to make this efficient. However, I shall benchmark the containers that support this operation:

```
List<T>
LinkedList<T>
C5.HashedLinkedList<T>
C5.HashedArrayList<T>
C5.LinkedList<T>
C5.ArrayList<T>
```

Apart from `LinkedList<T>` in the `System.Collections.Generic` namespace, all other containers listed previously have a method called `insert()` to insert an element at the mentioned index:

```
using System;
using SCG = System.Collections.Generic;
using System.Linq;
using System.Text;
using C5;

namespace PerformanceMap
{
  class Program
  {
    static void Main(string[] args)
    {
      SCG.Dictionary<int, double> perfMap =
        new SCG.Dictionary<int, double>();
      int N = 1000;
      //Change the container here and you should be done.
      //C5.HashedArrayList<int> nums = new C5.HashedArrayList<int>();
      C5.HashedLinkedList<int> nums = new C5.HashedLinkedList<int>();
      Enumerable.Range(1, 100).Reverse().ToList().
        ForEach(n => nums.Add(n));

      for (; N <= 20000; N += 1000)
      {
        DateTime start = DateTime.Now;
        for (int i = 0; i < N; i++)
        {
          nums.Remove(100);
```

```
            nums.Insert(new Random().Next(0,99),100);
          }
          DateTime end = DateTime.Now;
          perfMap.Add(N, end.Subtract(start).TotalMilliseconds );
        }
        foreach (int k in perfMap.Keys)
        Console.WriteLine(k + " " + perfMap[k]);
        Console.ReadKey();
      }
    }
  }
```

C5.HashedArrayList<T> and C5.HashedLinkedList<T> don't allow duplicate entries. So before inserting 100, we have to remove it. But since these are hash-based collections, removing items from these is a constant time operation. Thus, removing them doesn't have much impact on the overall performance.

The previous code will work for all except LinkedList<T> in the System.Collections.Generic namespace, as it doesn't offer any insert() method to directly insert elements. For LinkedList<T>, we have to use a different code for benchmarking:

```
using System;
using SCG = System.Collections.Generic;
using System.Linq;
using System.Text;
using C5;
namespace PerformanceMap
{
  class Program
  {
    static void Main(string[] args)
    {
      SCG.Dictionary<int, double> perfMap = new SCG.Dictionary<int,
double>();
      int N = 1000;
      SCG.LinkedList<int> nums = new SCG.LinkedList<int>();
      Enumerable.Range(1, 100).Reverse().ToList().ForEach(n =>
        nums.AddLast(n));
      for (; N <= 20000; N += 1000)
      {
        DateTime start = DateTime.Now;
        for (int i = 0; i < N; i++)
        {
          SCG.LinkedListNode<int> node = nums.Find(new Random().
Next(0, 101));
```

```
            if (node == null)
            {
              nums.AddFirst(100);
            }
            else
            {
              nums.AddBefore(node, 100);
            }
          }
          DateTime end = DateTime.Now;
          perfMap.Add(N, end.Subtract(start).TotalMilliseconds);
        }
        foreach (int k in perfMap.Keys)
        Console.WriteLine(k + " " + perfMap[k]);
        Console.ReadKey();
      }
    }
  }
```

As you run these programs for several containers and collect the data and put them on an Excel sheet, you will get an output similar to the following screenshot:

Attempts	List<T>	LinkedList<T>	C5.LinkedList<T>	C5.ArrayList<T>	C5.HashedArrayList<T>	C5.HashedLinkedList<T>
1000	0	0	0	0	15.625	0
2000	0	15.625	0	15.625	31.25	0
3000	31.25	78.125	15.625	15.625	46.875	15.625
4000	31.25	46.875	15.625	31.25	46.875	15.625
5000	62.5	250	15.625	62.5	62.5	31.25
6000	93.75	203.125	31.25	93.75	46.875	15.625
7000	125	828.125	31.25	140.625	109.375	31.25
8000	187.5	1093.75	31.25	187.5	93.75	31.25
9000	296.875	1375	46.875	281.25	125	46.875
10000	359.375	687.5	46.875	359.375	140.625	46.875
11000	453.125	1562.5	46.875	453.125	171.875	46.875
12000	593.75	3859.375	46.875	609.375	156.25	46.875
13000	750	2046.875	62.5	750	171.875	62.5
14000	906.25	3968.75	62.5	937.5	203.125	62.5
15000	1125	3578.125	78.125	1140.625	171.875	62.5
16000	1359.375	2531.25	62.5	1359.375	203.125	78.125
17000	1609.375	5640.625	78.125	1625	218.75	78.125
18000	1906.25	5953.125	78.125	1937.5	234.375	78.125
19000	2234.375	8562.5	93.75	2281.25	250	78.125
20000	2625	5750	93.75	2671.875	250	93.75

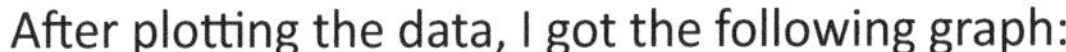

After plotting the data, I got the following graph:

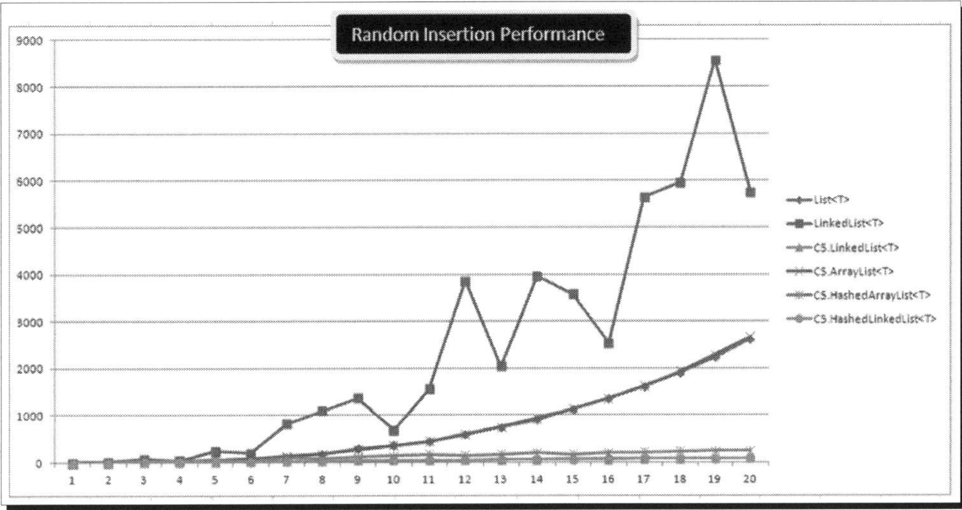

And the following shows how Wordle looks for the previous benchmarking test:

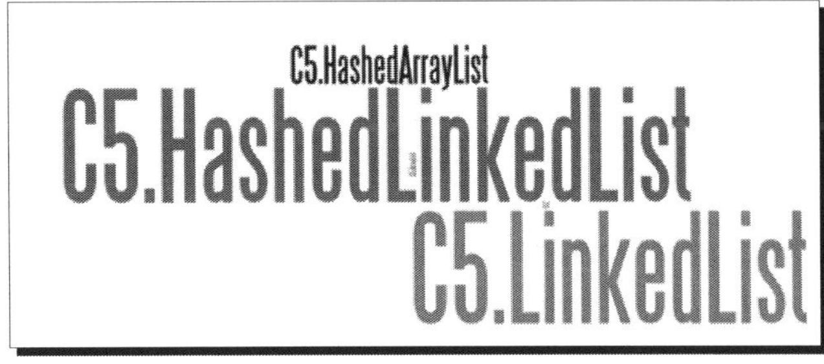

So, if your code demands a lot of insertions at random locations in the container, consider using C5.HashedLinkedList<T>, as that's the fastest you can get.

We can also tell from this tag cloud that List<T> offers one of the worst performances for random insertion. This finding is rather intuitive because containers that implement IList<T> generally use array as the internal data structure to offer native zero-based integer indexing. Therefore, inserting in a IList<T> implementation is actually inserting at a random location in an array. So, all elements after the location where the insertion happens have to be updated. Thus, inserting at a random index in an IList<T> implantation that uses array as the internal data structure is a O(n) operation in the worst case.

Benchmarking experiment 5

How much time does it take to delete a single element in a random location in a list-based collection?

Being able to delete at random locations is also a very important functionality sought by developers. Although it doesn't make much sense in IDictionary implementations and is advisable to avoid; it is almost taken for granted for an `IList<T>` implantation such as `List<T>`.

In this experiment, we shall try random deletions from `List<T>`, `LinkedList<T>`, `C5.LinkedList<T>`, `C5.ArrayList<T>`, `C5.HashedLinkedList<T>`, and `C5.HashedArrayList<T>` and see which one wins.

The following is the benchmarking code that will work for `LinkedList<T>` in `System.Collections.Generic`:

```
using System;
using SCG = System.Collections.Generic;
using System.Linq;
using System.Text;
using C5;

namespace PerformanceMap
{
  class Program
  {
    static void Main(string[] args)
    {
      SCG.Dictionary<int, double> perfMap
        = new SCG.Dictionary<int, double>();
      int N = 1000;
      SCG.LinkedList<int> nums = new SCG.LinkedList<int>();

      Enumerable.Range(1, 100).Reverse().ToList()
      .ForEach(n => nums.AddLast(n));


      for (; N <= 20000; N += 1000)
      {
        DateTime start = DateTime.Now;
        int x;
        for (int i = 0; i < N; i++)
        {
          nums.Remove(new Random().Next(0, 100));
```

```
            }
            DateTime end = DateTime.Now;
            perfMap.Add(N, end.Subtract(start)
            .TotalMilliseconds);
          }
          foreach (int k in perfMap.Keys)
          Console.WriteLine(k + " " + perfMap[k]);
          Console.ReadLine();
        }
      }
    }
```

For all other types, just change the highlighted part of the following line:

```
Enumerable.Range(1, 100).Reverse().ToList()
  .ForEach(n => nums.AddLast(n));
```

to

```
Enumerable.Range(1, 100).Reverse().ToList()
  .ForEach(n => nums.Add(n));
```

After running all the code snippets and collecting the data in the Excel sheet, you shall get a data trend similar to the following:

Attempts	List<T>	LinkedList<T>	C5.LinkedList<T>	C5.ArrayList<T>	C5.HashedLinkedList<T>	C5.HashedArrayList<T>
1000	0	0	0	15.625	0	15.625
2000	0	15.625	15.625	0	15.625	0
3000	15.625	15.625	15.625	15.625	15.625	15.625
4000	15.625	15.625	15.625	31.25	15.625	15.625
5000	15.625	15.625	31.25	15.625	15.625	15.625
6000	31.25	31.25	31.25	31.25	15.625	31.25
7000	31.25	31.25	31.25	46.875	31.25	15.625
8000	31.25	31.25	31.25	31.25	31.25	31.25
9000	31.25	31.25	46.875	46.875	31.25	31.25
10000	31.25	46.875	46.875	46.875	46.875	46.875
11000	46.875	46.875	62.5	62.5	31.25	31.25
12000	62.5	62.5	46.875	62.5	46.875	46.875
13000	46.875	46.875	62.5	62.5	46.875	62.5
14000	46.875	62.5	62.5	62.5	62.5	46.875
15000	62.5	62.5	78.125	62.5	46.875	62.5
16000	62.5	62.5	62.5	78.125	78.125	62.5
17000	62.5	62.5	78.125	78.125	62.5	62.5
18000	78.125	78.125	78.125	78.125	78.125	62.5
19000	78.125	78.125	93.75	93.75	78.125	62.5
20000	62.5	78.125	78.125	93.75	78.125	78.125

Using this data, I created the following plot:

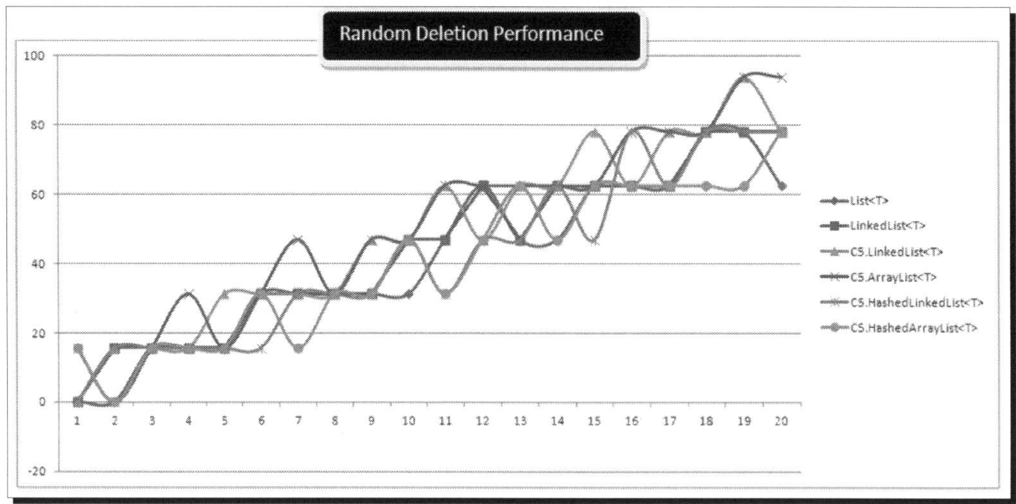

I think this is the fanciest looking graph so far! This means that all of these containers offer similar performance when it comes to random deletion. This statement is quite supported in the Wordle art too.

C5.HashedLinkedList
C5.LinkedList LinkedList
List C5.HashedArrayList
C5.ArrayList

However, array-based collections such as `C5.ArrayList<T>` and `List<T>` in `System.Collections.Generic` are trailing in this functionality too because of the same reason that in case of deletion, in an array worst case performance in `O(n)` there are `n` elements in the array.

Benchmarking experiment 6

How fast can we look up an element (or the unique key) in an associative collection?

IDictionary implementations are around for one good reason. They offer very good performance for unique key lookup. In this experiment, we shall see which of the IDictionary implementations is the best when it comes to key lookup. In this experiment, we shall limit our test with the following dictionaries:

```
Dictionary<TKey,TValue
SortedDictionary<TKey,TValue>
C5.HashDictionary<TKey,TValue>
C5.TreeDictionary<TKey,TValue>
```

The following benchmarking code is to be used for `C5.HashDictionary<TKey,TValue>` and `C5.TreeDictionary<TKey,TValue>`:

```
using System;
using SCG = System.Collections.Generic;
using System.Linq;
using System.Text;
using C5;
namespace PerformanceMap
{
  class Program
  {
    static void Main(string[] args)
    {
      string alphabets = "ABCDEFGHIJKLMNOPQRSTUVWXYZ";
      SCG.Dictionary<int, double> perfMap =
      new SCG.Dictionary<int, double>();
      int N = 100000;
      C5.HashDictionary<string, int> dic
        = new C5.HashDictionary<string, int>();
      alphabets.ToList()
      .ForEach(a => dic.Add(a.ToString(),
      alphabets.IndexOf(a)));
      for (; N <= 2000000; N += 100000)
      {
        DateTime start = DateTime.Now;
        for (int k = 0; k < N; k++)
        {
          dic.Contains("Z");
        }
        DateTime end = DateTime.Now;
        perfMap.Add(N,
        end.Subtract(start).TotalMilliseconds);
      }
      foreach (int k in perfMap.Keys)
      Console.WriteLine(k + " " + perfMap[k]);
      Console.ReadLine();
```

```
        }
      }
    }
```

For `Dictionary<TKey,TValue>` and `SortedDictionary<TKey,TValue>` in `System.Collections.Generic` change the following line:

```
dic.Contains("Z");
```

to

```
dic.ContainsKey("Z");
```

since the method to look up an item in these two IDictionary implementations is `ContainsKey()`.

After executing all the code snippets and entering the data in our Performance Excel Sheet, I got the following output:

Attempts	Dictionary<TKey,Tvalue>	SortedDictionary<TKey,Tvalue>	C5.HashDictionary<TKey,Tvalue>	C5.TreeDictionary<TKey,Tvalue>
100000	0	0	15.625	109.375
200000	15.625	15.625	31.25	218.75
300000	0	15.625	46.875	312.5
400000	31.25	15.625	62.5	453.125
500000	15.625	15.625	78.125	531.25
600000	31.25	31.25	93.75	640.625
700000	31.25	31.25	93.75	765.625
800000	31.25	46.875	125	843.75
900000	46.875	46.875	140.625	968.75
1000000	46.875	46.875	156.25	1062.5
1100000	46.875	46.875	156.25	1171.875
1200000	62.5	46.875	187.5	1281.25
1300000	62.5	62.5	203.125	1375
1400000	62.5	62.5	203.125	1484.375
1500000	62.5	78.125	234.375	1578.125
1600000	78.125	78.125	234.375	1703.125
1700000	78.125	78.125	265.625	1812.5
1800000	78.125	78.125	265.625	1906.25
1900000	93.75	93.75	281.25	2015.625
2000000	93.75	93.75	312.5	2109.375

Plotting the previous data, I got the following graph:

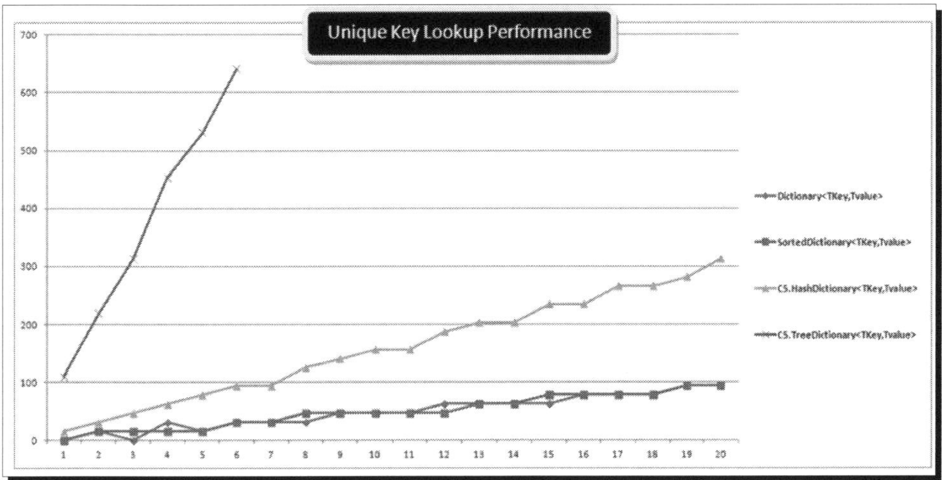

From the graph, it is evident that `C5.TreeDictionary<TKey,TValue>` is prohibitively slow and we have to limit our choice between `Dictionary<TKey,TValue>` and `SortedDictionary<TKey,TValue>`.

The following screenshot shows how Wordle looks:

There is something about the previous random word. As you can see, **Dictionary** not only has the highest font size, but it is also the first in the list. The second is **SortedDictionary** and the last is **C5.HashDictionary**. `C5.TreeDictionary` is so slow on key lookup that it almost didn't show up at all. So, the lesson learnt is if you just need a way to associate one type with another and no sorting, use Dictionary else use SortedDictionary.

Benchmarking experiment 7

How fast can we find the union of two or more sets?

Being able to find unions of large sets in a short time is what makes a 21st century algorithm click. We are living in a very interesting time and there is lot of data around us. Our applications have to deal with loads of data every day. But a seemingly simple task of keeping duplicate items at bay is a stupendously difficult task in practice.

To avoid this, we need quick set implementations. The .NET Framework and C5 offer a couple of set implementations. We shall put these containers under a lot of stress and find out how they perform.

The benchmarking code for `HashSet<T>` and `SortedSet<T>` available in `System.Collections.Generic` is as follows:

```
using System;
using SCG = System.Collections.Generic;
using System.Linq;
using System.Text;
using C5;

namespace PerformanceMap
{
  class Program
  {
    static void Main(string[] args)
    {

      SCG.HashSet<string> set1 = new SCG.HashSet<string>()
      { "A", "B", "C", "D", "E" };
      SCG.HashSet<string> set2 = new SCG.HashSet<string>()
      { "A", "D", "F", "C", "G" };
      SCG.HashSet<string> copyOfSet1 = new SCG.HashSet<string>()
      { "A", "B", "C", "D", "E" };
      SCG.Dictionary<int, double> perfMap =
        new SCG.Dictionary<int, double>();
      int N = 100000;

      for (; N <= 2000000; N += 100000)
      {
        DateTime start = DateTime.Now;
        for (int k = 0; k < N; k++)
        {
          set1.UnionWith(set2);
```

```
            set1 = copyOfSet1;
          }
          DateTime end = DateTime.Now;
          perfMap.Add(N,
          end.Subtract(start).TotalMilliseconds);
        }
        foreach (int k in perfMap.Keys)
        Console.WriteLine(k + " " + perfMap[k]);
        Console.ReadLine();
      }
    }
  }
```

The following is the benchmarking code for C5 set implementations. You can replace `C5.TreeSet<T>` with `C5.HashSet<T>` in the following code:

```
using System;
using SCG = System.Collections.Generic;
using System.Linq;
using System.Text;
using C5;

namespace PerformanceMap
{
  class Program
  {
    static void Main(string[] args)
    {
      C5.TreeSet<string> set1 = new C5.TreeSet<string>()
      { "A", "B", "C", "D", "E" };
      C5.TreeSet<string> set2 = new C5.TreeSet<string>()
      { "A", "D", "F", "C", "G" };
      C5.TreeSet<string> copyOfSet1 = new C5.TreeSet<string>()
      { "A", "B", "C", "D", "E" };
      SCG.Dictionary<int, double> perfMap =
        new SCG.Dictionary<int, double>();
      int N = 100000;

      for (; N <= 2000000; N += 100000)
      {
        DateTime start = DateTime.Now;
        for (int k = 0; k < N; k++)
        {
          set1.AddAll(set2);
          set1 = copyOfSet1;
```

```
            }
            DateTime end = DateTime.Now;
            perfMap.Add(N,
            end.Subtract(start).TotalMilliseconds);
          }
          foreach (int k in perfMap.Keys)
          Console.WriteLine(k + " " + perfMap[k]);
          Console.ReadLine();
        }
      }
    }
```

The following table has all the data collected from the previous benchmarking:

Attempts	HashSet<T>	SortedSet<T>	C5.HashSet<T>
100000	46.875	250	109.375
200000	78.125	421.875	171.875
300000	125	625	250
400000	156.25	843.75	328.125
500000	203.125	1046.875	421.875
600000	234.375	1265.625	500
700000	265.625	1468.75	578.125
800000	312.5	1687.5	656.25
900000	343.75	1890.625	734.375
1000000	390.625	2078.125	828.125
1100000	421.875	2296.875	890.625
1200000	468.75	2546.875	984.375
1300000	500	2765.625	1078.125
1400000	531.25	2906.25	1140.625
1500000	593.75	3140.625	1234.375
1600000	625	3343.75	1312.5
1700000	656.25	3546.875	1406.25
1800000	687.5	3781.25	1484.375
1900000	734.375	4031.25	1562.5
2000000	781.25	4234.375	1625

From the previous data, I got the following plot:

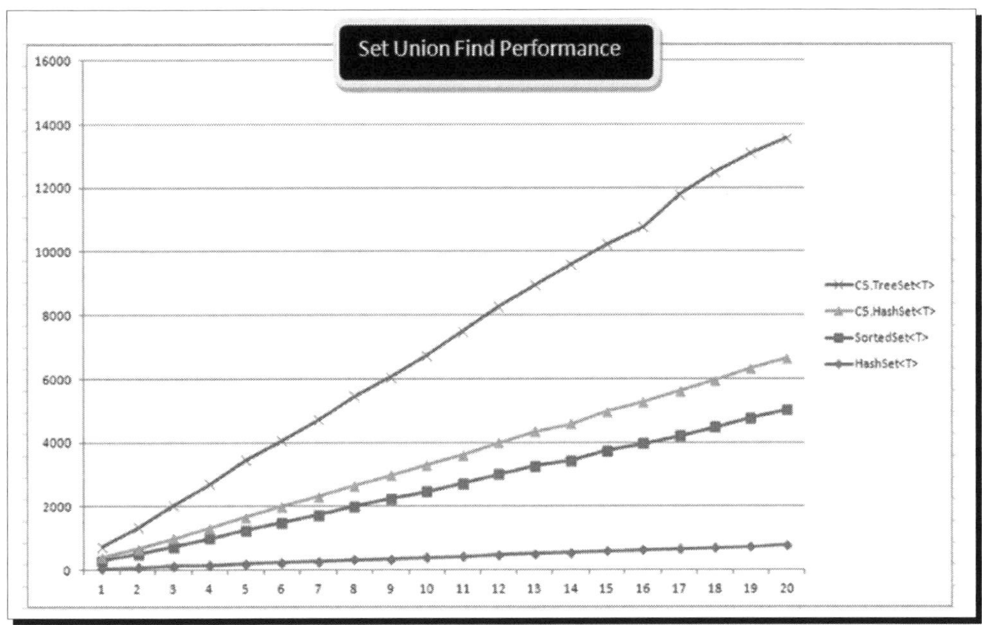

The result of this experiment is supportive of the result of experiment 1. In order to find the union of two sets, it is required to find whether a given element is present in either one or not. So, the container that offers the highest lookup speed for checking whether an element is present or not would intuitively offer the best performance for union also. That's exactly what the result of this experiment shows. `HashSet<T>` offers the highest lookup speed and also the best union find time.

My Wordle experiment with the data is as follows:

Benchmarking experiment 8

How fast can we find the intersection of two or more sets?

The result of this experiment is exactly the same as that of experiment 7 because intuitively finding a union is similar to finding an intersection. So, in this case, the order of performance is as follows:

`HashSet<T>` offers the best performance followed by `SortedSet<T>`, `C5.HashSet<T>`, and `C5.TreeSet.<T>`.

The following benchmarking code can be used with `C5.HashSet<T>` and `C5.TreeSet<T>`:

```
using System;
using SCG = System.Collections.Generic;
using System.Linq;
using System.Text;
using C5;

namespace PerformanceMap
{
  class Program
  {
    static void Main(string[] args)
    {
      C5.TreeSet<string> set1 = new C5.TreeSet<string>()
      { "A", "B", "C", "D", "E" };
      C5.TreeSet<string> set2 = new C5.TreeSet<string>()
      { "A", "D", "F", "C", "G" };
      C5.TreeSet<string> copyOfSet1 = new C5.TreeSet<string>()
      { "A", "B", "C", "D", "E" };
      SCG.Dictionary<int, double> perfMap =
        new SCG.Dictionary<int, double>();
      int N = 100000;

      for (; N <= 2000000; N += 100000)
      {
        DateTime start = DateTime.Now;
        for (int k = 0; k < N; k++)
        {
          set1.RetainAll(set2);
          //to make sure that we start
          //with the new set implementation
          //every time
          set1 = copyOfSet1;
```

```
            }
            DateTime end = DateTime.Now;
            perfMap.Add(N,
            end.Subtract(start).TotalMilliseconds);
          }
          foreach (int k in perfMap.Keys)
          Console.WriteLine(k + " " + perfMap[k]);
          Console.ReadLine();
        }
      }
    }
```

For `HashSet<T>` and `SortedSet<T>` in `System.Collections.Generic` just change the following line:

```
set1.RetainAll(set2);
```

to

```
set1.IntersectWith(set2);
```

As the results show a trend similar to the previous experiment, I didn't include the table values and the Wordle for this experiment.

Benchmarking experiment 9

How fast can we check whether a set is a subset of another set or not?

We shall benchmark the same four set implementations here.

The following code is to be used for `HashSet<T>` and `SortedSet<T>`:

```
using System;
using SCG = System.Collections.Generic;
using System.Linq;
using System.Text;
using C5;

namespace PerformanceMap
{
  class Program
  {
    static void Main(string[] args)
    {
      SCG.HashSet<string> set1 = new SCG.HashSet<string>()
      { "A", "B", "C", "D", "E" };
```

```
        SCG.HashSet<string> set2 = new SCG.HashSet<string>()
        { "A", "D", "F", "C", "G" };
        SCG.HashSet<string> copyOfSet1 = new SCG.HashSet<string>()
        { "A", "B", "C", "D", "E" };
        SCG.Dictionary<int, double> perfMap =
          new SCG.Dictionary<int, double>();
        int N = 100000;

        for (; N <= 2000000; N += 100000)
        {
          DateTime start = DateTime.Now;
          for (int k = 0; k < N; k++)
          set1.IsSubsetOf(set2);
          DateTime end = DateTime.Now;
          perfMap.Add(N, end.Subtract(start).TotalMilliseconds);
        }
        foreach (int k in perfMap.Keys)
        Console.WriteLine(k + " " + perfMap[k]);

        Console.ReadLine();
      }
    }
  }
```

For `C5.HashSet<T>` and `C5.TreeSet<T>` the benchmarking code has to be modified by changing the following line:

```
set1.IsSubsetOf(set2);
```

to

```
set1.ContainsAll(set2);
```

When the details are copied to our performance spreadsheet, we get data similar to the following screenshot:

Attempts	HashSet<T>	SortedSet<T>	C5.HashSet<T>	C5.TreeSet<T>
100000	31.25	703.125	31.25	0
200000	31.25	1375	62.5	15.625
300000	46.875	2078.125	93.75	15.625
400000	62.5	2781.25	125	15.625
500000	78.125	3437.5	156.25	15.625
600000	93.75	4140.625	203.125	15.625
700000	109.375	4828.125	218.75	31.25
800000	125	5531.25	250	46.875
900000	140.625	6203.125	281.25	31.25
1000000	156.25	6906.25	328.125	46.875
1100000	171.875	7562.5	343.75	46.875
1200000	187.5	8281.25	359.375	46.875
1300000	218.75	8953.125	421.875	46.875
1400000	218.75	9640.625	421.875	62.5
1500000	234.375	10343.75	468.75	62.5
1600000	234.375	11031.25	500	62.5
1700000	281.25	11734.38	531.25	62.5
1800000	281.25	12421.88	562.5	93.75
1900000	296.875	13093.75	593.75	78.125
2000000	312.5	13812.5	625	78.125

Plotting the previous data, I got the following graph:

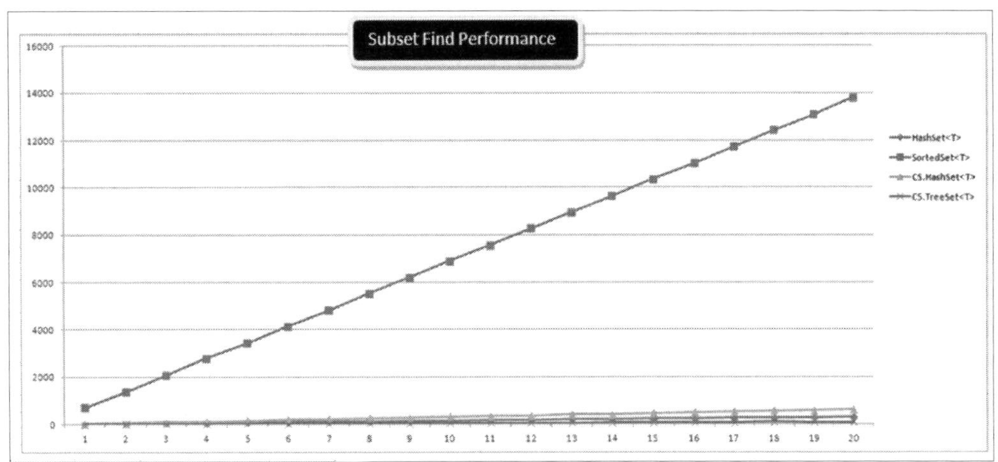

And the Wordle for this benchmarking looks similar to the following screenshot:

We have come to an end with our experiments for this chapter. I hope you got an idea how to benchmark your collections for several needs. It is very interesting that while `C5.TreeSet<T>` is almost unusable for a union or an intersection, it outperforms other set implementations when it comes to the finding subset functionality.

So, the lesson learnt is one size doesn't fit all. Learn what works best for the job at hand by benchmarking it against several options.

Summary

We have come a long way and now know with confidence which container is better in a given situation than another, even though theoretical time complexity for the mentioned operation in question is the same.

I hope the guidelines mentioned in this chapter will help you steer clear of pitfalls that can appear easily while dealing with code involving Generics.

You can download an Excel Workbook with all these benchmarking details from the book's website.

A

Performance Cheat Sheet

List<T>

Methods	Complexity (for n elements and count m)
`Add`	O(1)
`AddRange`	O(n + m)
`AsReadOnly`	O(1)
`BinarySearch`	O(log n)
`Clear`	O(n)
`Contains`	O(n)
`ConvertAll`	O(n)
`CopyTo`	O(n)
`Exists`	O(n)
`Find`	O(n)
`FindAll`	O(n)
`FindIndex`	O(n)
`ForEach`	O(n)
`GetRange`	O(n)
`IndexOf`	O(n)
`Insert`	O(n)
`InsertRange`	O(n + m)
`LastIndexOf`	O(n)
`RemoveAll`	O(n)
`RemoveAt`	O(n)
`RemoveRange`	O(n)
`Reverse`	O(n)
`Sort`	O(n log n)

Methods	Complexity (for n elements and count m)
`ToArray`	`O(n)`
`TrimExcess`	`O(n)`
`TrueForAll`	`O(n)`

Stack<T>

Methods	Complexity (for n elements)
`Clear`	`O(n)`
`Contains`	`O(n)`
`CopyTo`	`O(n)`
`Peek`	`O(1)`
`Pop`	`O(1)`
`Push`	`O(1)`
`CopyTo`	`O(n)`
`ToArray`	`O(n)`
`TrimExcess`	`O(n)`

Queue<T>

Methods	Complexity (for n elements)
`Clear`	`O(n)`
`Contains`	`O(n)`
`CopyTo`	`O(n)`
`Dequeue`	`O(1)`
`Enqueue`	`O(1)`
`Peek`	`O(1)`
`ToArray`	`O(n)`

HashSet<T>

Methods	Complexity (n and m are number of elements)
`Add`	`O(1)`
`Clear`	`O(n)`
`Contains`	`O(1)`
`CopyTo`	`O(n)`
`ExceptWith`	`O(n)`
`IntersectWith`	`O(n + m)`
`IsProperSubsetOf`	`O(n)`
`IsProperSupersetOf`	`O(n)`
`IsSubsetOf`	`O(n + m)`
`IsSupersetOf`	`O(n + m)`
`Overlaps`	`O(n)`
`Remove`	`O(1)`
`RemoveWhere`	`O(n)`
`SetEquals`	`O(n)`
`SymmetricExceptWith`	`O(n + m)`
`TrimExcess`	`O(n)`
`UnionWith`	`O(n)`

SortedSet<T>

Methods	Complexity (for n elements and count m. l is lower bound and u is upper bound of the view)
`Add`	`O(log n)`
`Clear`	`O(n)`
`Contains`	`O(log n)`
`CopyTo`	`O(n)`
`ExceptWith`	`O(n)`
`GetViewBetween`	`O(u - l)`
`IntersectWith`	`O(n)`
`IsProperSubsetOf`	`O(n)`
`IsProperSupersetOf`	`O(n + m)`
`IsSubsetOf`	`O(n + m)`
`IsSupersetOf`	`O(n + m)`
`Overlaps`	`O(n)`

Methods	Complexity (for n elements and count m. l is lower bound and u is upper bound of the view)
Remove	O(n)
RemoveWhere	O(n)
Reverse	O(1)
SetEquals	O(n + m)
SymmetricExceptWith	O(n + m)
UnionWith	O(n)

Dictionary<TKey,TValue>

Methods	Complexity (for n elements)
Add	O(1)
Clear	O(n)
ContainsKey	O(1)
ContainsValue	O(n)
Remove	O(1)
TryGetValue	O(1)

SortedDictionary<TKey,TValue>

Methods	Complexity (for n elements)
Add	O(log n)
Clear	O(1)
ContainsKey	O(log n)
ContainsValue	O(n)
Remove	O(log n)
TryGetValue	O(log n)

Parameters to consider

The following are the top 20 parameters to consider when selecting a generic collection:

1. Simple or associative
2. Random access capability
3. Lookup speed
4. Random insertion speed
5. Edge insertion speed
6. Random deletion speed
7. Edge deletion speed
8. Speed to empty
9. Time to count
10. Zero-based indexing
11. Native sorting capability
12. Thread safety
13. Interoperability
14. Platform portability
15. Memory requirement
16. Construction versatility
17. Native bsearch support
18. Speed of set operations
19. Code readability
20. Least effort to migrate

None of these facilities come in a single collection. So you need to deal with calculated tread-off and strike a balance between computational cost and optimum performance.

The parameters are explained as follows:

1. **Simple or associative:**

   If you want to store a few elements in a random order then you don't need an associative collection. Simple lists are `IList<T>` based where as associative collections are `IDictionary<TKey,TValue>` based.

2. **Random access capability:**

   If you regularly need to access elements, you would need a collection that supports this functionality to boost performance. Mostly, random access capability is offered by zero-based indexing. Containers that implement `IList` offer this functionality.

3. **Lookup speed:**

   Lookup speed can be crucial in the selection of associative containers. More the speed, the better. Normally, hash-based implementations outperform tree-based or list-based implementations. Thus, accessing an element in `SortedDictionary<TKey,TValue>` is faster than `SortedList<TKey,TValue>`.

4. **Random insertion speed:**

   If there are a lot of insertions at random locations in the collection, then you should consider how fast you can insert a few elements at arbitrary locations inside the collection. `LinkedList<T>` offers faster random insertion than `List<T>`.

5. **Edge insertion speed:**

   If you know that there will be many insertions at the edges (start or end) of the collection, choose one that is programmed to offer a faster speed. For example, `Stack<T>`, `Queue<T>`, or `LinkedList<T>`. Inserting in an array-based container, such as `List<T>`, offers the worst performance as all the elements beyond the point of insertion have to be shifted.

6. **Random deletion speed:**

   If there are a lot of deletions at random locations in the collection, then you should consider how fast you can delete a few elements at arbitrary locations inside the collection. `LinkedList<T>` offers faster random deletion than `List<T>`.

7. **Edge deletion speed:**

   If deletions occur only at the extreme ends of the collection, then you should consider collections optimized for that, such as `Stack<T>`, `Queue<T>`, or `LinkedList<T>` over `List<T>`.

8. **Speed to empty:**

   In many situations, you need to clear all the elements of the collection, perhaps inside a loop. In such situations, you should consider collections that take minimum time to clear all the elements.

9. **Time to count:**

   It is crucial to count how many elements there are in the collection. If it takes `O(n)` that's not good. In such situations, resort to collections that offer constant time-count operations. Luckily most of them do.

10. **Zero-based indexing:**

    Zero-based indexing has become the habit of programmers of our time, thanks to C arrays and C++ vectors. If you need random access on a simple sequential collection, resort to the one that offers this, such as `List<T>`, rather than using the `ElementAt()` method.

11. **Native sorting capability:**

    If you need to sort the collection every now and then, you can consider those that offer native sorting capabilities such as `List<T>` or resort to a sorted collection such as `SortedSet<T>`. It is better than using `OrderBy()` because a Lambda expression evaluation is generally slower.

12. **Thread safety:**

    If your collection will be used in a multi-threaded environment, it is better to use new concurrent collections than a primitive locking mechanism.

13. **Interoperability:**

    Use collections that are more flexible, or in other words, that implement more interfaces. For example, if you need associative storage, then you can use `SortedList<TKey,TValue>`. However, `SortedDictionary<TKey,TValue>` is also good because it supports serialization. So, in future, it would be easy to serialize.

14. **Platform portability:**

    If you are programming for a platform limited by memory, then some part of the framework will be absent. Be sure to check for the availability of the collection in the framework targeted to the hardware you are using.

15. **Memory requirement:**

    If you are in a memory-crunched system, you should also check the storage requirement of the collection. If it takes up too much memory, you might have to resort to something else. For example, if all you need is to add elements at the end and process them from the front, a `Queue<T>` would do just fine and you don't need a `List<T>` which is more heavyweight.

16. **Construction versatility:**

    The easier it is to create the generic container, the better. It's better if a collection offers more variations in constructor, because you always remain prepared for unprecedented situations. You would never know how much information you would need to create a collection.

17. **Native bsearch support:**

    Binary search is crucial to finding an item in a long list. You can always use the `BinarySearch()` method of an `Array` class; however, if native support is available, that's better. You would save a couple of boxing and unboxing calls.

18. **Speed of set operations:**

    Although you can perform all set operations via LINQ, resort to one proper set implementation if you need a set.

19. **Code readability:**

    Make sure to choose a collection that signals your intent more obviously than others, resulting in more readable code.

20. **Least effort to migrate:**

    Remember that the element of least surprise always works. Select collections that are available conceptually in several other languages.

B

Migration Cheat Sheet

STL to Generics

STL	.NET Generics class	Comments
vector	List<T>	
deque	LinkedList<T>	deque allows addition and deletion at both ends in constant time.
list	LinkedList<T>	list also allows addition and deletion at both ends in constant time. Thus, that is what is best mapped to these two containers.
stack	Stack<T>	
Queue	Queue<T>	
priority_ queue	Not available	You can use PriorityQueue<TKey,TValue> described in Chapter 3, *Dictionaries*.
set	HashSet<T>, SortedSet<T>	Use SortedSet<T> if you always want the set to be sorted.
multiset	Not available. You can use OrderedBag from PowerCollections.	Can be modeled as Dictionary<T,int> or SortedDictionary<T,int> if you want entries to be sorted.
map	Dictionary<TKey,TValue> SortedDictionary <TKey,TValue>	Use SortedDictionary<TKey, TValue> if you always want entries to be sorted.
multimap	Dictionary<TKey, List<TValue>>	You can also use OrderedBag in PowerCollection
bitset	List<bool>	

JCF to Generics

Java Collection Framework (JCF)	.NET Generics class	Comments
LinkedList	LinkedList<T>	
ArrayList	Not available	Use ArrayList<T> in C5 Collections.
HashSet	HashSet<T>	
TreeSet	Not available	Use TreeSet<T> in C5 Collections.
HashMap	Not available	Use HashDictionary <TKey,TValue> in C5 Collections.
TreeMap	Not available	Use TreeDictionary <TKey,TValue> in C5 Collections.
LinkedHashMap	HashDictionary<TKey,TValue>	
Vector	List<T>	
HashTable	Dictionary<TKey,TValue>	
SortedSet	SortedSet<T>	
SortedMap	SortedDictionary<TKey,TValue>	
PriorityQueue	Not available	Use PriorityQueue <TKey,TValue> described in Chapter 3, *Dictionaries*.
Deque	LinkedList<T>	

Power Collections to Generics

Power Collection Class	.NET Generics class	Comments
Pair<TKey,TValue>	KeyValuePair<TKey,TValue>	
Set<T>	Set<T>	
MultiDictionary <TKey,TValue>	Not Available	You can use the MultiDictionary we have created in Chapter 3, *Dictionaries*.
OrderedSet<T>	SortedSet<T>	
Bag<T>	List<T>	
OrderedBag<T>	Not available	This is basically a sorted list where duplicates are allowed.
Deque<T>	List<T>	You can add/remove from both ends of a List<T>.
Triple<T1,T2,T3>	Tuple<T1,T2,T3>	This is a special case of a Tuple.
BigList<T>	List<T>	

.NET 1.1 to Generics .NET 4.0

Non-generic collection	Generic collection (available from .Net 2.0)	Thread-safe generic collection
ArrayList	List<T>	ConcurrentBag<T>
Stack	Stack<T>	ConcurrentStack<T>
Queue	Queue<T>	ConcurrentQueue<T>
HashTable	Dictionary<TKey, TValue>	ConcurrentDictionary<T>
SortedList	SortedList<TKey, TValue>	ConcurrentDictionary<TKey,TValue>
BitArray	List<bool>	ConcurrentBag<bool>

C
Pop Quiz Answers

Chapter 2

Lists

1	numbers.Find(1), 3
2	3
3	{2}
4	{d}
5	{a,b,c,d,e}

Chapter 3

Dictionaries

1	a
2	b
3	stockPrices["MSFT"]["June2011"]

Chapter 4

LINQ to Objects

1	◆ Where(x=>x%2==0 && x<10) ◆ Where(x=>x<10) However remember that many where clauses can result in the same query as with if-statements.
2	c
3	a (It will throw an exception as there is no such element present in the collection)

Index

Symbols

A

E

F

G

H

M

N

O

T

U

V

W

Z

[PACKT] PUBLISHING

Thank you for buying .NET 4.0 Generics: Beginner's Guide

About Packt Publishing

Packt, pronounced 'packed', published its first book "Mastering phpMyAdmin for Effective MySQL Management" in April 2004 and subsequently continued to specialize in publishing highly focused books on specific technologies and solutions.

Our books and publications share the experiences of your fellow IT professionals in adapting and customizing today's systems, applications, and frameworks. Our solution-based books give you the knowledge and power to customize the software and technologies you're using to get the job done. Packt books are more specific and less general than the IT books you have seen in the past. Our unique business model allows us to bring you more focused information, giving you more of what you need to know, and less of what you don't.

Packt is a modern, yet unique publishing company, which focuses on producing quality, cutting-edge books for communities of developers, administrators, and newbies alike. For more information, please visit our website: `www.PacktPub.com`.

Writing for Packt

We welcome all inquiries from people who are interested in authoring. Book proposals should be sent to `author@packtpub.com`. If your book idea is still at an early stage and you would like to discuss it first before writing a formal book proposal, contact us; one of our commissioning editors will get in touch with you.

We're not just looking for published authors; if you have strong technical skills but no writing experience, our experienced editors can help you develop a writing career, or simply get some additional reward for your expertise.

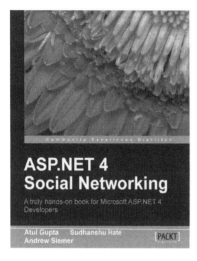

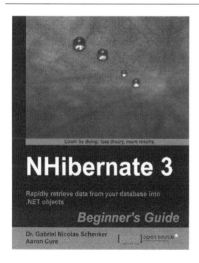

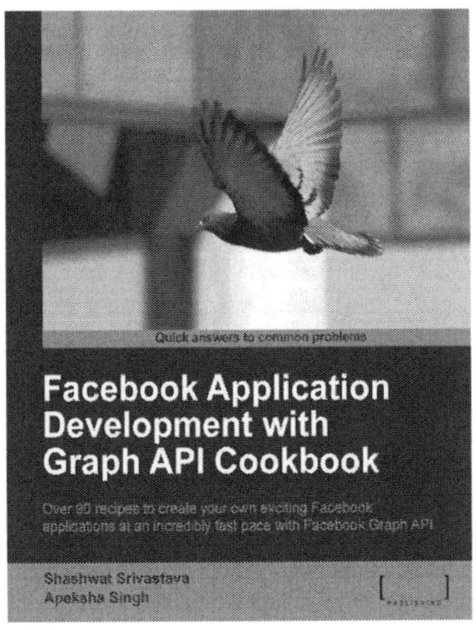

Facebook Application Development with Graph API Cookbook

ISBN: 978-1-84969-092-8 Paperback: 350 pages

Over 90 recipes to create your own exicting Facebook applications at an incredibly fast pace with Facebook Graph API

1. Dive headfirst into Facebook application development with the all new Facebook Graph API
2. Packed with many demonstrations on how to use Facebook PHP and JS SDKs
3. Step by step examples demonstrating common scenarios and problems encountered during Facebook Application Development
4. Houses an exquisite collection of ready to use Facebook applications

---

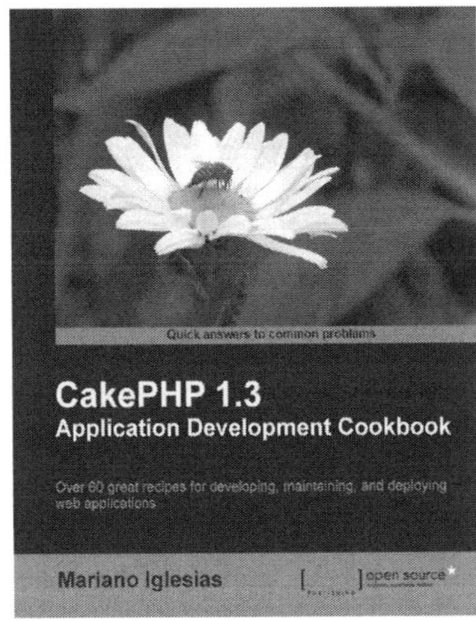

CakePHP 1.3 Application Development Cookbook

ISBN: 978-1-84951-192-6 Paperback: 360 pages

Over 60 great recipes for developing, maintaining, and deploying web applications

1. Create elegant and scalable web applications using CakePHP
2. Leverage your find operations with virtual fields, ad-hoc queries, and custom find types
3. Add full internationalization support to your application, including translation of database records

Please check **www.PacktPub.com** for information on our titles

Made in the USA
San Bernardino, CA
15 February 2014